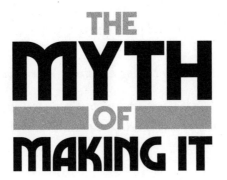

THE MYTH OF MAKING IT

THE
MYTH
OF
MAKING IT

A Workplace Reckoning

**SAMHITA
MUKHOPADHYAY**

RANDOM HOUSE
NEW YORK

Published in the United States by Random House, an imprint and division
of Penguin Random House LLC, New York.

RANDOM HOUSE and the HOUSE colophon are registered trademarks of
Penguin Random House LLC.

Library of Congress Cataloging-in-Publication Data
Names: Mukhopadhyay, Samhita, author.
Title: The myth of making it: a workplace reckoning / by Samhita Mukhopadhyay.
Description: First edition. | New York: Random House, [2023] | Includes index.
Identifiers: LCCN 2024009818 (print) | LCCN 2024009819 (ebook) |
ISBN 9780593448090 (hardcover) | ISBN 9780593448106 (ebook) |
Subjects: LCSH: Work—Psychological aspects. | Work-life balance. | Success.
Classification: LCC BF481 .M84 2024 (print) | LCC BF481 (ebook) |
DDC 158.7—dc23/eng/20240322
LC record available at https://lccn.loc.gov/2024009818
LC ebook record available at https://lccn.loc.gov/2024009819

Printed in the United States of America on acid-free paper

randomhousebooks.com

2 4 6 8 9 7 5 3 1

FIRST EDITION

Book design by Ralph Fowler

For Baba and Toto

1. Whatever the work is, do it well—not for the boss but for yourself.
2. You make the job; it doesn't make you.
3. Your real life is with us, your family.
4. You are not the work you do; you are the person you are.

—Toni Morrison, The New Yorker, 2017

Be ruthless with institutions. Be kind to each other.

—Michael Jamal Brooks

CONTENTS

INTRODUCTION

The show was about to start. My heart was pounding with the music as I tried not to topple over in my heels while looking for my seat. The fake fur draped over my shoulders was threatening to fall off. I found my seat: front row, midway down the catwalk. Attendees were dressed to the nines, and I was prepared. I religiously followed Fashion Week street-style blogs, and I knew the drill—the more outrageous, the better. (A neon-green one-shoulder top, striped pants, and heels so tall I can barely walk? Sure, why not!) There was a party around me. Compliments: *Kiss kiss. OMG, you look incredible.* And side-eyes: *Who is that again?*

I had just turned forty and was six months into my job as executive editor of *Teen Vogue*. I'd been a feminist writer and critic for almost fifteen years, and even though I'd always been interested in fashion, I'd also been vocally critical of its untenable standards. Still, here I was— a fat, brown feminist writer turned fashion magazine editor, sitting in the front row of Fashion Week. I posted endless selfies on Instagram ("Baby's first #NYFW"), tagging the brands of my group-text-approved outfits, welcoming the "yasss queens" in my comments. I felt hot, uncomfortable, and a little ridiculous, but it was worth it. I was participating in something I had secretly fantasized about—the upper echelon of New York City life and culture. After years of criticizing the elitism and exclusiveness of these very spaces, I was sitting in the belly of the beast.

This, I told myself, *is what making it feels like.*

Teen Vogue had recently started covering feminism and social justice in earnest, and I'd gotten hired to polish the coverage. Fashion Week wasn't exactly an essential part of my job, but I felt pressure to not only be part of this new group but also be seen in it. Attending felt like another way to stretch myself in my career, meet new people, and belong to another community. And let's be honest: It was *fun*. I was ascendant. I was becoming someone more momentous and more exciting than just an editor.

I can now see that this fabulous story I had been telling the world wasn't particularly true. I felt out of place at that fashion show, like I was watching myself in a movie about someone else's life. The veneer of social media often glosses over what's really happening in people's lives, and I was no exception. Posting those pictures allowed me to deflect what was actually going on.

The real story was that the previous year I had been let go from a job, which had led to months of depression and uncertainty about my career and financial future. My dad's health was in bad shape, as were my parents' finances. I regularly took time out of my "glamorous" New York City life to head upstate on Metro-North and visit my dad in depressing hospital rooms or in our cluttered house in the exurbs. I resented how anxious, exhausted, and worried it made me. I hadn't dated in months, and I was often too tired to catch up with friends. Instead I stayed at the office until well past dinner. And my feet always hurt. I was at the apex of my career, but I was dissociated from the reality of my actual life. As I sat in the front row that day, I was 80 percent faking it with a 100-percent-real Gucci bag.

When I think of that era, the very real highs—there was a lot I loved about the job, and I felt fiercely loyal to my team—are coupled with the unavoidable lows of limping home at night, struggling to keep my eyes open after back-to-back days full of meetings and managing difficult personalities with few breaks. I told myself, though, that this was what making it meant. It meant you were tired. Frazzled. That you sacrificed friendships and resented your family for needing you. That you stress-ate and paid too much for lattes and ignored it when your doctor was alarmed by your latest bloodwork. It meant you worked twelve hours a day and came home with painful feet.

This was simply what it cost to flourish. To be a "success story."

I never would have called myself a girlboss—I am too old for that, and the pink "she-conomy," Type-A, organized, SoulCycle devotee was never my style. I would have never claimed to be "leaning in"—it is too neoliberal for my leftist tastes. But what's inescapable to me now is how thoroughly I had bought into certain myths about what it means to be a woman who is "getting ahead at work." I told myself I was loving it. I was like a coach who couldn't stop giving pep talks: "This is awesome" or "I'm so happy to be here." And sometimes it was even true. If work meant sacrificing everything, then I'd sacrifice.

Then, one day, it all came crashing down.

I'm not alone. Millions of women and nonbinary people in the past decade—and especially during and after the pandemic—have looked at their lives and said, "What the fuck?"

Why are we working all the time to make less than our male counterparts?

Why are we doing most of the childcare even when our partnerships are "equal"?

Why have we sacrificed so much of our personal happiness to be driven by these undefined measures of success?

Why are we spending more time with our coworkers than with anyone else in our lives?

Why are we tired all the time?

For a while there, many of us faithfully followed a certain vision of what it meant to be killing it at work. Want to earn more? Want to get ahead? It was nothing a little girlbossing, leaning in, and hustling couldn't help you achieve. If you worked hard enough, you could overcome any obstacle in your way. It was just a matter of putting in the time, working your network, and being smart and hyperorganized about it.

But recently we've seen the cracks start to show. What this ethos leaves out is the many, many roadblocks women face that can't be hustled through, no matter how hard they work. Things like unequal pay, cost-prohibitive child- and medical care, lack of affordable housing, and student debt. If you're a person of color, poor, disabled, queer, and/or gender nonconforming, the walls you may hit at work are likely to be even more complex. During the past few years, many of us woke up to the reality that we were trying to find individual solutions for systemic issues. So, we sit now at a career crossroads, wondering what our next move is.

The truth is we still have to navigate these imperfect systems. We have to find ways to earn money while maintaining some sense of morality but *also* while being able to pay our rent or our parents' rent or to have a child and put them through college or, I don't know, finally go on that vacation.

But despite knowing that we can't push ourselves and our bodies any harder and knowing that if we lean in any further we'll break our faces on our desks, we are still ambitious, we still dream, and we still want to do great things. Even while intimately knowing about all those structural barriers, we still want to build full, free, satisfying lives for ourselves.

The question is, How do we do that?

Perhaps the first step to answering this is figuring out, as the philosopher Brian Massumi calls it, our "margin of maneuverability." The Canadian philosopher suggests that, rather than giving in to pessimism and inaction when the events of the world feel dreadful, a person ought to turn their attention to what *is* possible. He suggests that uncertainty is, in fact, an opportunity to give a person space for optimism, for possibility, for hope, and for making empowering decisions.

This is the same uncertainty in which many of us stand today. Every day, we are faced with the horrors of everything from skyrocketing inequality to unregulated guns to racial injustice to never-ending wars to climate catastrophes to ongoing threats to our bodily autonomy. And, in the middle of all that, the way we work has become untenable, both personally and globally. We are craving something more and something better.

What is the space between what we can actually do in our lives and what is insurmountable or unattainable without collective effort? We have an opportunity to rethink what ambition means, and, contrary to the hustle mantras on which we were raised, we can't do it alone.

This book is not a how-to manual. What I explore instead are the bigger questions that undergird our desire to get ahead: What fuels our aspirations, and what keeps us yearning for more? I start by considering how corporate feminism set us up to fail. I then examine the roots of the myths we buy into about work and revisit what hasn't worked and what we can learn from that. The second half of the book is about my own experiences as a manager and as a woman of color navigating environments that are often inherently unequal. About when diversity and inclusion is important but also when it is not enough. I reckon with our relationship to burnout and the corresponding pressure for self-care. Finally, I consider what ambition ultimately means and where it is leading us.

But I also consider where we have had small wins and how they can add up to a bigger one—making it possible for all of us, despite our different places in the economy, to fight for global worker solidarity—and how we can become radicalized workers or leaders, while also prioritizing happiness in our own humble lives. What, ultimately, does real success look like? What does it truly mean to make it? Think of this book as the friend and mentor you've needed, who's trying to help you answer those questions.

I'm not coming to you as someone who has it figured out. Quite the opposite. I wrote this book because I've done this and that job, and I wanted to share what I've learned and talk to other people about what they see, too. I wanted to feel heard and seen in my experience, which is both unique to me and also very not unique at all. I was shocked to learn that those in my life who look like they have it all were either unhappy, stressed, anxious, or in constant fear of things falling apart. And all I could think was, *This is not normal. There must be a better way.*

My hope is, together, we can find it.

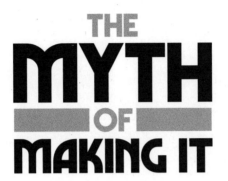

YOU CAN'T HAVE IT ALL

I am not free while any woman is unfree, even when
her shackles are very different from my own.

—Audre Lorde

The year 2015 was poised to be a great year for ambitious women: We were nearing the end of the Obama years and steadily coming out of the economic upheaval that had plagued a generation's job prospects. Sexism was being called out in Hollywood. We weren't yet at the reckoning that would come in 2018, but it was the year that many of the women who accused Bill Cosby of sexual assault came forward, with an unforgettable image on the cover of *New York* magazine—thirty-five of his accusers in black and white, looking straight at the camera, ready for justice.

The show *Younger* had just hit TV screens, starring Sutton Foster as a fortysomething stay-at-home mother named Liza Miller who, recently divorced, is preparing to get back into her career. She assumes (probably rightly) that she's aged out of entry-level jobs in the publishing industry, so she pretends to be a twentysomething to be taken seriously, and hijinks ensue. With friends' help, she gives herself a fashion-of-the-moment makeover: She dons perfectly frayed skinny jeans, ankle booties, and mixed prints, or cropped floral dresses and moto jackets. The perfect girlboss attire: casual but put together, high-low combinations, the nineties throwback but formfitting (these Laura Ashley–type dresses had *waists*).

Her work wife, Kelsey Peters—played by Hilary Duff, an actual twentysomething millennial—captured the spirit of the mid twenty-teens, embracing feminine chic tousled blond hair with an edge, skinny jeans paired with sensible blazers, and a chunky heel. She had a conventionally attractive boyfriend *and* a great career, but she could also and regularly would do shots. Miller learns quickly that this generation believes they can have it all and have it all in pink: enjoy the wins of corporate feminism and chic city life while espousing a type of traditional femininity.

The year before *Younger* premiered, Nigerian writer Chimamanda Ngozi Adichie published *We Should All Be Feminists*, a book-length essay based on a talk she had given, and Beyoncé—who had sampled Adichie's talk for her single "***Flawless"—performed at the 2014 MTV Video Music Awards, her unmistakable silhouette appearing under a white blaze of letters spelling it out: feminist. An indelible image, and it seemed like, in public and in private, more and more women were embracing the identity. Meanwhile, big tech, acting on the deep inequality rife in their companies, had started to broaden their parental leave policies. Women-owned and -led businesses were being invested in, and women entrepreneurs were encouraged to take the leap. In 2015, Elizabeth Holmes was named by *Forbes* as the youngest self-made woman billionaire. In politics, Hillary Clinton was poised to be the front-runner in the next presidential election, and Elizabeth Warren was gearing up to be her most serious opposition. (Donald Trump? He'd announced his run, but it seemed like a long shot.)

We had christened 2014 a certifiable year of women (*Time* magazine called it the best year for women "since the dawn of time"), and we were only going up from there. Adichie's *We Should All Be Feminists* joined Sophia Amoruso's *#Girlboss* on the shelves—one of many books advising women on how they might take their feminist principles to work. In a pithy review for *The New York Times,* Erin Gloria Ryan observed, "Being anti-establishment is the old cool. The new cool is playing by your own rules and still winning by their standards."

Sexism was *out;* women's ambition was *in.*

At the time, I was working at the National Women's Business Council—a federal advisory council to the Obama administration that ensured that federal money was being directed to women-owned businesses. The stats were exciting: As of 2014, 9.1 million women were running their own businesses, and that number was getting bigger every day. While women struggled to earn as much investment as their male counterparts, the "she-conomy" was growing, and lady-led, "girl power"–vibed enterprises were coming into being. The girlboss era was upon us, and we were swallowing it hook, line, and sinker.

When I think about this era, what I remember is a heady and very sincere optimism about what the future held. Even I, an often-cynical Gen Xer about the same age as Sutton Foster's character in *Younger,* was giddy about it. It felt like a time when my fellow women, femmes, and I might do anything and have anything. And if there were things we didn't have, well, that's because we'd chosen not to have them. *No partner? That's my choice! No baby? Chose that, too.*

In this period the stuffy idea of acting like a man to win in a man's world registered as blaringly outdated—in offices around the country, women were embracing a new aesthetic of femininity, born out of the belief that women would and should be recognized in the workplace. Hustling was no longer just for men in finance but also for women who worked in corporate jobs and hit that hot-yoga class in the morning—*every* morning. We were standing on the shoulders of the women who came before us, but the pantsuit was out, and frilly dresses paired with blazers were in. We were ready to work all day and all night. We had smartphones and social media and Uber and time-management software . . . and Zappos. We were literally *unstoppable.*

The Sexy Gal Who Can Have It All

It was hardly the first year, first decade, or even the first generation of women who believed that they could have it all and have it all while wearing pink. "Having it all"—these three words have had an outsized impact on how we have talked about women, work, family, and everything else for decades. The phrase itself was popularized—if not coined—by proto-girlboss Helen Gurley Brown in her 1982 book, *Having It All: Love, Success, Sex, Money—Even If You're Starting with Nothing*. At the time the book came out, Brown was sixty and famous for her long reign as editor of *Cosmopolitan* magazine (which under her tenure had been revamped into a type of work-and-play bible for young working women) and for her book *Sex and the Single Girl*, which had launched her to fame in 1962.

A slight, waiflike woman with dark hair and eyes, she often described herself as "an ugly duckling." And she aimed *Having It All* at women she termed *mouseburgers*: regular—or what she called unexceptional—women who didn't believe they could have the things that beautiful, talented women with rich husbands had. (It was a decidedly groundbreaking message at the time.)

Gurley Brown certainly had her own rags-to-riches story. She was born in 1922 in Green Forest, Arkansas, where her father was involved in local politics. He moved the family to Little Rock before dying tragically when she was ten years old. He left her mother behind to parent two children with no solid income. Devastated by the loss, her mother moved the family to Los Angeles, California. The move changed the young girl's life. As journalist Suzi Parker writes in *The Washington Post*, "Brown knew she didn't have looks on her side . . . but she had brains." In 1939, Brown graduated as valedictorian of her Los Angeles high school.

Bright and unstoppable, Brown—still Gurley at that point—skipped college but worked her way up the corporate ladder, first in secretarial jobs and then as an advertising copywriter. By early 1960, she was the highest-paid female copywriter in California. As one of her biographers, Brooke Hauser, detailed, Brown had a slew of love affairs and was unapologetic about sometimes having sex with colleagues or even the boss, if needed. One of her married bosses paid her rent for a stint, which helped her support herself, her struggling, widowed mother, and her sister, who had been paralyzed by polio.

The weaponization of her sexuality, as she saw it, was core to her self-expression and identity. As she often wrote about herself, she was not considered particularly attractive—an opinion that's repeated ad nauseam in anything written about her or her life.

Eventually, a movie producer and former managing editor of *Cosmopolitan* named David Brown, who was twice divorced and known to date starlets, ended up on her radar. After a career as a journalist, he had been hired in the early 1950s at Twentieth Century Fox to head up the story department. After Gurley asked a friend for a setup, they dated and eventually married in 1959, when she was thirty-seven. David encouraged her to pursue her passion for writing and consider publishing an advice book, so she wrote and published *Sex and the Single Girl*—her first book, twenty years prior to *Having It All*—despite not being single or really a "girl."

Sex and the Single Girl was a guidebook for unmarried working ladies on how to become financially independent and use their sexuality for that independence if needed. The book was both highly controversial and wildly successful, selling two million copies in the first three weeks of its release, and was made into a 1964 movie of the same name starring Natalie Wood. In her book, Gurley Brown said something that hadn't really been said before, astutely observing that sex outside of marriage and financial independence were fundamental parts of women's freedom. But while this sounds very much like the core of second-wave feminism, her obsession with both beauty standards and providing sexual pleasure to men led the feminists of the time to be skeptical of her work, with one journalist dubbing her brand of women's empowerment "deep-cleavage feminism."

But, as the feminist historian Jennifer Scanlon notes, Gurley Brown spoke to the women who the more elite feminists perhaps didn't reach: working-class, pink-collar women without college degrees. When questioned about the cultural significance of her work, Gurley Brown retorted in a 1963 interview with *Playboy* magazine, "Well, it's just because nobody ever got off his high horse long enough to write to single women in any form they could associate with."

Indeed, outside their roles as wives and mothers, it was rare for women then to be addressed at all by books that attempted to wrestle with the challenges (as well as the delights) of their lives. Betty Friedan's *The Feminine Mystique* came out in 1963, just a year after *Sex and the Single Girl*. *The Feminine Mystique* would be a landmark book, no question, but one deeply symbolic of a split that was happening in feminism at the time, around women and work—especially for women of color and working-class women. While Gurley Brown's idea of "having it all" focused on career and sex, Friedan offered another insight: Turns out many women who gave up their careers to focus on family instead were *miserable*. These insights were not in opposition so much as speaking to two different classes of women. While the expression "having it all" wasn't yet in popular usage in the 1960s, conversations about women, work, and family were ratcheting up in earnest. The questions of what it meant to have "it all" and who gets to have "it" were yet to be answered.

. . .

Two decades after *Sex and the Single Girl* and *The Feminine Mystique* came out, Brown published *Having It All*. In her thirty-year reign at *Cosmopolitan*, she had made *Cosmo* a brand synonymous with women's sexuality (and inducing male pleasure), birthing the "Cosmo girl." But that young woman was suddenly facing a new set of conundrums that came with the eighties: more sexual freedoms but also a backlash against the wins of feminism.

Having It All reads like a parody today. A sampling of sections includes "Virtually everybody has to diet, so stop thinking you're special" (complete with a tuna fish salad recipe) and "You Got Some Color!" admonishing the presumably all-white readers about the hazards of sunbathing and premature aging. In the chapter on sex, she has a section called "The Specialty," writing that, while a man should never leave you unsatisfied, "it's not a bad little specialty to have—bringing a man inexorably to climax—and I'd like to encourage you to have it," boasting about her skills as a fellatio queen.

True to its title, the book literally had it *all*—and, like her previous work, was impressively sex positive, even if a lot of it reads as stubbornly regressive today. She was also playing with a pop-culture feminism, merging feminism and capitalism in a way that would continue for the next three decades. Yesterday's tuna fish salad recipe and beauty tricks became today's keto diet and hot-yoga classes.

The irony, of course, is that today "having it all" means balancing a career, a relationship, a personal life, and motherhood, but *Having It All* was not about having kids and a career. Brown didn't have children, and her writing and interviews seem almost hostile toward the idea of motherhood. Judith Thurman wrote that, while Brown was sympathetic to single mothers—especially because she saw firsthand how her mother struggled as one—she "alienated subscribers with her frank animus towards motherhood, which she equated with drudgery, and towards pregnancy, which made you fat."

Despite this, the slogan "having it all" was pitched as a feminist rallying cry, but if anything, it was a strategy to make feminism impossible by muzzling ambitious women with the threat that they would be seen as bad mothers. The ideal woman was no longer just a great wife and mother or a career woman; she had to be both, and exceptional at both, while being a fit, beautiful sex goddess. She had to be the superwoman—a mythical creature, a fantasy comic-book character who could overcome adversity with the right day planner and Tupperware set. It also shaped the public perception of feminism as a culture war between women who supposedly wanted only to be career women and those who wanted only to be moms, rather than a movement deeply rooted in material considerations.

But as much as "having it all" has come to stand in for the problems faced by mostly white-collar working moms, according to *The New York Times,* Brown never actually wanted it to be the title of her book. In a letter to her editor, quoted in the *Times,* she wrote, "I've always visualized this as a book for the downtrodden, a book by a near loser who got to be a winner, instead of somebody who sounds—based on the title—like a smartass all-the-time winner from the beginning."

Still, this style of "feminism" laid the groundwork for a defanged workplace politics that moved away from the quest for structural equality and justice and asked women to fetishize gender inequality as something you could overcome with quirky personality traits, disarming oppressive men with a twinkle of the eye and a touch on the arm. As broad as the book's reach was, women, even at that time, felt conflicted about Brown's message—especially feminists.

In a 1982 *Washington Post* feature on Brown, Carol Krucoff notes that the contents of her book are no longer in vogue, as women were trying to get away from the myth of the superwoman. Gloria Steinem tells Krucoff, "I appreciate her as a pioneer, she was the first woman editor of a woman's magazine, and *Cosmo* admitted women could be sexual beings . . . but she's fooling herself if she thinks her message is a feminist one." After following Brown around for a day, Krucoff concludes, "underneath her obsession with male approval, Brown is a bright, complex woman trying to blend traditional ideas of femininity with modern, liberated reality."

Brown's book resonated during a period in which women wanted to embrace the hard-fought wins of the feminist movement at home and in the workplace . . . but they didn't want to be perceived as sexless, anti-man, or politically rigid while doing so. Moira Weigel writes at the *Times,* "She offered a blueprint for success in a sexist world, telling readers how to game a system that was set up to exploit them."

Two Women, One America

It was instead Friedan's *The Feminine Mystique* that set the tone for what the mainstream American feminist movement of the sixties and seventies would be focused on: releasing the housewife from the oppression of the nuclear family and encouraging her to join the workforce. Friedan famously called it "the problem that has no name": that women in American society were largely miserable in their role as wives and mothers. She writes, "As she made the beds, shopped for groceries, matched slipcover material, ate peanut butter sandwiches with her children, chauffeured Cub Scouts and Brownies, lay beside her husband at night—she was afraid to ask even of herself the silent question—'Is this all?'"

The way we talk about women and work is rooted in the postwar nation-building projects of the second half of the past century. Middle-class women played a key role in the development of the nation's economy through unpaid labor and childbirth so that men could focus on accruing wealth. This was at least true for predominantly white families in the middle of the past century, but it also became the blueprint for all American families: a working father, stay-at-home mother, two or more children. Anything that deviated from this model was labeled "broken" or antithetical to American values—including divorce, single-parenting, poverty, being childless, or having too many children. Marketing strategies and economic textbooks alike furthered the idea of the family as an economic unit replete with Oreo cookies, family vacations, and two-car garages as essential must-haves for modern life. What was pushed as a cultural and gendered expectation—the stay-at-home wife—was an economic imperative, one where families became products *and* consumers.

The middle-class nuclear family, a concept that dates back thousands of years but was added to the dictionary in the 1920s, would be the pinnacle of what is considered a successful life in the modern United States. As a society, in the middle of the past century, we moved from a family structure that included extended relatives to one that narrowed down to parents and children, which had profound implications, especially around labor and care work.

That pressure to maintain a "traditional" family structure continues today. For example, a 2011 report sponsored by the right-leaning group National Marriage Project asserts that the "long-term fortunes of the modern economy rise and fall with the family"—meaning two straight parents in a married household with children. But despite being a long-standing conservative talking point, there is debate about the role of the nuclear family in organizing our culture and economy. Columnist David Brooks writes in *The Atlantic* that the move from an extended family to a nuclear family "ultimately led to a familial system that liberates the rich and ravages the working-class and the poor."

The hegemony of the idea of a nuclear family as the standard to which we would be held remained in place, despite the form successfully existing for only fifteen years, as Brooks points out.

It was this pressure that Friedan was responding to. Her research for *The Feminine Mystique* had started a few years before its publication, during her fifteen-year class reunion at Smith College in 1957. She learned from talking to the women who had graduated with her that many of them were dissatisfied with their lives. Women who were initially afraid that their college degrees would prohibit them from success in marriage and family were instead frustrated by the push into domesticity. Her inquiry birthed a movement, and the discussion around women in the workplace became less about necessity and more about the yearning of educated women stuck at home.

Of course, housework is also work. As feminist scholar Silvia Federici has long argued, women's unpaid domestic work—caretaking and child-rearing—is the invisible labor upon which capital accumulation has been built. She writes in *Caliban and the Witch* that despite this devaluation, "women have been the producers and reproducers of the most essential capitalist commodity: labor-power." And if women were going to stop performing this type of labor at home, their husbands would have to pick up the slack . . . and most of them were unwilling to do so.

And so, if middle-class women were going to enter the workforce, poorer women—often women of color, who had already been working "out of the home" but perhaps would have welcomed the opportunity to stay home and look after their own families—entered white-collar working women's homes as domestic care workers, from housekeepers to nannies. Feminist progress for white women created an underbelly economy for working-class women and women of color who would start to do the majority of their care work. The labor that was assumed to be a housewife's duty was simply outsourced to other women.

Most women have always labored, even though that experience hasn't informed the dominant discourse on women and work. Care work, child-rearing, and household maintenance are labor; enslaved people were forced to work, and poor and many middle-class women had to work. Most women never had the luxury of simply staying home and taking care of their children—even if many of them would have loved to. Historian Alice Kessler-Harris writes in *Women Have Always Worked* that to suggest that housework and childcare are unpaid support work ignores their value. "To describe women's work as incidental or a matter of choice ignores the history of women's consistent need to earn incomes, and the role of work in shaping expectations and the aspirations of women as well as men," she writes.

Of course, our entire economic system in the United States was built on the unpaid labor of enslaved people. While wealthier white women first demanded entry into the workplace in the mid-nineteenth century, Black women didn't have the same option, because, having been forced into chattel slavery, their labor was both mandatory and unpaid. Under slavery, Black women were tasked with working inside the house and in the field. As Angela Davis has written, Black feminists' priorities did not include getting out of the house to work, because they had almost always had to work. In fact, Michelle Wallace points out, the myth of the superwoman means something different for Black women, who are expected to be of "inordinate strength, with an ability for tolerating an unusual amount of misery and heavy, distasteful work. This woman does not have the same fears, weaknesses, and insecurities as other women, but believes herself to be and is, in fact, stronger emotionally than most men."

Instead, Black women's feminism was fighting for an end to race-based and economic terrorism in their communities, among other issues. It is well documented that American suffragists made the choice to exclude Black women's right to vote, because they saw the opposition to it as a matter of race and not of gender, but what is less known is that, within that movement, there was always a divide between working-class women and middle-class women as well. As bell hooks writes, "From the onset, reformist white women with class privilege were well aware that the power and freedom they wanted was the freedom they perceived men of their class enjoying."

In 2018, Kimberly Seals Allers wrote in *Slate* about the contemporary goals of work/life balance,

> Simply put, the labor of Black, Hispanic, and Asian American women has raised white women's standard of living . . . there was a time when the only work options available to women of color were doing the work that white women of means did not want to do. White women needed us and we needed them. So we breastfed your babies. We raised your children. We cleaned your houses. We did your laundry. We cooked your food.

While the feminists of Friedan's time were largely criticized for this schism, it's worth noting that, in her youth, Friedan was a Marxist (and even attempted to join the Communist Party) and had worked as a labor journalist after her time at Smith College and later at the University of California, Berkeley. In 1966, she founded the National Organization for Women, which campaigned for equal rights, access to abortion, and fair pay, and was also heavily rooted in labor politics. But throughout her time at NOW, she made a strategic decision to focus on recruiting elite straight white women in an appeal to the center, which alienated some Black and brown feminists from the organization.

The Feminine Mystique is regularly regarded as one of the foundational texts for second-wave feminism, but it was Friedan's legacy of
speaking to affluent white women that led bell hooks, in her 1984 book
Feminist Theory: From Margin to Center, to begin with a dissection of
this long-heralded classic: "She made her plight and the plight of white
women like herself synonymous with a condition affecting all American women."

American feminism splintered, as a tale of two women in the modern era emerged: the working woman and the comparatively more
affluent, most likely stay-at-home, woman. Both women worked, whether
inside the house or outside of the house, but they played different roles
in the economy and the public imagination. Whereas Gurley Brown's
woman was single and trying to manage a career and a love life, these
women were trying to be great at being either a career woman or a parent. There was no having it all. Not yet, anyway.

Working Women Were Always Doing It All

In the end, the 1980s were largely defined by the regressive economic
policies of the Reagan administration. It was a disastrous decade for
women of color (and Black women in particular), for working women
in general, and especially for working mothers. Women were still making much less than men on average, they were virtually absent from
boardrooms, and they were often relegated to or pushed into "feminine" jobs such as retail, fast food, teaching, nursing, and social work;
all while Reagan was cutting much-needed social services for poor
Americans—especially poor women, Black women and women of
color, and single mothers.

After reading Brown's book, I couldn't help but consider how my
mother might have engaged with Brown's manifesto had she read it.
(She hadn't even heard of it, and I can guarantee she would have been
shocked by its contents.) My mother was born the youngest daughter
in a middle-class Brahmin family in the suburbs of Kolkata in the In-

dian state of West Bengal. Her father was a college professor who became a school inspector and relocated the family to Darjeeling in the
north of India. Her mother was a certified midwife and volunteered
for the Red Cross. They had three boys and one girl before my mom.
My mother was a talented musician and eventually went to college in
Kolkata to study music. In 1973, she and my father were wed in an arranged marriage, with the hope that she would continue her education
and become an accomplished musician and singer. She never thought
she would have to get a job outside of singing and being a housewife.
When she immigrated to the United States in 1974 with my father at
the age of twenty-three, she was hit by a cold reality: She would have
to find work. She told me that, for their first wedding anniversary, my
father bought her a typing manual so she could get a clerical job, which
was *not* what she had signed up for.

By the time Brown's book came out in 1982, my mother was raising
two small children, working full time as a bank teller, sending money
to India, helping my father build his business, managing the schedules
and concerns of various family members who were coming in from
India to stay with us, and maintaining a very vibrant social life—
including leading the choir at our Upper East Side temple.

My family was eking their way into the middle-class at the time, but
she—along with many, many women like her—was emphatically left
out of the bigger conversation about what "having it all" meant for most
working women. Most of them were just trying to make ends meet.

Working women were, in fact, always doing "it all"—because they
had to. According to the Bureau of Labor Statistics, as of 1980, 52 percent of women were in the workforce, a number that increased to 58
percent in 1990 and 60 percent in 2000. Black women have always had
higher rates of workplace participation. The Center for American
Progress observed that, as of 2017, "Black women's labor force participation rate was 60.3 percent, compared with roughly 56 percent for
white women, Asian American women, and Latinas." (Since February
2023, the labor force participation rate of women between the ages of
twenty-five and fifty-four has reached a historic high: 77.8 percent.)

These women are rarely touted as "having it all," even though many of them have successfully done it all—work, raise kids, go to college, and have a relationship or relationships—while suffering from higher rates of poverty, a lack of resources, and an even more extreme wage gap compared to white women. Add to this that women of color are often doing the work that allows white women to "have it all."

The factors that lead to lower wages for women vary but include a confluence of sexism, racism, classism, age, ability, and education. What underpins such low wages for women in general, however, is a false belief that women's work isn't valuable (or should be free) and the continuing myth that women don't need to work to support themselves and their families the way men do, but rather choose to work out of a desire for fulfillment—and, by doing so, create an impossible situation for themselves.

The fault lines that Brown perhaps indirectly uncovered in the 1960s largely remained unchanged by the eighties, even if the precise terms of the fight had changed. Feminism lite (of which Brown was hardly the only purveyor) was bubbling up at the same time that a war against some of the feminist movement's biggest wins of the previous decade was beginning. As Susan Faludi asked in her 1991 book, *Backlash*, which details the different ways Americans were sold a false bill of goods on women's liberation, "If women 'have it all,' then why don't they have the most basic requirements to achieve equality in the workforce?"

In her book, Faludi argues that, while the press decided women had won the battle for equality, it also claimed that this was why women were so miserable. She writes, "They hold the campaign for women's equality responsible for nearly every woe besetting women, from mental depression to meager savings accounts, from teenage suicides to eating disorders to bad complexions."

Generation Anita

By the time I went to college in 1996, there was a new wave of feminism that was both markedly antiestablishment and considered largely frivolous (as we—late Gen Xers and early millennials—were seen as unserious by many older feminists). While popular culture was grap-pling with the gains of feminism, *Time* magazine was criticizing the state of the movement. But these aren't the only cultural touchstones that define a given moment. In her 2020 book *They Didn't See Us Coming: The Hidden History of Feminism in the Nineties*, Lisa Levenstein writes, "As nineties feminism became ever more diversified and ubiq-uitous, much of the movement became almost wholly invisible to the public . . . few people in the 1990s understood who most feminists were or what they were doing."

They were us. The nineties were teeming with alternative-subculture babies: slackers and hackers, riot grrrls and b-girls. Our feminism was born of a skeptical distrust of institutions, from marriage to corporate workplaces. We were not the generation of "having it all"; we were the generation of making our choices.

When I eventually ended up a women's studies major, discussions of feminism in the larger world were predicated on the right-wing back-lash of the 1980s—but academia was interested in its own battles and in a postcolonial, postmodern feminism. Academic feminism was, at that time, going through a long-overdue shift in the understanding of the idea of *woman* toward a varied conception of womanhood, based on a slew of differing identities and genders. A new generation of fem-inists was fighting against both the patriarchy and the version of wom-en's liberation that had been popularized—that of mostly privileged white women. There was a recognition that the systems that we hoped to game could no longer serve us.

We were also the generation that watched the incredibly successful and poised Anita Hill humiliated in front of the Senate Judiciary Com-mittee and disbelieved in public about Clarence Thomas's alleged un-wanted sexual advances in the workplace. If there is an image that defines a generation, it's the one of Hill with her hand raised high as she was sworn in before her testimony in front of the committee (as the image of Christine Blasey Ford testifying is likely to be for the teens coming up today). Hill wore a tailored turquoise suit dress with gold button details and minimal gold jewelry. Her lips had a lightly stained berry gloss, and her hair was perfectly coiffed. Her face was calm.

Everything about her felt measured—she was the epitome of a professional woman working in a conservative profession (law).

Hill became the face of the modern working woman and all the
obstacles she faces, whether she wanted to or not. She hailed from
Oklahoma, where her parents had been farmers, and her grandfather
and great grandparents had been born into slavery. She was the youngest of thirteen children. Her parents raised her as a Baptist. She was
always studious, eventually becoming the valedictorian of her high
school. She made her way to the University of Oklahoma, where she
studied psychology. In 1980, she headed to Yale Law School and, upon
graduation, began her law career in D.C. Talented and precise, she first
worked with Clarence Thomas at the U.S. Department of Education's
Office for Civil Rights, where he had been an assistant secretary. In
1982, he became the chairman of the U.S. Equal Employment Opportunity Commission, where Hill worked as his assistant. She had dreamed
of working on civil rights. But her career as a lawyer was cut short
when, in 1983, she quit after being hospitalized for what she later said
were "stress-related stomach pains." Instead, she became a professor,
first at Oral Roberts University in Tulsa and later at the University of
Oklahoma College of Law, where she remained for ten years before
Thomas's nomination to the Supreme Court.

In 1991, when Thomas was nominated by then President George H. W.
Bush, Hill came forward with her story. She said that Thomas regularly
asked her out despite her lack of interest and refusals. When she would
not see him outside of work, he turned to lewd comments in the office,
describing graphic sex acts and pornography he had watched, and
speaking of his own "sexual prowess."

She was invited to testify before the Senate Committee on the Judiciary, where she was mocked, humiliated, and disbelieved. Senator
Orrin Hatch suggested that her testimony was politically motivated
and bolstered by "slick lawyers." She was questioned about why she
followed Thomas to another job (she responded that she thought the
sexual advances would stop) and about the accuracy of her testimony,
given how many years had elapsed.

Thomas further politicized the moment by claiming he was the victim of a "high-tech lynching" by white liberals who were afraid of what his tenure on the courts would mean.

Hill's courage and the corresponding response from political leaders became a clarion call for feminists at the time to push back against the idea that women should just endure the harassment they experience in the workplace. A year later, public opinion turned in her favor. As Rebecca Traister writes in *All the Single Ladies,* by the early nineties she was no longer being pushed out of the public sphere; instead, "a generation of women was, like Hill, living, working, and occupying public space on its own."

In contrast to the fantastical *Sex and the Single Girl* woman of the sixties and seventies, Hill embodied the real obstacles facing working women. Dare to enter the men's chambers, suffer the consequences of their unwanted sexual advances. Also, Hill, as a Black woman, did not have access to those same narratives of sexuality and power that someone like Gurley Brown may have had, especially in the workplace. Instead, Black women are routinely sexualized or disbelieved when they come forward with stories of harassment or sexual abuse—even when they are presented in the most respectable possible way. Hill was the perfect victim. In addition to her impeccable appearance, she was soft-spoken, she played by the rules, and she was a manifestation of the type of professionalism that women were told would be able to overcome obstacles like sexism and racism. Hill was the American dream.

Conversely, Gurley Brown had widely espoused the idea that any sexual advance toward a woman from a man was a compliment—experiences like Hill's visibly proved that Gurley Brown was wrong and a new generation wasn't having that shit. Donning our "I Believe Anita Hill" Sonic Youth T-shirts, we were reading *To Be Real,* a book of essays edited by the activist and writer Rebecca Walker, Alice Walker's daughter, and diligently attending Eve Ensler's *The Vagina Monologues.* Hill's humiliation felt like an attack on all of us. Young feminists were firmly of the belief that we should not have to sleep our way to the top and that, when we were sexually harassed in the workplace, the perpetrator should be held accountable.

But while there was a vibrant feminist subculture—through music and poetry, riot grrl, and hip-hop—the covers of magazines were still celebrating our demise. Anita Hill was but one example of how the modern working woman and the progress she represented was considered a joke. On a 1998 cover of *Time* magazine, three faces were shown in black-and-white cutouts—Susan B. Anthony, Betty Friedan, and Gloria Steinem—next to a color photograph of the actor Calista Flockhart. Under her image, readers were asked in bold red letters, "Is feminism dead?"

At the time, Flockhart was known for being the lead in the newest legal drama, *Ally McBeal.* The show was supposed to be a fresh new take on the workplace, complete with genderless bathrooms, and its hot mess of a main character was ostensibly the newest face of feminism. *Ally McBeal,* which ran five seasons, closed out the nineties with a lead who was a messy accidental career woman (having followed her boyfriend to Harvard law) and was so fixated on finding love in her life that she was caught up in sexy or baby-focused daydreams all the time and could never really focus on work, which she mostly managed to be pretty good at (Gurley Brown's dream realized). Her anxieties about love, sex, and marriage dominated the dialogue, and it was hard to keep track of what she was saying out loud and what was going on in her head.

Its pop feminism was perfect for getting the older feminists angry. Ginia Bellafante—who, frustrated by the show and its characters, wrote the infamous *Time* cover story—called the show "it's all about me" feminism, arguing that it reduced serious concerns to self-absorbed musings that distract from the bigger fight for women's equality. Her critique feels harsh and dated considering all the ways feminism would make its way into popular culture, but watching *Ally McBeal* today, it's hard to parse how much was a backlash to feminism and how much was the mostly male writers and network TV executives trying to grapple with new, feminist characters. But Bellafante and the feminists she interviewed then were not convinced of the latter explanation. "It's easy to dismiss the voices of Old Guard feminists as the typical complaints of leaders nostalgic for their days at center stage," she writes. "But is *Ally McBeal* really progress? Maybe if she lost her job and wound up a single mom, we could begin a movement again."

By the time I graduated from college in 2000—three years after *Ally McBeal* premiered—it was understood that, if you went to college, your next step was to find yourself and to figure out what career to pursue, at least for a certain set of women. Partners would come later; the priority was exploring your dreams, whether that meant figuring out what job you wanted or which grad school to go to or how to join the Peace Corps, finally spending that year backpacking in Europe, etc. The next step was not getting married and settling down—not for single, educated city girls. We had our thirties for that.

Still, when I graduated with that women's studies degree, I was qualified for nary a job. So, I joined AmeriCorps and worked in underserved public schools. Later, I'd do a short stint on Pete Seeger's boat on the Hudson teaching inner-city youth about the history of our mighty river—a type of experience that wasn't uncommon among my cohort, because "finding yourself" had become the postgraduation norm. We were the first graduating class of the new millennium, and I had no idea what I wanted to do with my life; I just knew I needed to get a job, and that one day, that job would have to turn into a career. Looking back, I was on a career path that had only just emerged: I was in the same cohort as the new generation of "professional feminists" that Levenstein details in *They Didn't See Us Coming*. The work we were doing, both in academia and in nonprofit and organizing spaces, was laying the groundwork for feminism to enter multiple domains, from social movements to nonprofits to the corporate sphere. Connections that feel obvious today—like *of course* feminism should be considered in the fight against climate change—were normalized in progressive and feminist work then (and, of course, building on the work of the women-of-color feminists of the sixties and seventies, but later for that).

We were also making different choices because of the newfound freedoms of feminism—we marry when we want to, not when society tells us to. And the idea of having children young became almost absurd: Sure, you could have it all, just not at the same time and certainly not in that economy. I didn't fully realize until later in life that we were also telling ourselves another "having it all" story, just a delayed one. Having children was sold to us as exceedingly difficult without two solid incomes, which was both true in a technical sense, given the economic insecurities most people face now, and a way of using the stories of poor people to scare us. (Many of us had also internalized the message that it was incumbent upon us not to get pregnant "too young," or else we would be deemed irresponsible about sex and contraception.) Our negative perception of settling down or having children too young was a result of the demonization of both poor, young, often Black or Latine mothers, and motherhood in general, in the eighties and nineties. (Lest we forget, Reagan may have laid the groundwork for the vilification of "welfare queens," but it was former president Bill Clinton who signed the Personal Responsibility and Work Opportunity Act of 1996, effectively pushing single mothers off much-needed financial assistance.)

These narratives deeply impacted the decisions we made and, even while we recognized that these cautionary tales were racist and sexist, they still dominated our sense of selves as young women of color. My friend Syreeta, who is now in her late forties, told me that being one of the only people in her family to leave her working-class hometown of Milwaukee to attend Columbia University made her believe that she could "have it all" but do it differently—as in, have both a career and a family. "Everyone around me was having kids young, and I knew I wanted to go to college and do all that stuff later," she told me.

For a 2002 study, published by the *Harvard Business Review*, the economist Sylvia Ann Hewlett surveyed educated women in two middle- and higher-income brackets who were not having children. In interviews, she found that those women wanted to have children but found it very hard to navigate, both because of the pressure from the office and because their partners didn't pull enough weight at home. So they were, at that point, postponing getting pregnant.

In her summary, Hewlett wrote, "In the words of one senior manager, the typical high-achieving woman childless at midlife has not made a choice but a 'creeping nonchoice.'" The idea of prioritizing your career over having children is still a reality for working women twenty years later. Consider the popularization of egg- and embryo-freezing, lest their eggs "going bad" be a reason women defer career advancement.

"Having it all" was never about women actually having it all, and it was never about women having choices. It instead became a way to make women feel culpable for the choices they made, rather than helping them decide among the choices that were available to them. And the result was a lot of women who never felt like they could keep up, or who felt like failures because they weren't great at everything they touched.

Despite being about the experiences of a narrow, privileged segment of the population—the few women who choose to work but don't economically need to—the "having it all" debates have defined how we talk about women and work in the media for decades. This conversation has left most working women and working mothers high and dry, because it rests on a narrative that fails to reckon with the real factors that women are up against at work: sex discrimination, harassment, low pay, being locked out of senior management, or being pushed into lower-paying pink-collar jobs.

A movement that had the potential to unify women across class and race and geography was instead reduced to a fitness routine and a lunch on the go. This became very clear in the years that followed: Workplace feminism shifted from a philosophy that demanded the eradication of oppressive systems to one that was trying to work within the system.

Of course, one of those kinds of feminism was more acceptable to the mainstream than the other.

2

TRICKLE-DOWN FEMINISM

Some women being empowered does not prove the patriarchy
is dead. It proves that some of us are lucky.

—Roxane Gay

When Sheryl Sandberg started at Facebook in 2008, the company was four years old and had already taken the market by storm as a major player in social media. At thirty-eight, she walked into the belly of Silicon Valley's male-dominated world of start-up tech. Mark Zuckerberg, who was twenty-three when Sandberg joined the company, told *The New Yorker* in 2011 that, after a series of meetings, he knew Sandberg would be a "perfect fit."

"There are people who are really good managers, people who can manage a big organization," he told Ken Auletta. "And then there are people who are very analytic or focused on strategy. Those two types don't usually tend to be in the same person."

In 2008, Facebook had only just barely become a platform for people other than college students to connect with their friends and family. You could write on people's "walls," send them messages, and "poke" people. (Who can forget that weird function we have collectively decided to pretend never happened?) It wouldn't be until 2009 that you could post to the wider public—those people whom you weren't "friends" with on the platform. Facebook wasn't the first social media platform where you could connect with people and send them messages or write on their walls; Friendster, MySpace, and LiveJournal were there first. But Facebook was the most enterprising—the first to bring a level of uniformity to the look of people's profiles and provide a very easy-to-use interface.

And our moms loved it.

To users, Facebook became about community, friendship, and reconnecting with people that you probably never would have otherwise. It took us from an era where you had only an IRL circle of friends to one where you had a virtual network. People were writing poems and essays about how much they loved the connections that Facebook was bringing to their lives—rekindling old flames, reuniting long-lost friends, bringing together families across geographies. How could something that Auntie Uma was using possibly be a nefarious technology?

The soft, dewy entry of Facebook into our lives brought with it a couple of things: the normalization of social media as a way to express ourselves and connect with people, first in our personal lives and soon in our professional; and the rise of the rock star tech entrepreneur who brought this new "social economy" to our computers and mobile phones.

Within three years of Sandberg joining as the chief operating officer, Facebook became profitable. Sandberg was born in Washington, D.C., to upper-middle-class parents and grew up in North Miami Beach. She was a good student, ending up at Harvard. She started her career in 1996 interning at the World Bank for her mentor Larry Summers (who infamously said the lack of representation of women in the sciences was due to biological differences in ability), working on social issues like the spread of HIV in India. He had been her advisor for her undergraduate thesis, which was about the role economic inequality plays in domestic violence. Later, she earned her MBA at Harvard Business School, and after graduating, she wanted to make a difference, but ended up working in management consulting at McKinsey.

In 2001, she joined the advertising team at Google. Sandberg excelled at scaling business: She took Google's ad-and-sales team from four to thousands after building their two most lucrative programs, AdWords and AdSense, which, according to *The New York Times,* accounted for a sizable chunk of Google's $16 billion–plus revenue in 2007. After she'd had several meetings with Zuckerberg, he convinced her to come join the team at Facebook and do the same thing there. And grow they did—beyond what anyone could have imagined a social media entity could become.

In making Facebook one of the largest and most profitable social media companies in the world, Sandberg also became one of the first recognizable female tech leaders, the model for "she can do it and so can you" in both that industry and the larger corporate world. She became cited as evidence that the playing field was now level and women could overcome any barrier. She was polished, feminine, married, a mother, *and* a cutthroat businesswoman. What better person to redefine what women are capable of in their careers?

Sandberg's energy took the company by storm: She surveyed her colleagues, making sure she wasn't spending all her time in the C-suite. She was committed to giving younger employees face time with senior management (something she'd done in jobs before). She hadn't yet laid claim to the mantle of feminist but had identified what she believed was holding women back in the workplace. In a 2010 TED talk, she walked the stage in five-inch stilettos, her signature blown-out brown bob, and a tailored peplum top cut just low enough to avoid being stuffy without being inappropriate. She told the crowd that we have more opportunities than the women who came before us, but "we still have a problem. Women are still not making it to the top of any profession."

Then, in 2013, she wrote a book sharing her own experience of climbing the corporate ladder and what she learned from it—a book that kicked off another decade of debates around whether women could have it all or not: *Lean In: Women, Work, and the Will to Lead.* The book has nary a tuna salad recipe in sight; it does, however, feature Sandberg on the cover smiling with her brown bob, minimalist jewelry, and a soft, white V-neck sweater. She, like the message she was proselytizing, was intended to look modern but *accessible.*

And Sandberg's manifesto felt as friendly as Facebook itself felt in 2013. She acknowledges at the book's very beginning that the idea of "having it all" is a myth, calling it "the greatest trap ever set for women." She continues, "Because no matter what any of us has—and how grateful we are for what we have—no one has it all." But her public persona, her well-buffed appearance, and her wealth belied this admission. This was a woman who clearly had it all—or at least most things any working woman would ever want. And, whether she intended it or not, "leaning in" became a shorthand for a path to "having it all."

We Could All Be Feminists

In 2009, at a bar in Austin during the South by Southwest Interactive Conference, I started chatting with a young woman who was interested in what the conference was about. I was there to talk about my work at the blog *Feministing;* back then, conferences were inundated with panels about the lack of women in various fields, especially in tech. When she asked me what I did for a living, I told her with embarrassing earnestness that I was a "professional feminist." She made a face and got uncomfortable and spat out, "Oh my God, are you, like, a lesbian or something?" I was perplexed and said, "Well, not *exactly,* but . . . there's nothing wrong with being a lesbian?" It was an odd thing to hear; I thought that surely this woman knew feminism was not a synonym for lesbianism.

For decades, calling yourself a feminist made you a punch line at best, and reviled and castigated as a "femi-Nazi" at worst. But by the 2010s, it felt like more and more women were embracing the mantle of feminism in a way that hadn't been seen since the seventies.

Female celebrities, who had long dodged the "Are you a feminist?" question, started donning the identity—from Katy Perry to Emma Watson to Taylor Swift. With that came the increased prominence of feminist activists such as Malala Yousafzai, Tarana Burke, and a slew of youth activists like Greta Thunberg, X González, and so many others.

Feminists also showed up as a core constituency during Hillary Clinton's 2016 presidential run, which is why the reaction to Clinton's loss and Trump's ascendance came to a head with the Women's March in 2017, the largest gathering of women in American history. It was rooted in a kind of women's rage and openly cloaked in feminist symbology, like the now infamous pink pussy hats. (Incidentally, Merriam-Webster's 2017 word of the year was *feminism*.)

Seven years have passed since then, and I can still remember vividly the clash of feelings at the time. There was real rage, real sorrow—and a real feeling of momentum, too. I had spent so many years watching people slide away from me at the very use of the word *feminist,* and there it was being embraced by women from all over the country. And not only were they using it but they were also actively engaging in feminist organizing. It felt like forward momentum. *Now regular women were embracing it! Pussy hats? Surely, this is good for the movement!*

But the popularization of any movement can also lead to the dilution of its messaging and aims. It's not that any of these women weren't feminists or weren't allowed to call themselves feminists if they didn't understand or embrace certain aspects of the larger organized movement. Women, young and old, have collectively endured decades of sexism in politics, education, business, Hollywood, and the music industry, to name just a few domains. And feminism is and should be open enough to include women who are new to it or don't appear to fit the mold of a long-term committed feminist. What is the point, otherwise?

But while feminism was being absorbed by the mainstream culture—politically and economically—it was also being repackaged to be more accessible. Soon after it was more widely embraced by political and cultural icons, a movement that aimed to measurably make women's lives better turned into an identity marker—a vague Instagram post about women, a T-shirt, a media opportunity—and a marker that was sometimes divorced from the political and cultural aims of the movement itself.

Whatever it was, it seemed like, if a woman was doing it, that thing was considered feminist—especially if women were doing it in traditionally male power structures. The pantsuit feminism of the 1980s, with its shoulder pads and briefcases that encouraged women to "act like men" to get ahead at work (but not too much like men, lest they stop being sexy!), was replaced with a new, more feminine aesthetic: power suits with a girl-power edge.

Reagan had embedded the seeds for what an individualistic society should look like, and as our social safety nets began to unravel and the country's economic system moved more and more toward neoliberalism, so did our feminism. In response to this trend in feminism and the role *Lean In* played in it, the scholar Catherine Rottenberg writes, "The neoliberal feminist subject is thus mobilized to convert continued gender inequality from a structural problem into an individual affair." Similarly, in a devastating review of Sandberg's manifesto, Susan Faludi writes, "The movement originally forged to move the great mass of women has been hijacked to serve the individual (and privileged) girl." To many, *Lean In* was ultimately less a feminist manifesto than a symbol of the corporatization of feminism.

Neoliberalism (to define a term that itself is often divorced from its original context) is an individualistic understanding of traditionally liberal ideals, filtered through a dogged faith in the healing power of capitalism. Adherents posit an Adam Smith–like vision of rational actors who believe capitalism is a fundamentally fair system in which all people are producers and consumers, subject to the ebbs and flows of what its defenders believe is the evenhanded, unrestricted marketplace. Competition, they believe, will lead to rational and equitable ends, because actors will act in their best self-interest, which is also in the interest of the greater good.

However, not all actors are rational, and neoliberalism in action has simply valued people by how much they can work, how much they can earn for that work, and how much of that money they can spend, while self-interested business owners have consolidated their wealth by relying on legacy and other people's labor. As environmental activist and writer George Monbiot writes in *The Guardian,* "Neoliberalism sees competition as the defining characteristic of human relations. It redefines citizens as consumers, whose democratic choices are best exercised by buying and selling, a process that rewards merit and punishes inefficiency."

Some philosophers argue that neoliberalism has infiltrated our political systems and culture, a theory that French philosopher Michel Foucault was the first to deeply investigate. The philosopher Wendy Brown writes, "Neoliberal rationality disseminates the *model of the market* to all domains and activities—even where money is not at issue—and configures human beings exhaustively as market actors, always, only, and everywhere."

A neoliberal narrative of professional development is extremely compelling, because who wants the disempowering narrative that you can't control your own financial destiny? Neoliberal capitalism engenders the belief that if you dream it, you can have it, and that there's nothing a little hard work can't get you—and that there is no need to give too much consideration to cultural, institutional, or financial barriers that mean some people can work the same amount but be rewarded differently.

For all that conservatives like to scream about the "rise of socialism," the reality is that most liberal Democrats (who also regularly espouse their belief in the superiority of the capitalist system) are best thought of as neoliberal, or traditional liberals with a strong belief in the power of individualism.

And so, now, are most mainstream—call them "girl-power"— feminists.

The popularization of "girl power" coincided with a broader appetite for a type of accessible, less threatening feminism. (In fact, *girl power* was first used in a feminist zine from nineties riot grrrl band

Bikini Kill, before the Spice Girls brought it to the mainstream.) Andi Zeisler, a writer and cofounder of *Bitch* magazine, calls this "marketplace feminism"—or "branding feminism as an identity that everyone can and should consume." In her book *We Were All Feminists Once,* she writes, "It kicks the least sensational and most complex issues under a rug and assures them that we'll get back to them once everybody's on board."

Part and parcel of the concept of "marketplace feminism" is the idea of individual choice—if a woman chooses something, whatever that thing may be, it is feminist, because feminism is about our choices. On its face, this doesn't feel wholly inaccurate: Much of feminism has been about the expansion of women's choices and fighting for their ability to make those choices. But even if feminism facilitates a woman's ability to make a choice, it doesn't necessarily follow that said choice is feminist (as in, reliant on the fundamental belief that women should be equal participants in society).

For example, accepting and trying to emulate normative beauty and body standards is now often peddled as a choice. As modern women and femmes, we can find empowerment in the decision to dress according to society's standards around femininity, and while there can be power in this, that choice won't necessarily change the objectification of women's bodies or how femmes are broadly treated in a sexist society. As Zeisler argues in her book, focusing so much on the choices we make pushes us further into a model of empowerment that is focused on buying things to feel good.

When people criticize "corporate feminism," what they are often referring to is this idea that feminism—a radical, multigenerational movement fighting for the improvement of women's lives through reproductive rights, the elimination of sexual assault, equal pay, and other issues—has been exploited for capitalist gain and reduced to a "Sisterhood Is Powerful" T-shirt sold by Christian Dior. (Side note: I have this T-shirt. But in my meager defense, it was gifted to me.)

It's clear that corporations' efforts to embrace feminism are often purely for their bottom lines, not necessarily to elevate the status of women in work or in society. In an essay for the Brookings Institution (written prior to her joining the Biden Administration as treasury secretary), Janet Yellen writes that women in the workplace were a major reason why the United States became an economic power in the past century, and for this reason, we should celebrate the wins of women in the labor market. In laying out what women face in the workplace, she writes, "If these obstacles persist, we will squander the potential of many of our citizens and incur a substantial loss to the productive capacity of our economy at a time when the aging of the population and weak productivity growth are already weighing on economic growth."

She's right in that women's participation in the labor force makes them not just essential workers but a necessary part of our economy. But she also inadvertently suggests that equality for its own sake isn't reason enough to support women's entry into the workplace; rather, she argues that it serves the marketplace and is good for the global capitalist economic system.

This type of economic justification is used a lot in the business sphere: You will regularly hear research quoted by business leaders about how diversity helps a company's bottom line. McKinsey & Company has been a leader in this, regularly publishing reports about the economic benefits of diversity. For instance, they found in 2020 that "the relationship between diversity on executive teams and the likelihood of financial outperformance has strengthened over time." And the reason it's circulated so often is that it's an argument that's proven persuasive with CEOs and the other gatekeepers of workplace advancement for women and people of color at big companies. A bottom-line case for increased diversity is a much easier sell than convincing these mostly male corporate leaders that ensuring that your company doesn't have discriminatory hiring practices is the ethical and right thing to do. (In fact, researchers Robin J. Ely and David A. Thomas found that diversity doesn't automatically engender benefits to a company's bottom line without shifts in culture and actively fighting bias and discrimination in the office, something I'll discuss at length in Chapter 6.)

Corporate feminism also fits easily into a system that elevates individuals and makes examples of them—especially when it's so easy to marry a shallow identity politics with the quest to get ahead. Everything we do in a neoliberal economic system can become a commodity, exploited for personal gain, including our own identities. As Jia Tolentino writes in *Trick Mirror* on being adjacent to what she calls the "scam" of corporate feminism: "I benefit from it—even if I criticize its emptiness; I am complicit no matter what I do."

As am I, whether I want to be or not: My identity is a compelling part of selling my story. ("It's a great time to be South Asian in publishing," an editor once told me.) And because I'm a "professional feminist," on some level my identity and what it stands for are a type of cultural currency—and that's not necessarily always bad. It's important to recognize and include women and people of color in institutions to which they have been historically refused access, but what does it mean if our membership is solely rooted in our identity?

The scam in this is that, despite making a nice hashtag, girls (and women) don't actually have a lot of power, even when we have a seat at the table.

For this reason, many of us have grown weary of mainstream, corporate, neoliberal feminism, as in the idea that women's equality is rooted in our individual advancement in existing structures. "If I can do it, so can she and she and she and she" doesn't really work as a rallying cry without any recognition of the structural barriers we all face to get ahead. Consciously or unconsciously buying into the idea that our advancement in the workplace relies on our ability to hustle, grind, and, yes, "lean in" sets us up to lose sight of the "we" as we focus on the "I, I, I" of our lives—both in our professional ambitions and in the amount of responsibility we agree to shoulder.

Lean In, Ten Years Later

As Obama entered his still-hopeful second term in 2013, the effects of the 2007 recession eased and women started to make small gains in the corporate workplace. There were glimmers of excitement. *Perhaps, now,* we thought, *we are seeing the fruits of feminism's labors?*

But in reality, it was the popular strain of corporate feminism that was becoming ascendant—and it soon became clear why. For one thing, a lot of women have to interact with the workplace, so we're inherently invested in how feminism might play out there. And for another, our society is a competitive one: We value achievement, and corporate feminism is often about how to get ahead.

Corporate feminism emphasizes the individual over the communal and is neoliberal at its core, which seemingly makes it a perfect mode to flourish in our age. It's always been really easy to make women feel bad about their own experiences in any environment, so why not carry that feeling to the workplace? And why try to alter or rethink entire institutions, let alone social structures, when you can demonstrate that women are progressing by highlighting the success stories of a few special actors?

It is within this context—a defanged, neoliberal feminism—that Sheryl Sandberg's *Lean In* found its wide audience in 2013. Sandberg spoke to the women who'd had enough of getting paid less for equal (or even more) work than their male counterparts, and being locked out of the boardroom and upper management.

She rightfully points out all the systemic barriers women face in the workplace, from low pay to being looked over for promotions to being pushed out of the labor market entirely after having children. However, her solution—or rather, "the revolution" she saw—is designed to come from individual women: Ask for more, find your voice, visualize your future, don't be forced into decisions you don't have to make yet (like deciding not to put yourself up for a promotion because you want to have a baby soon), build relationships with other women in the workplace (i.e., Lean In Circles), and so on.

In and of itself, nothing about this advice was particularly wrong-headed. Most women need to work and would benefit from insight on how to operate within these imperfect systems. For instance, women (and really everyone) should be negotiating their salaries more aggressively. Ashley Louise, the cofounder of Ladies Get Paid—which trains women on financial literacy, including how to negotiate employment contracts—told me that, while there are many structural changes that need to happen in workplace policy, she will never "apologize for teaching women how to negotiate their salaries," because "that is net positive, no matter what way you cut that."

Sandberg, like many corporate feminists, writes that more women at the top means things get better for women overall: "If we can succeed by adding more female voices at the highest levels, we will expand opportunities and extend fairer treatment to all."

There is also *some* truth to this idea: Examining data from LinkedIn, the World Economic Forum found that, when women are in senior leadership positions, they are likely to hire other women. This is partly because those with the power to do so hire people like themselves, so white women with power end up reproducing the same dynamics, if not the same results, as white men: They hire other white people of their gender, class, and educational backgrounds. So, in and of itself, having diverse leaders does have some type of a relationship to how diverse your company is.

Still, as Faludi points out in her critique, Sandberg's view of success for women left a lot of women out, and in the months after the book's publication, opinion began to coalesce around what exactly a book like *Lean In* was telling us about the realities of the American workplace— specifically, how class and race impact what kind of access women have to the spaces where they can lean in at all. Sandberg's model of feminist advancement assumes a playing field in which women are already doing relatively well on the corporate ladder. But what about women who are poor? What about queer women? What about women of color? Different groups have different access to the levers of power. Is simply seeing ourselves in management enough?

Women from communities that have long been locked out of the boardroom, whether for racial, cultural, socioeconomic, or geographic reasons—or any reason, really—have an entirely different relationship to work. Our comfort with advocating for ourselves is different, as is the reception we get. In an interview with *Forbes*, Minda Harts, author of *The Memo: What Women of Color Need to Know to Secure a Seat at the*

Table, says, "These labels like 'angry Black woman,' 'docile Asian,' 'feisty Latina,' all these things were put on us before we even got to say, 'my name is.'"

These additional experiences with othering and discrimination in the workplace aren't accounted for in a model that assumes you can get ahead on your own merits, on your ability to build relationships, or by networking your way to the top.

bell hooks even felt the need to grapple with both the criticism and the idolatry of Sandberg, writing, "To women of color young and old, along with anti-racist white women, it is more than obvious that, without a call to challenge and change racism as an integral part of class mobility, she is really investing in top-level success for highly educated women from privileged classes."

According to hooks, Sandberg's promise of corporate power is "whites only."

hooks was not alone in her critiques of leaning in. As Melissa Gira Grant wrote in *The Washington Post,* "This is simply the elite leading the slightly-less-elite, for the sake of Sandberg's bottom line," and that "there's simply no way for women to lean in without leaning on the backs of other women." Even Maureen Dowd called her "the It Girl of Silicon Valley," writing, "She has a grandiose plan to become the PowerPoint Pied Piper in Prada ankle boots reigniting the women's revolution—Betty Friedan for the digital age."

Anne-Marie Slaughter, one of Sandberg's most vociferous critics, writes in *Unfinished Business,* "Plenty of women have leaned in for all they're worth but still run up against insuperable obstacles created by the combination of unpredictable life circumstances and the rigid inflexibilities of our workplaces, the lack of a public infrastructure of care, and cultural attitudes that devalue them the minute they step out, or even just lean back, from the workforce." Five years later, even Michelle Obama, on tour for her book *Becoming,* chimed in: "I tell women that whole 'you can have it all'—mmm, nope, not at the same time, that's a lie. It's not always enough to lean in because that shit doesn't work."

Much of the criticism of Sandberg and *Lean In* was thoughtful and sharp, especially on the book's blind spots, but some of it also seemed to be taking part in the age-old sport of tearing down a woman for not having a perfect message that checked every single box (which is an impossible task). Feminist writer Jessica Valenti wrote in *The Washington Post,* "The feminist backlash against Sandberg . . . reveals a big and recurring problem within the movement: We hold leaders to impossible standards, placing perfection over progress." *Jezebel* founder and writer Anna Holmes wrote in *The New Yorker* that many of the book's detractors relied on out-of-context quotes for their critiques and that the majority of them hadn't even bothered to read it in the first place. (In my observation: correct.) She writes, "But anyone who had read her book would have known that Sandberg herself is the first to acknowledge the debts she owes to the women who came before her, not to mention her youthful naïveté and eventual engagement with gender politics."

As I write this in 2023, it's been a decade since *Lean In*'s publication, and like my time at *Teen Vogue,* there are certain aspects of it that are clearer in hindsight. One of them is how Facebook—which even in 2013 still retained the feel of an approachable, fun, nerd-squad-y company, though its revenues then were already in the billions—has been revealed as a threat to our democracy. Sandberg's message of corporate feminist empowerment and her role at the company have been eclipsed by the much more troubling misdeeds of Meta itself, including the wild spread of misinformation that has led to the increased polarization of the American public and distrust of the media (not to mention a complete deterioration of privacy standards)—in which she played a part. The behemoth company has had profound global power yet has failed to be truly accountable for its role in increasing polarization and weakening democracy.

The main critique from hooks (who also noted that most people who criticized the book hadn't read it) was perhaps the one that still rings the truest. She wrote, "No matter their standpoint, anyone who advocates feminist politics needs to understand the work does not end with the fight for equality of opportunity within the existing patriarchal structure."

Some of the criticism of Sandberg may have felt overwrought at the time, but it has since become very clear that any kind of feminism in the service of reckless corporate profits is probably not much of a feminism at all. (Right-wing politicians are probably far worse for women than leaning in is good for them.)

But despite losing credibility with certain audiences, the book's message still resonated. *Lean In* sold four million copies and continues to be in the top ten most bought business books for women. And Sandberg's mission to create Lean In Circles was somewhat successful, boasting membership around the world in countries such as India and Brazil.

Whatever you may think of it, "lean in" remains one of the *only* things people bring up when you talk about women and the workplace. You can't really argue with the premise that more women should be ascending to senior positions—if you believe in the maintenance of such hierarchies. The deeper question is, What does a workplace look like without such stark power differentials? What is possible if we were to dismantle what hooks calls "the structures of imperialist white supremacist capitalist patriarchy"?

The debate over *Lean In* was ultimately less about the actual words in the book than about which approach women and feminists think is more effective: to work within the system to effect change, or to destroy that system and rebuild it in an entirely different way. But that has pushed us into an impasse, because rebuilding the system is not exactly something that can happen overnight and, while we focused on the number of women who might lean in, we forgot that the largest swath of women are either just in an ambition echo chamber or unable to move forward at all. Or, you know, have literally never heard of "leaning in."

And, lucky for you, you don't have to like or dislike Sandberg's faulty approach: Leaning in hasn't ultimately worked, and women are still left behind in the workplace despite their best intentions and efforts.

Wokeplace Feminism

In late 2017, I got a LinkedIn message from the HR department at Condé Nast. They wanted to talk to me discreetly about a position that had opened at *Teen Vogue*. They couldn't tell me what it was, they said, but it was "very senior." I was fresh off a layoff and in the middle of promoting my second book, so I had the mindset of someone who had been dumped by a partner at the end of a relationship they knew wasn't working. *I am doing fine. Great, even! How dare they dump me? I didn't love them anyway!*

Still, I had no plans to interview for the job. I had already decided I didn't want to work in media again, and I certainly didn't want to work for The Establishment™ and everything that came with that. But my friend Lauren sat me down and said, "I totally get that you are distrustful, but you *have* to take this opportunity seriously." Lauren was never one for shiny objects, so I took her advice to heart and went in for the introductory interview for what turned out to be the executive editor job. The parent company had recently decided to shutter the print version of the magazine, which led to the departure of their inspiring editor in chief Elaine Welteroth. They were looking to beef up the digital operation, which was my area of expertise. So, I went back for the follow-up interview.

My second interview was with *Teen Vogue*'s newly promoted chief content officer, Phillip Picardi. Phill was a wunderkind, a rising star at Condé, bright and unafraid to take risks. (Just the month before, he was dealing with the fallout from publishing a how-to guide for anal sex on the site—something that led to much pearl clutching. It was, after all, a *teen* brand!) He pushed against my perception of what it meant to work in fashion. Yes, he was stylish (and sometimes bitchy), but he did not take the power of his perch lightly and wanted to make a significant impact on politics and culture. Phill rose through the ranks at *Teen Vogue* quickly and helped the digital property pivot to cover substantive issues to serve an increasingly politicized generation.

I knew right away I wanted to work with this beauty editor turned journalist-activist. The interview went well; I'd say we vibed, even though he has long claimed that I didn't bring a résumé and told him he shouldn't need one from me. (Let the record state: I never said that, and what actually happened was that I had been begging his assistant to print my résumé out before he saw me, because I was a forty-year-old without a printer at home.) As we wrapped up the interview, he casually mentioned that the next one would be "with Anna."

"Wait, Anna *Wintour*?"

He looked me dead in the eyes—a tactic I would realize was his whole shtick—and said, "Yup!"

And then he giggled demonically while I all but shit my pants.

It's hard to conceive of meeting with someone whose persona is as larger-than-life as Wintour's. Originally hailing from London, Wintour is nothing short of a publishing legend, regularly called "the last of her kind"—an iconic editor who is more institution than person. Her unapologetic ambition and remarkable talent led to her quick rise through the fashion and magazine worlds. She became the editor in chief of American *Vogue* in 1988, a position in which she has stayed for over three decades. Throughout that time, her personality has been a subject of intrigue and interest—the stuff of documentaries, articles, books, and, most notably, fictionalized accounts that have served as cultural milestones. Everything from her alleged steely attitude toward colleagues to her precise editorial process and even her diet and exercise routine are the subjects of speculation and obsession.

And whether you believe any of that or not, Wintour is one of the people who has determined what is fashionable for decades. Who could forget the words of Miranda Priestly (played by Meryl Streep) in *The Devil Wears Prada* (which was based on the book of the same name, written by Wintour's former assistant Lauren Weisberger), when admonishing Anne Hathaway's Andrea for believing she is above fashion in her "lumpy blue sweater." This blue, she says, "represents millions of dollars and countless jobs, and it's sort of comical how you think that you've made a choice that exempts you from the fashion industry when, in fact, you're wearing the sweater that was selected for you by the people in this room from a pile of *stuff*."

Despite the movie being a fictional account, I still went into a panic—the same panic any mortal would face at that moment: *What the fuck was I going to wear?*

What does one don to meet with the woman who has decided what women should wear for the last thirty-plus years? I had always fancied myself an amateur style girl, but meeting with her and her team was another level. And I am a plus-size woman: Designer clothes literally don't fit me. Either I had to figure out a way to lose a lot of weight before our interview (thanks to winter break, I had four weeks), or I had to walk in there with my head held high.

Obviously, I chose the latter.

I also chose to buy myself a Gucci purse. I had already been planning to treat myself to one as a present for my fortieth birthday but decided if there was ever a reason to give myself an early birthday present, interviewing with Anna Wintour was it. (I have no regrets.)

I walked into her office in the January cold—the bag practically hanging from my neck—wearing what I considered a fashionable plus-size dress that perfectly matched the bag. I was sweating through my white wool coat; I had never been that nervous for a meeting in my life.

I don't remember what she was wearing, but I do remember what she was not wearing: sunglasses. Long rumored to rock large black sunglasses everywhere from the front rows of fashion runways to meetings, she was, to my surprise, not wearing them on that day. I later learned she does not regularly wear her sunglasses at the office—at least not in most meetings with her employees, and definitely not when you are meeting with her one-on-one. The first myth was busted.

The room was neat, almost sterile, and bright. We sat at a round wooden table with a bouquet in the center. Behind her was a breathtaking view of the entire city. Maybe she noticed my clothes, and maybe she didn't, but it didn't matter: Upon meeting her, I felt stupid to have bought into the hype that it would. She was there to talk about what I'd be bringing to *Teen Vogue,* what I thought was most interesting in the culture right now, and why I wanted the job. I barely remember what I said that day, but I know I told her I had a lifelong commitment to infusing feminism and politics into popular culture, and that we had long been underestimating the power of teen girls. And I said, as a born-and-raised New Yorker, I also loved the arts and fashion. I also mentioned I was once an "aspiring fashion designer" but the truth was that, when I lived in the Bay Area, in the early 2000s, I used to make clothes to wear to raves and eventually to Burning Man. (Not exactly the stuff of high fashion.)

Despite her reputation and notoriety, she was actually very nice. She seemed to like that I was originally from New York. She listened intently and asked tough questions (or maybe they weren't even tough, and I was just in the middle of a panic attack), but she also smiled and chuckled a lot, which put me at ease. As I walked out in a daze, unclear on what had just happened, her assistant whispered something to the effect of "Wow, she really liked you! FYI: She doesn't always laugh like that."

Excuse me, what? I thought to myself. I was excited. I already knew I wanted the job, but I had told myself it didn't matter what happened in that meeting. This was a huge moment for my career: Samhita, state-school graduate, scrappy feminist blogger, interviewing with one of the most powerful women in media. Whatever had happened, I made it here. That was exhilarating.

You're probably judging me: Little miss feminist falls apart at the chance to talk with a famous fashion editor. Heck, I judged myself. I had long criticized institutions like Condé Nast; I was, I believed, at my core, antiestablishment and anticorporate. I told myself, *I know who I am and what I need to get out of there. Make no friends! Taking the job is a strategic play.*

Beneath that, though, there was another layer. (Isn't there always?) I'd been working as a writer since my midtwenties, a lot of the time scrambling and feeling unsure about what I was doing or how I'd earn any money. Now I was being invited to sit at the table at the company that, whatever its faults, employed some of the greatest writers, editors, and creatives in the world. The attention and the prestige of a job like executive editor of *Teen Vogue* were intoxicating. I knew this would be a unique opportunity, unlike any I'd ever had.

I was ready to lean in.

Phill texted me that night to tell me Anna loved me and they'd be in touch with next steps soon. A few days later, I got the offer. It felt like a dream. After a very quick negotiation, I accepted the job. I was elated—I couldn't believe I'd be working at this legendary place.

I went to Condé to work for a brand that had pivoted from covering only fashion to covering culture and politics, through a leftist lens. They went from being a teen girls' fashion magazine to being an important outlet for young people to find their voice in a changing world. This inclusive vision of the world ran through our entire edit project, from photoshoots to articles. We regularly featured diverse talent on our covers as a corrective to the women's magazines of the past. We were "woke," right before the concept went mainstream (and long before it became an insult that adults used to criticize young people's way of seeing the world), and doing things in a way that felt in alignment with our progressive values.

Working as the executive editor from 2018 to 2021, I first reported to Phill, who had led the charge on digital to make *Teen Vogue* more than just an entry point to the flagship publication. He left shortly after I arrived; I then worked for Lindsay Peoples, an exceptionally talented young Black fashion editor from *The Cut* who had made waves pointing out the whiteness of the fashion industry. She came in as the editor in chief—armed with a clear vision and the work ethic to make it happen. Together, we hired a diverse staff—predominantly young people of color—and we led that team through the changing political landscape, a pandemic, an uprising around race, several editorial pivots, and layoffs. We continued to elevate the stories we cared about—the ones that we saw as being left out of mainstream media—that would resonate with a new, inclusion-minded generation.

Lindsay and I became fast friends (and later longtime collaborators) as we worked together within a storied institution that was often difficult to navigate. We worked toward a singular mission: This would be the place we'd needed when we were teen girls. It would be politically aware and culturally relevant, both fashionable and inclusive. The role that women's magazines have played in how women feel about themselves, see themselves, and decide what they yearn for is not small. This was our chance to reach young women who wanted more than what women's magazines had given them to date.

I learned fast that it's easy to criticize institutions from the outside, but it is quite different to be navigating them internally or to predict how you might act while in a position of some power in a given institution. Organizations are full of people—cool people, shitty people, checked-out people, burned-out people, awesome people, extremely not cool people. Navigating that ecosystem gave me a unique insight into how hollow other people's perceptions were of what makes a place what it is.

Getting the job at Condé was like being inducted into a secret society of women who weren't all outright feminists but had carved out an alternative path to female-based power by taking what real women cared about and building an empire around it. But working for women doesn't mean that your workplace is inherently good for women or is uniquely feminist, or collaborative, or nurturing. The remnants of act-like-a-man corporate behavior laced the air as thoroughly as the scent of Chanel No. 5.

They had leaned in before leaning in was even a thing. Suddenly, I felt like I should do that, too.

It wasn't easy to manage a team that wanted more out of an institution that wasn't going to give them or me any more. And despite *Teen Vogue* being characterized as woke as a brand, as managers, we couldn't be that woke. Our priority was making sure we met our corporate goals, even when that meant negotiating about stories deemed offensive for advertisers (or our higher-ups) or making sure we were covering topics that would generate traffic. I felt pressure to be a good corporate soldier, so that the team could have the runway to be as creative as they wanted to be.

Juggling the requirements of my job and my personal values gave me a lot of food for thought. Sometimes I'd leave the office giddy at what we'd accomplished that day. Other times, I'd limp toward my Uber (when I should have been taking the subway) and blearily ride home over the Brooklyn Bridge, brooding over the latest HR struggle from that day or week. Was it possible for us to be subversive in the context of a corporation led by its bottom line and defined by a type of exclusive elitism? Was I a part of a great change in media, or was I complicit in the same politics of neoliberal individualism that I deplored when I saw it elsewhere? Was *Teen Vogue* now popular simply because we prioritized identity—the "I" over the "we"—when that was something everyone realized they needed? I'd stare out the window but find no easy answers.

What I can now see (with the distance of perspective and some sleep) is that all these things were true at the same time. *Teen Vogue* was subversive, and we created a publication that went against the grain of what fashion magazines are supposed to do: We were inclusive, body-positive, diverse; we decentered the thin white bodies that dominated our industry before other publications did. But despite efforts to create its own world, *Teen Vogue* was still subject to the discretion of its parent company and the broader marketplace. Decisions about its future were not ours to make: They were based on anxious advertisers and what our parent company had decided to prioritize. Despite all the buzz, *Teen Vogue* had a fraction of the money other bigger publications had. And it's also worth mentioning that, in general, the budgets that magazines historically had no longer exist, so ignoring profit was not an option; profit made it possible for us to stay afloat.

That was part of the deal. We published content reflective of what we saw as the values of our readers—equality, collective organizing, fair working conditions, racial justice, body inclusivity, and more. But as employees we couldn't fully embody or express many of those values in our actual workplace. It felt deeply contradictory. (It's worth noting that in the fall of 2022, Condé Nast employees unionized.)

Where I differ from the most unyielding critics of corporate or neoliberal feminism is that I see value in learning how to navigate these environments, because they exist and affect people now. Pop-culture feminism can be a stepping stone to greater awareness of gender inequality that leads some women to become more politicized—a trend we've seen in the last few years. Mainstreaming feminist and leftist values can absolutely be a pipeline to deeper political commitments.

But I have learned that you can't sustain even a version of feminism at work without a vested interest in equality from the top, or without equal pay for equal work. And the challenge for me was, while I was fully aware of those bigger considerations, I was also fighting my own battles. I had been passed over for promotion and there were no other opportunities for me at the company, so my commitment to stay faded.

Despite everything I loved about my job, the team, and our ability to meet the moment, my priorities were shifting, my interest in working myself to death was waning, and I was exhausted. I was also straddling two worlds: I had one foot in the communities that were growing increasingly agitated with the structure of work, and the other beneath a desk at a very old and established seat of power in the media behemoth Condé Nast. And I couldn't face the split within myself anymore.

So, I did the unthinkable. I got on a call with Anna (it was during the early years of the pandemic, so there wasn't another sweaty office visit), and I thanked her for the incredible opportunity and explained that it was time for me to move on. She understood and thanked me for my leadership. She told me, should I ever need anything, not to hesitate to reach out. "I mean it, OK?" she said. I nodded as I logged off in a post-quitting haze.

We Still Need a Feminism of the Workplace

A trickle-down, neoliberal feminism of the workplace is compelling but doesn't ultimately address the needs of all women. Such a feminism relies on the good faith of a few actors—usually women or people of color who relate to and understand the needs of their employees and act accordingly. Elevating a few women or people of color to positions of power, or achieving that power as individual women, is not systemic change; it is individual change that, while important, also runs the risk of propping up existing systems of inequality.

That does not mean increased diversity doesn't make a difference, or that it can't change systems, or that it can't sometimes just make our day-to-day lives a little bit better. Binary thinking will not give us space to come up with creative solutions within systems most of us have to navigate to eat and to live. The question we need to ask ourselves is, how do we navigate these existing systems while keeping a bigger, grander political vision in our hearts and our minds? What is our "margin of maneuverability," or the space between working at a job to pay the bills and actually changing conditions for all women?

Constantly expressing disappointment with existing models for workplace equality and advancement can only get us so far. Even though corporate feminism has been the predominant model of work-place feminism, that does not mean an alternative is not possible. Instead, we need to ask ourselves who we have to blame for it. Is it the fault of the worker who is just trying to get by? The middle manager who is just taking orders? The woman asking for more money when approached for a new job? Are we complicit by simply buying into the idea that we deserve to get paid more, and that the pay gap should be eliminated?

Or is the problem systemic, and neoliberal feminism a way to distract us all from a solution?

What I do know is what is often lost in the theoretical conversation about workplace feminism: There are material considerations to a short-term, local workplace feminism, corporate or not. Workplace equality and changing women's material conditions have been long-standing and essential tenets of feminist activism.

Early feminists fought for women's right to work to allow them more autonomy and independence, to make them less reliant on an actual patriarch who had control over their physical, mental, and spiritual destinies. "We are entering a significant period," the suffragist Anna Howard Shaw wrote in her 1915 book, *Story of a Pioneer,* about women joining the industrial revolution one hundred years prior. "Around me, I saw women overworked and underpaid, doing men's work at half men's wages, not because their work was inferior, but because they were women."

As we debate the efficacy of corporate feminism, women's advancement in the workplace hasn't gotten much better. Women's participation in the labor force still lags behind men's and saw a major downward shift during the pandemic when 1.8 million more women than men left the workforce, most of them mothers (but by 2023, women and mothers had reentered the workforce to record levels). White women still make seventy-nine cents to the men's dollar. For Latine women it's fifty-seven cents; for Black women, sixty-four cents. Asian women make eighty cents to the dollar for white men, but this doesn't account for the vast differences in class experience among Asians. Interestingly, one study found that lesbian and bisexual women make slightly more than straight women, but gay men and transwomen on average make less to the dollar than the average straight white man.

There is also still a leadership gap between women and men at the top: As of 2023, women make up 10.4 percent of the CEOs of *Fortune* 500 companies (a huge jump in recent years). No Black women headed a *Fortune* 500 between 2016, when Ursula Burns left Xerox, and 2021, when Rosalind Brewer was named CEO of the Walgreens Boots Alliance in March and Thasunda Brown Duckett became the CEO of the Teachers Insurance and Annuity Association in May of the same year (making her the fourth ever Black woman to head a *Fortune* 500 company). Women of color represent only 4.7 percent of executive or senior-level managers in these companies, and corporate boards remain overwhelmingly white and male. And that's just in the big companies. Smaller companies and other industries have profound leadership gaps as well.

Reaching women in the workplace is an important goal of feminist organizing; the reality is, women need economic security to live full, free, and self-determined lives. Without access to money, women can't get healthcare, childcare, reproductive care, or food. They can't leave violent situations; they can't keep their families safe. Women are also disproportionately impacted by poverty in most places in the world and have increasingly become the primary breadwinners in their families.

Workplace organizing is unifying because reaching women where they work is an opportunity to connect them to a story of global worker solidarity. But that's not been how corporate feminism has metastasized; instead, it's collected itself around the idea that an overt focus on individual behavior versus larger policy issues would lead to a broader collective advancement. It's hard to see that as a coincidence.

In thinking about this, it might be helpful to look at the parallels with another big issue of our time—climate change. There, too, we see tensions around strategies of change that put all the onus on the individual to combat this issue. The emphasis on the individual has been routinely criticized in both cases, as individual actors are imperfect and cannot be relied on to do what is necessary for the upliftment of an entire group of people. There is no guarantee that your female (or queer or person-of-color) boss will be any more supportive, or advocate for you, just by virtue of their identity; in fact, many of us have stories to the contrary.

That doesn't mean there isn't some relationship between increased diversity at the top and increased support for workers who have had similar experiences, especially in male-dominated fields—though it is perhaps not as direct as is often touted. And it doesn't mean that, like individual actions to combat climate change, diversity can't lead to increased awareness and activism for the necessary systemic change.

We need more than one on-ramp for women. The problem was never about women being at the top. It was that there seemed to be only one way of getting there, and one way of behaving once you were there.

My friend Susie recently pointed out that the irony of *The Devil*

Wears Prada is that it was supposed to be a cautionary tale of a woman giving in to unfettered ambition (she might be rich and powerful, but she ends up alone, unhappy, divorced, and bitter), but its lasting legacy was a fetishization of what it takes to be successful. And as the era of the girlboss would show us, that came with some major downsides.

GIRLBOSS, INTERRUPTED

You choose courage over comfort. You choose what is right
over what is fun, fast, or easy. And you choose to practice
your values rather than simply professing them.

—Brené Brown, *Braving the Wilderness*

Considering how ubiquitous the term has become—from earnest
Instagram posts to cutting X chatter—it's not always clear what
we mean when we say *girlboss*. Does it refer to an ambitious
woman with a can-do attitude? A corporate hustler? A woman CEO?
Is it just a meme? Is it feminism? Is it the death of feminism? And why
are we calling women "girls"?

The concept now feels largely dated, but for a moment there seemed
to be a lot riding on the word.

When Sophia Amoruso published her book *#Girlboss* in 2014, she
was known primarily as the founder of Nasty Gal, a fast-growing retail
line that sold vintage and vintage-inspired clothes for young women.
She writes, "A #GIRLBOSS is someone who's in charge of her own life.
She gets what she wants because she works for it." *#Girlboss* was the

millennial pink version of Helen Gurley Brown's "having it all," and the living embodiment of Sheryl Sandberg's order to "lean in." While *Lean In* was for an older, midcareer audience, *#Girlboss* was seen as younger and more "for misfits."

Girlboss also became synonymous with hustle culture: the optimistic, almost religious desire to get ahead at work and in life. The ethos suggests that, structural inequality be damned, there is nothing a little elbow grease and the right shade of lipstick can't overcome.

In her book, Amoruso was talking specifically about women entrepreneurs, but the concept of the girlboss quickly expanded to include any earnestly ambitious woman trying to make it, be it in her own business or at her marketing job. Girlbosses can work anywhere, but they shine brightest in lifestyle businesses like fashion, media, and luxury goods. The girlboss espouses a feminized hustle: You may be ambitious, but (just like a girl!) you are neither masculine nor threatening. She also has the new version of "it all": body, face, outfit, and a career. This millennial caricature doesn't need to wear a pantsuit, and if she does, it's going to be *pink*. Everything she does is *empowering*, including unapologetically embracing capitalism.

#Girlboss, like *Lean In,* was addressing a real concern: The game is rigged against women, who are by all measures as capable as men. Why should any of us be held back from being our own boss and starting our own business?

• • •

As I mentioned earlier, I never really considered myself a girlboss—not just because I refused to SoulCycle but also because I'm kind of old for it, and unless you count my ill-fated foray into making my own clothes and wanting to start my own "fashion" brand in 2002, I am not an entrepreneur. (Other people have disagreed. "Editor at a fashion magazine? That's a girlboss hero," a friend once told me.)

That said, I did take one significant dip in the entrepreneurial world, when I worked for that federal advisory council, the National Women's

Business Council (NWBC). I took the job both as a way out of another job and because I was deeply inspired by their Obama-appointed chair, Carla Harris. Harris, a Black woman, is a veteran Wall Street insider, an author, a motivational speaker, *and* a gospel singer. She is also a force. Born and raised in Florida, she pursued a career in finance after attending Harvard for her undergrad and then Harvard Business School for her MBA. In 2013, at the age of fifty, Harris was promoted to vice chairperson of wealth management at Morgan Stanley.

One of her goals in life, she once told me, was to get as many people of color, especially women, into the upper echelons of finance as possible—a concrete and material way to redistribute wealth. Harris was not exactly a not-for-profit leader, but she was rooted in mission and purpose and an unapologetic authenticity I hadn't seen in other leaders. In our first ever phone call, I was anxious, having read about her formidable career; but she was remarkably warm and engaging, and I was immediately put at ease. Working as the NWBC's communications and engagement director wasn't exactly my dream job (I wanted to be writing full time), but I took the job because I needed to work and wanted to learn from Harris and the other women in the council, who were mostly all successful small-business owners. I was intrigued: Maybe women-owned businesses *were* a path to equity.

The NWBC's mission was to advocate for women-led and women-of-color-led businesses. Additionally, they were a research entity putting out an annual report on the state of women's business leadership. My job was to elevate both our research and the stories of women's successes.

And—I say this seriously—these bosses were *inspiring*. For one thing, though the idea of girlbosses has been quite influential, women founders have a very hard time building and sustaining their businesses. As of 2021, women founders raised only an estimated 2 percent of all venture capital money (Black and Latine women raise even less)—numbers that have stayed stubbornly steady for years.

But that doesn't mean women aren't starting businesses: According to the World Economic Forum, in 2021 women founded 49 percent of all new businesses (up from 28 percent in 2019), generating approximately 1.8 trillion dollars per year—and, in that job, I heard about their experiences firsthand. The stories I heard from women founders were usually some version of "I kept being looked over for promotion, so I broke out on my own"—and this was especially true for women of color.

This trend has only continued in the years since I left the NWBC: Many young people have turned to entrepreneurship because they haven't been able to find work elsewhere, or out of a desire for more flexibility at work—a desire that has been on the rise since COVID changed our relationship to the office.

The Demise of the Girlboss

When Audrey Gelman founded the Wing—a women-and-nonbinary-people-only coworking space—in 2016, she was hoping to create a place where people could come together and work, build community, make a difference, network, *and* fix their hair. With pink exteriors, tasteful snacks and wines, feminist memorabilia, and well-lit bathrooms—perfect to fix up your makeup or spritz on one of their Maison Margiela perfumes (who doesn't love Beach Walk?)—the Wing marketed itself with a message of feminist empowerment. It was a millennial woman's room of her own.

"We're a coven, not a sorority," stated one 2016 Instagram post on the Wing's account.

The Wing was both a caricature of the millennial woman and a completely savvy recognition of its target clientele. I was never a member (I had a full-time office job), but many smart, creative, innovative women liked the space and found value in what they were offering. One woman, Noël Duan, told me that as an entrepreneur she really looked up to Gelman, and when she was invited to be a founding member, she felt like she was being inducted into a "close-knit community of women."

The Wing found a niche in the market, and it grew quickly; it seems Gelman and her cofounder, Lauren Kassan (the founder of the exercise-class access app ClassPass), were an investor's dream, as they represented a much-neglected demographic in venture capital: women founders. By 2019, they had raised $118 million.

For Duan, that intimacy she felt at the outset didn't last through the height of the business's popularity. "By 2019, I couldn't get a seat on a Wednesday morning, couldn't find an outlet, and it was super, super noisy," she says. Duan was hardly the only disillusioned Wing-er.

In an investigation for *The New York Times Magazine,* Amanda Hess found that many of the employees—especially support staff—had been excited about the potential of a feminist workplace, only to find the culture toxic and unsupportive. She writes, "Members and their guests could be casually racist. One eyed a photo board of Wing employees and remarked, 'There's a lot of colored girls that work here.'" Other staffers were promised promotions they never got, or saw their job duties inexplicably changed. "Some staff members hired to work the front desk or run events saw their job duties inflated to include scrubbing toilets, washing dishes, and lint-rolling couches," Hess writes.

The idea the Wing sold—that capitalism and feminism could have a totally functional baby—turned out like many such myths to be possible through the labor of an underclass of poorly treated employees.

The Wing, however, was hardly the only business that marketed an ethos of girlboss feminism but failed to live up to what it promised. Starting in 2019, continuing into the COVID pandemic's early months, and cresting with the uprisings of 2020 following the police killing of George Floyd, what began as a sprinkling of stories alleging toxic workplaces and racist behavior in women-led, mission-driven start-ups turned into a wave of high-profile exoduses from these companies.

In 2019, luggage company Away, which had put at the core of its brand the idea of a new generation of inclusive travelers, was one of the first to face reports that it had created a toxic and aggressive work culture, especially for employees of color. According to a report on the technology website *The Verge,* the culprit was one of their female founders, Steph Korey, who eventually had to step down.

Then editor in chief Christene Barberich left the buzzy, feminist-leaning digital women's publication *Refinery29* in June 2020, following accounts that the publication was a hostile work environment for Black women and other women of color.

Also in June 2020, Leandra Medine, a cofounder of the feminist fashion blog *Man Repeller,* stepped back from her role. A year later, in an ill-fated and viral interview with designer Recho Omondi, Medine said that, despite reports of favoritism toward white employees, she didn't see herself as a racist. "I'm an equal-opportunity asshole. Like, I sucked as a leader," she said.

Around the same time, at Reformation—a sustainable-clothing company marketed to smart, liberal, stylish, and thin women—CEO and founder Yael Aflalo stepped down after the brand had posted a message supporting Black Lives Matter on Instagram and employees came forward saying they had experienced racism at work.

All these resignations had to do with workplace behaviors, including insensitivity to racial dynamics, office microaggressions, troubling management decisions, and thoughtless HR policies. The subjects of these investigations represented a particular archetype: wealthy, white, college-educated women who were both leaders and the faces of their brands, with large social-media followings, influential relationships, and celebrity endorsements.

The companies they helmed were also eerily similar: entities that promised new, disruptive visions for business, rooted in inclusion—positing women's leadership as a sign of the glass ceiling shattering, and often using feminist themes in their branding. When these ideals were not made good on, the leaders took swift and often dramatic falls. And our eagerness to punish them was also revealing: Women are encouraged to behave like men at the office, but punished for still being women in the end.

And what followed the Great Girlboss Reckonings of 2019 and 2020 was a cacophony of criticism about the girlboss ethos itself. Think pieces decried the end of the moment, and memes like "girlbossing too close to the sun" and *girlboss, gatekeep,* and *gaslight* emerged as pointed criticism of hustle culture and the women who bought into it. *Girlboss* quickly went—at least among certain women—from an empowering idea celebrated as the next wave of feminism to shorthand for a type of faux-woke white feminism that failed to reckon with inequality in the workplace.

It turns out that workplaces led by "women acting like men" are not always just or fair workplaces, nor are they necessarily feminist. But it also became too easy to conflate criticism of certain "girlbosses" with criticism of women's leadership and women's ambition in general. What gets lost is both the opportunity that entrepreneurship might present to women leaders and workers, if done mindfully, and the many young women who are drawn to starting their own businesses.

That said, a toxic workplace is a toxic workplace, regardless of the gender of your boss. Yes, diverse talent at the top does have a relationship to the diversity of talent throughout the organization or company. But are women automatically uniquely qualified to lead? Or do some of them emulate troubling patriarchal leadership dynamics?

· · ·

Perhaps nothing rang the death knell for the concept of the girlboss more firmly than the criminal charges brought against Theranos founder Elizabeth Holmes, who was arguably not really a girlboss but whose gender was the subject of much scrutiny and obsession. The self-made billionaire of 2015 took a swift fall from grace in the years that followed. Holmes's mission at the health start-up was to revolutionize the process by which blood is tested. She hated having her blood drawn from her arm and wanted to disrupt the medical system with what she claimed was her innovative new finger-prick system that required less blood to test for a variety of conditions. Unfortunately for nearly anyone who used the product, the system didn't work, regularly giving false blood-test results.

After a series of investigations, Holmes was charged by the SEC and found guilty on four federal counts of defrauding her investors in early 2022, after a trial in which she accused business partner Ramesh "Sunny" Balwani of emotionally abusing, controlling, and manipulating her in their romantic relationship and of being the real captain of the company she'd so publicly helmed. She was sentenced to eleven years in prison and started serving her time in May 2023.

But before all that, to her investors, Holmes was considered a refreshing, long-overdue face in a sector of the economy that trumpeted diversity but had no idea how to get it. She herself was an obvious caricature of the Silicon Valley founder: dressing like Steve Jobs, infamously modulating her voice, and sticking to a rigorous tech-productivity-hack-type schedule that included waking up at four a.m., workouts, preplanned meals, and meditation.

Journalists (most notably John Carreyrou, who turned his investigative work for *The Wall Street Journal* into the book *Bad Blood: Secrets and Lies in a Silicon Valley Startup*), documentarians (Alex Gibney, director of *The Inventor: Out for Blood in Silicon Valley*), and even television writers and producers (Elizabeth Merriweather, creator of *The Dropout*, starring Amanda Seyfried) have all pondered what went wrong with Theranos, how Holmes made it so far, and whether the debacle would be a wake-up call for Silicon Valley, where exaggerating what your company is capable of is par for the course.

But some felt—despite her company's egregious lies—that Holmes's treatment by the industry and the press highlighted an unfair double standard for women founders. At her criminal trial, she was followed by a group of young women who dubbed themselves "the Holmies." A photo of them sporting blond wigs and black turtlenecks was posted to the Instagram account @elizabethholmesupdates captioned, "In solidarity w Elizabeth Holmes put on your best black turtleneck. United we slay, divided we fall." There was merch with her face on it, along with slogans like "They hate to see a girl boss winning," viral Tik Tok videos of people imitating her voice, and Facebook groups defending her.

Some of it, of course, was parody—jokes from young women who understood that she represented the worst of start-up culture and Silicon Valley—but some of it came from ardent supporters who felt she was being held to a tougher standard because of her gender.

Onetime Reddit CEO Ellen K. Pao (who herself violated the unspoken rule of brushing Silicon Valley sexism under the table when, in 2012, she filed a gender discrimination lawsuit against her employer, the venture capital firm Kleiner Perkins) wrote in *The New York Times*, "Indeed, as Ms. Holmes's trial for fraud continues in San Jose, Calif., it's clear that two things can be true. She *should* be held accountable for her actions as chief executive of Theranos. And it can be sexist to hold her accountable for alleged serious wrongdoing and not hold an array of men accountable for reports of wrongdoing or bad judgment."

Others felt she signaled that the idea of the girlboss was an abject failure and had an unfortunate impact on women entrepreneurs. One woman founder, Alice Zhang, told *The New York Times* that when she was trying to raise money for her own medical start-up, investors would ask her about Theranos and about Holmes rather than focusing on the business she was pitching. "I could see no similarity besides the fact that we're both women in the hard-science space," Zhang said.

Parsing out what was sexism and what was Holmes's own wrongdoing would be both challenging and futile. If anything, her gender may have softened others' treatment of her, because people were trying to overcompensate for their own sexism and the industry's lack of women founders. It's possible that her being a woman blinded some investors to the shortcomings of the company that, at face value, would have seemingly been easier to vet. On the other hand, perhaps the desire to prosecute her (and her male business partner) more aggressively than, say—as Pao points out—the CEOs of Uber or WeWork for similar potential fraud is an overcompensation based in the bitterness of men having been scammed by a woman.

Ultimately, the lesson shouldn't be that women are bad leaders but that growth-at-all-costs capitalism is ripe for corruption. Start-up companies are not particularly conducive to making good on one's goals of diversity and equality. Women-led or not, they are notorious for propagating toxic work environments just by virtue of their structure: They reward bombastic personalities, innovators, entrepreneurs, and people that can sell a clear vision and point of view, but not necessarily those who have what it takes to be good or ethical leaders.

Maurice Schweitzer, a professor at the Wharton School of Business at the University of Pennsylvania who studies emotions, ethical decision-making, and the negotiation process, says this is part of what makes navigating start-ups challenging. "You need to make quick decisions, you have less structure, you have less hierarchy. And so, there are more ways for people to feel like they're in a stressful situation, making quick, difficult decisions," he told me.

The focus on women tech entrepreneurs, then, can feel pointed when you consider that toxic leadership is an industry-wide issue. Tesla/SpaceX/X CEO Elon Musk, Uber cofounder Travis Kalanick, and Meta's Mark Zuckerberg are all tech-industry leaders who believe their work makes the world a better place (whether it does or not is another question) but have overseen or contributed to toxic workplace behavior—turning a blind eye to harassment and labor issues—or had a hand in the weakening of American democracy.

The culture in Silicon Valley has a long documented history of hostility, especially to women. Anna Wiener writes in her searing memoir *Uncanny Valley:*

> Being the only woman on a nontechnical team, providing customer support to software developers, was like immersion therapy for internalized misogyny. I liked men—I had a brother. I had a boyfriend. But men were everywhere: the customers, my teammates, my boss, his boss. I was always fixing things for them, tiptoeing around their vanities, cheering them up. Affirming, dodging, confiding, collaborating. Advocating for their career advancement; ordering them pizza. My job had placed me, a self-identified feminist, in a position of ceaseless, professionalized deference to the male ego.

Schweitzer has said there are three things that happen when someone is put in a leadership role with unchecked power. One is that they develop a sense of exceptionalism: They may often "feel as though the rules don't apply to them" or believe they have "special privileges." Second, they have what he calls "diminished perspective taking," which means that, as they attain more power, they begin to lose empathy for other people's points of view—especially people who work under them. Lastly, he says, leaders, and especially entrepreneurs, are more likely to have an "approach orientation," meaning, "if they want something, they're going to go do it," irrespective of how other people feel. Given these tendencies, it's not hard to imagine how toxicity can flourish in a start-up environment.

If the girlboss reckoning has taught us anything, it's that, without a shift in power, putting women or people of color in leadership positions runs the risk of them reproducing those very current inequalities. The demise of the girlboss was, of course, inevitable—even Amoruso admits it's a dated term now and acknowledges things are "much more nuanced" today. But how much of our newly negative fixation on girlbosses is about the troubling workplace dynamics they replicate, and how much of it is our ceaseless enjoyment in pillorying women?

All this can be true: Women can be bad leaders, and they can also be held to unfair double standards. Focusing so much on the demise of the rockstar image of the girlboss fails to address the bigger problems: the system that produces them, the investors that suggested they use their gender to tap into the women's market, and the expectation that women will be better than men on issues of diversity and inclusion, even though (as Schweitzer also noted) they often aren't and may act like their male counterparts once they get to the top.

What Comes After the Girlboss?

I suppose it's easy to just say the girlboss is dead (the term certainly is) and we don't need any more of them, but that does a bit of a disservice to the potential for women to be successful business owners who create their own companies and products. With the right support, women entrepreneurs could be antiracist and equitable and create feminist workplaces—if we could all navigate and be honest about the ridiculous pressure to "perform" our feminism rather than simply living it.

Part of this is acknowledging and even celebrating that not every company needs to grow at a breakneck pace, and that there are successful business leaders who choose a more mindful path, despite the financial incentive to grow. Renée Rouleau is the Austin, Texas–based founder of her own eponymous skin-care line that now employs fifteen people. She started as an aesthetician, but eventually the brand became what is today: a direct-to-consumer e-commerce business with customized skin-care products that have a devoted following. And, despite offers to buy her company or give her investment money to go bigger faster, she chose to stay small and grow at a slower pace.

She told me that people would tell her, "Renée, you could be a gazillion-dollar company, right now." But no one could answer her question: "Please tell me why bigger is better. Tell me. Other than it just being an American ideal." She wanted to maintain control of her product—partly because she was passionate about it, but also because it was important to her to create a happy workplace.

"In the early years, I just wanted to be able to pay my bills, not have financial stress, create a great work environment for my team, and that was it," she says. "It was just wanting everyone to be happy."

It worked: In 2020, Renée Rouleau, Inc. was voted one of the best places to work in Austin.

It might not be the best path for every business, but there is a lesson here about what it could mean for entrepreneurs and small-business owners to prioritize management, culture, and creativity over accelerated profit. Everyone wants to make money, but the question is, Does everyone need to raise $180 million to fund exponential growth before having their ducks in a row from a management-and-culture perspective? Probably not.

Another lesson for all entrepreneurs is that you shouldn't build a

large business (or really, any business at all) where you have to be accountable to the needs of your team if you are not interested in being
accountable for the needs of your team. Starting a company of more
than one means being beholden to workers, and that should be codi-
fied in how we think about starting businesses and understood as part
and parcel of the process.

· · ·

When our admiration for girlbosses started to unravel, I certainly
sighed with relief; I, too, was ready to do away with the ungodly pressure to be not just wildly successful but well coiffed, thin, able-bodied,
constantly motivated, and driven by purpose every moment of my life.
But I also knew from my experience working with younger women
that hustle culture was the water in which many of them—and especially women of color—swam.

When I worked at *Teen Vogue,* young women who hadn't even graduated from college showed up to our events with résumés in hand.
Aspiring entrepreneurs emailed me regularly, voraciously networking
to start their businesses. Women I worked with—who got up at the
crack of dawn to get to the gym, who worked on their side hustles after
hours, who were motivated by something deeper than the credit or the
cover of a magazine—earnestly posted serif-font graphics on their
social-media accounts about how "it's not luck, it's hard work."

Young women believed working hard was the only way out of the
conditions they were living in or were born into and, for them, there
were few alternatives.

So, while much of the criticism of girlbosses has been focused on
extremely successful women tech start-up entrepreneurs, the larger
backlash against the girlboss also became a way to criticize a certain
type of woman: one who unapologetically displays her ambition in
public, one who hustles, one who isn't afraid to be caught trying.

As the backlash against girlbosses—or, really, "bossy" girls—took
off, I kept thinking back to the young women I had worked with over

the years. They weren't the faces of companies, but they had bought into the girlboss ethos of unrelenting femininity-forward ambition.

Cristina Flores, the director of scheduling for the U.S. Department of Education (who I worked with at the NWBC) told me that, despite the criticisms, she identifies with being a girlboss and attributes that, in part, to her parents having come here from Mexico to build a better life for her and her siblings. "I see it as an empowering term," she says. " 'I'm a girlboss, I got this, nothing's going to stand in my way.' "

Despite its many flaws (and being a little cheesy), the spirit of the girlboss—stripped of Instagram follower counts and untenable investment dollars—does provide an on-ramp for young women into bigger questions about their vision of career success that is cognizant of gender, equality, and justice. And I knew firsthand that many young women, especially the ones who were less privileged, needed to believe they could get ahead in order to do so.

With the girlboss backlash, it felt like young women, heretofore encouraged to give in to unfettered ambition, were now being chastised for wanting to get ahead. Women in my life started to whisper about how some of the callouts, while justified, also felt unfairly targeted—more at the women's ambition than at how they implemented it. "Why should I hide that I work hard?" said one. "I hope no one is ever interviewed about *my* management," a former coworker said to me.

On the other hand, young fashion designer Sky Conner has internalized many of the girlboss callouts and says it's given her a real awakening on the importance of living your brand values, especially around diversity (to which she is committed). Despite that, however, she told me she still worries she "could get canceled or attacked" just for doing her job—i.e., being a boss. Other women entrepreneurs may be rethinking how fast or big they want their businesses to grow: Duan, the entrepreneur and founding member of the Wing, said watching the anti-girlboss reckonings has made her rethink if she wants to have a large profile at all.

Then there's Ladies Get Paid (LGP), the organization that holds training and conferences for women on financial literacy, including how to ask for a raise. In 2020, they were gearing up to publish their book, but they decided to reframe it. "We wanted to get ahead of any girlboss backlash," Ashley Louise, the cofounder and CEO, told me. "We felt we had to defend what we do." They didn't want to defend the idea of the girlboss but did want to defend women's ambition.

Claire Wasserman, the other founder of LGP and author of the book *Ladies Get Paid,* writes in the introduction, "There are also those who call this corporate feminism and say that it is performative at best and perpetuating systemic inequalities at worst. I hear you." She continues on to explain that "helping women move up in their companies and make more money (which men have done since the beginning of time) is, on its face, not a bad thing."

There is also something about the girlboss backlash that feels snobbish. Louise agreed: "I'm not saying that it's good to simp for these elite female professional-success people, but there are so many women everywhere who just want to do better and move up," she said. "The anti-Girlboss thing feels really elitist to me."

Perhaps the broad idea of a girlboss is in need of reinvention, not a funeral—one that is cognizant of its drawbacks but acknowledges its power and the need for an alternative path. The girlboss identity was, in part, a survival mechanism for women in a brutal and taxing work world that puts inordinate amounts of pressure on women to succeed and stereotypes them as not feminine enough when they do. But, like any other corporate feminism, it also functioned in part by convincing women that the onus is on them (and them alone) to make their lives better, rather than asking that we all work to change structural inequalities and fight together to better the lives of women.

In the last few years, many of us are rethinking what ambition means to us, where it has gotten us, and how much we really need to or even want to work. Younger women in particular are consciously talking about issues outside of career ambition, like mental health, self-care, and work-life balance, in ways my generation did not. "Having it all" means something different for younger women: It means getting

ahead in your chosen work, but also enjoying your life and not sacrificing everything to a career or a family the way that previous generations
of working women had to (and that many working women still do
today).

Yes, we should critique a system that requires inhumane sacrifice
disguised as aspiration. And we should certainly hold toxic, problem-
atic, unethical leaders accountable. But the girlboss backlash makes
clear that ambitious women still make people uncomfortable. It seems
to say that there is something crass—even "common"—about wearing
your ambition on your sleeve, and about being honest and forthcom-
ing about wanting to change the economic circumstances that have
been handed to you.

There is a very narrow path set out for women's success, and limited
conditions under which we allow it. We insist that women should hustle and get their bag and all that, but then we punish them severely if
they do it without being perfect. But people are not perfect—and neither is the capitalism under which we live.

We know the "hustle harder" ethos of girlboss culture is not the
stuff of righteous political goals, but it has also been one of the few
paths out of marginalization for women—especially those often left
out of economic progress. And as we push for equitable workplaces
and continue to galvanize our collective power, it is imperative that we
cast a wide net when inviting people to that party.

4

THE END OF THE HUSTLE

It seems like nobody wants to work these days.

—Kim Kardashian, billionaire

*H*ustle has a lot of different meanings. As a verb, it means "to crowd or push someone"; as a noun, it can denote anything from "energetic activity" to a "dishonest plan to get money." The hustle was also a dance of the disco era, and a hustle can refer to any criminalized activity, such as stealing or sex work.

In the late 1800s, the word *hustle* began to be used in reference to working hard—or, really, hard *enough*. According to Isabella Rosario at NPR, the word was used to admonish workers—specifically Black workers. She writes,

> Hustle—or a lack thereof—was invoked to make an association between blackness and laziness. "The average colored man does not know how to hustle," Timothy Thomas Fortune wrote for *The Southwestern Christian Advocate,* a Methodist African American newspaper, in 1888. Fortune, a black economist himself, argued that black men enjoy "exceptional opportuni-ties," like public libraries and free night schools, but were too

"ignorant" to take advantage of them. In short, he concluded, "colored men have themselves oftenest to blame." (For what? He doesn't say.)

However, the Emancipation Proclamation was only signed in 1863; the Civil War ended in 1865. Juneteenth, when the final 250,000 enslaved Americans in Texas learned they were free, happened June 19 of that year. Fortune was writing just a couple decades later, and his observation that "the average colored man does not know how to hustle" is endlessly complicated by the context in which he—as Rosario points out—was writing. The very roots of "hustling" are tied to the standards of success set by a white-dominated culture that had been enslaving Black people just twenty-five years before he was writing.

In the following century, the word *hustle* would alchemize, shift, and take on new meanings and nuances.

In his 2015 book, *Knocking the Hustle: Against the Neoliberal Turn in Black Politics*—the title is a reference to the 1996 Jay-Z song "Can't Knock the Hustle" about his come-up as a rapper—Lester K. Spence writes, "For a variety of reasons we've been forced to hustle and grind our way out of the post–civil rights era, and it is this hustle and grind in all of its institutional manifestations that's resulted in our current condition."

Spence documents the ways the hustle mentality infiltrated rap music and other forms of popular culture to reinforce the message that surviving and thriving are based solely on how hard you work. And to be sure, rap music often both glorifies and makes very cool the idea of hustling in all its incarnations. Who among us hasn't put on Nicki Minaj to shake off a rejection or to amp us up for a battle ahead? Whether it's Rick Ross's hypnotic but shallow anthem "Hustlin'" or Jay-Z's autobiographical telling of his rags-to-riches story, a hustle mentality is a thematic core in rap music and, therefore, in popular culture. Spence writes, "Much of rap explicitly exalts the daily rise-and-grind mentality black men with no role in the formal economy need to possess in order to survive and thrive." And failure has less to do with how the system is set up than with what you can personally do to overcome it.

"Indeed," he writes, "under the neoliberal turn, arguably the most important figure is the figure who consistently works." He continues, "Black elected officials and civil rights leaders reproduce these ideas, participating in a remobilization project of sorts, one that consistently posits that the reason black people aren't as successful as their white counterparts [is] because of a lack of hustle, is because they don't quite have the work ethic necessary to succeed in the modern moment."

Similar narratives are spun about the working poor. Embedded in the grift of bootstrap theory is the idea that "if there is a will, there is a way": if you want to be successful, the only thing getting in the way is you and your laziness. But if you bought the right suit, organized your life, and motivated yourself, you'd make it.

The idea that hustle is a necessary aspect of surviving under and thriving in capitalism was, of course, absorbed by the millennial-branded, entrepreneur-led work culture of men and girlbosses alike. Hustle has come to mean an almost religious obsession with getting ahead, to the point where overexertion on behalf of a company or project without any work/life boundaries is just part of the process of success.

That's not new in the business world—Wall Street has certainly been all about that kind of hustle for decades—but its ubiquity certainly is.

• • •

One conservative anxiety laid bare during the COVID-19 pandemic was the idea that too much economic support—which is a truly laughable concept, given the cost of rent or groceries—meant that people would lose their incentive to work. In response to President Biden's COVID relief bill, the conservative publication *National Review* wrote that, not only was it bad policy, "the continued elevated unemployment payments make unemployment more lucrative than employment for many people and will discourage a return to work at the margins."

COVID was not the first time the belief in this myth had revealed itself. People across the political spectrum fundamentally buy into the unsupported-by-evidence idea that if you give people enough support to keep their heads above water financially, they will inevitably lose all motivation to work. This is largely untrue for many reasons, among which is that workers can rarely just quit and collect a government check in America. (That's literally not how unemployment insurance works.)

And employers are not powerless in creating workplaces that can retain workers—whether it be service or office work. Companies have the choice to pay workers appropriately, they can have flexible family leave policies, and they can develop paths to help employees feel like their hard work means something and give them real opportunities to advance in their careers. A workplace doesn't have to be inherently challenging and unjust, demotivating workers and forcing them out in droves—that is a *choice*.

The widespread belief is that you must always hustle—both at work and in your all-but-necessary side hustles—and to keep you hustling, you need to be kept hungry, metaphorically and literally. This belief underlies the reality that many jobs expect you to work (or be available to work) all the time, despite many important battles fought for us to have fair wages and parameters around the workweek. There no longer *is* a workweek: Every moment needs to be maximized for earning, whether as a wage worker or a salaried employee. In fact, even our free time is maximized and often focused on producing *something*. Jenny Odell writes in *How to Do Nothing*, "Many of us find our every last minute captured, optimized, or appropriated as a financial resource by the technologies we use daily. We submit our free time to a numerical evaluation, interact with algorithmic versions of each other, and build and maintain personal brands."

In a 1930 essay entitled "Economic Possibilities for Our Grand-children," the economist John Maynard Keynes hypothesized that by

2030, our wealth would have grown so much that, as a people, we'd only be working fifteen-hour weeks. Here we are in 2024, and I can only look at that and think: *Fifteen hours?*

For example, the typical knowledge worker in New York City starts their day around seven or eight A.M., responding to emails from bed while drinking coffee. Their days are filled with meetings, tasks, deliverables, and lunch meetings; evenings can often be taken up by work-related dinners or events, capped off with a few final emails or notes sent in bed, perhaps after they've put children to bed and as they fall asleep . . . only to wake up and do it all over again. Slack, email, and productivity software are all available through our mobile devices to make life "convenient" and keep us chained to this hostile cycle, often resulting in twelve-to-fifteen-hour work*days*—forget *weeks.* Maybe not every day but enough days for it to be the norm. As Ezra Klein remarks, speaking about Keynes's predictions, "In an inversion of past history, the more money you make now, the more hours you generally work." Or as my friend Steven Thrasher says, "We worked really hard so now we can work even harder."

Today, there is certainly a class of idle rich, but the ethos for most people is that you work to earn money and, we are told, accrue wealth. And if you are not a salaried worker, you're likely trying to do this across multiple jobs and shifts with little security or benefits, and no ability to advance. For her book *Nickel and Dimed,* Barbara Ehrenreich traveled around the United States, taking "unskilled labor" jobs and attempting to survive on those salaries. Throughout her experiment, she worked hard to find a balance between earnings and the cost of living, but despite her best efforts, she almost always came up short, even when making the best possible (and available) choices in terms of rent and transportation. She says, "Something is wrong, very wrong when a single person in good health, a person who in addition possesses a working car, can barely support herself by the sweat of her brow. You don't need a degree in economics to see that wages are too low and rents too high."

After a successful fight for a minimum-wage increase in New York

State, a fast-food worker in New York City, if they work full time, makes an average of about $33,000 a year. The average cost of a studio apartment in NYC is $2,600; that obviously goes up if you have a family or need more space. Most people are working more than one minimum-wage job or have a side hustle that helps with the exorbitant cost of living. But it's hardly enough money to live on, let alone save for the future, own a home, or put a child through college. And despite these criminally low wages for what are often essential services, little has changed for those trying to work their way out of poverty. Corporations run these enterprises at staggeringly low wages because, as Ehrenreich writes, "employers resist wage increases with every trick they can think of and every ounce of strength they can summon."

Perhaps the greatest hustle of all is that many of these companies in and outside New York City that employ low-income, "unskilled" employees rely on their employees' use of Medicaid, food stamps, and other government services to avoid raising wages to a livable standard. A 2020 study by the Government Accountability Office found that corporations such as McDonald's and Walmart were the largest beneficiaries of these programs, making their exploitative wages possible with taxpayer dollars. Who is demotivated now?

Yet, the welfare system itself operates on the logic that if you give people barely enough (or not enough) to survive, they will want to work. (To be clear: It's also like that because some people have to be poor so that the rich can stay rich.) But instead of providing people with the means to survive or thrive, whether by wages or through support from the state, we dole out the ethos that personal failure is what causes poverty rather than structural inequality and government policies designed to keep people poor.

That allows us, as a society, to justify being so angry about the idea of people getting things we don't believe they earned, rather than considering what everyone ought to have. The government enshrines this sentiment in policy, but we as individuals often believe this, too. Just think about all the old grumps who have said, "I paid off my student loans; they should have to, as well!" And this is a particularly egregious sentiment considering the 2023 Supreme Court decision that struck down President Biden's student loan forgiveness program, shoving younger people back into a cycle of debt they had a short respite from during the pandemic.

Americans have a very punitive sense of what is fair, but fairness itself is just one big lie.

. . .

Embracing a "get yours" culture of hustle is extremely compelling. It feels much more empowering to believe that you have a say over your own fate than to accept the harder truth that most of our successes and failures are determined by structural realities: policies that don't give workers enough support; discrimination in the workplace; lack of access to necessary education, training, and professional networks. And a hustle mentality is not without merit. Often, it helps with the goals you may have set for yourself. There is still a need to find our "margin of maneuverability": the space between the realities we face and what is possible within them.

Believing that you can get ahead if you hustle just enough is a survival mechanism in the face of insurmountable barriers. Part of hustle culture is this massive industry of books, courses, and motivational speakers that sell us on the idea of hustling—everything from *Hustle Believe Receive: An 8-Step Plan to Changing Your Life and Living Your Dream* by Sarah Centrella to Chris Guillebeau's *Side Hustle: From Idea to Income in 27 Days* to the bible of hustle culture, *Hustle Harder, Hustle Smarter* by Curtis Jackson, aka the rapper 50 Cent. There is no shortage of business books about how to work harder to get what you want in the workplace—hack your schedule, multitask, build relationships—or learn how to outwit the competition. Brand it any way you want, but ultimately, most business advice is about how to hustle *every day*.

If our bookshelves show us anything, it's that endemic to American idealism is an infatuation with people who have made it. We are obsessed with "self-made" successes: Jeff Bezos, Bill Gates, Steve Jobs, Barack Obama, Oprah Winfrey. Fundamental to President Obama's appeal was the fact that he came from humble origins, raised by a single mother, but through hard work and perseverance, he attended Ivy League schools and ended up in the highest office in the land: a true testament to the American Dream. Or consider Oprah's rise to stardom: Born into poverty in rural Mississippi to a single mother, she faced abuse in the farming town where she was growing up and eventually moved to Nashville, Tennessee, to live with her father. From there she went to Tennessee State University and started to work in radio in Nashville, which led to her career in journalism. Over time, she built herself into a media mogul, brand, and one of the richest, most powerful people on the planet. Both stories are remarkable: people overcoming insurmountable odds and doing it with grace and style and to tremendous success.

But we fetishize these stories rather than acknowledging that they are rare, if not nearly impossible, and that people like Obama and Winfrey are two among millions. And often these stories, rather than being inspiring, make you feel like you can never measure up; that constant feeling of failure is a byproduct of an economic system that devalues you. Society perpetuates this, but so do we as individuals. I've done it to myself: pushing myself to work beyond what is reasonable and considering it a failure when I haven't accomplished something that was likely unrealistic or damn near unachievable. I've also done it to others, pushing down the never-ending stress I was feeling while joking with similarly-aged colleagues about how "these kids will never make it" because they weren't willing to sacrifice as much as I had. "They actually log off at five P.M. Good luck!"

And my initial reaction to my younger colleagues' attempts to preserve their work/life balances, while knee-jerk, wasn't totally wrong, either. To function in the type of economic system that we have right now, there is an expectation that sacrifice to the company is normal and to excel at anything, you have to go as far as you are physically able and emotionally willing. And also, not every negative experience necessitates a "mental-health day"—and sometimes it can feel like an absurd excuse to get out of a work obligation. (We used a fake cough.)

If you are lucky, when you do sacrifice your time and sanity for your employer's bottom line, you are rewarded for it. And sometimes you are lucky. As much as I want to throw the whole idea of hustling away, it's also worked for me. I am good at the low-key side hustle (which is to say that I have zero boundaries with work and am great at making myself feel bad if I'm not always working). I blogged and wrote books on the side while managing completely different careers—teaching, community organizing, and then digital communications. I didn't even get a job in journalism until I was thirty-seven, but because I'd been freelance writing and editing for free on the side, I qualified for a senior-level job when I did.

I am still working on figuring out where I'll land, but I'd be disingenuous not to admit that my hustle helped me get to a place where I could have more control over what I was doing with my life. And I've seen young women around me—especially other women of color—who hustled and overcame barriers to get where they are. They hustle because their day job isn't paying them enough, or they hustle because they are not getting promoted fast enough and want to get ahead, or they hustle because they don't feel inspired by what they are doing, and they seek inspiration elsewhere. They hustle for so many reasons. And I can't knock their hustle! But I know firsthand what all of us have sacrificed to get where we are in the face of a system and society that doesn't have our backs. And I also know that my own success is the exception, not the rule.

Younger generations are saying no to the hustle and showing less of a commitment to working themselves nearly to death than older generations. I am jealous of the young people that can say no to late nights at the office, because it's so not in my DNA to even utter the word in a work context. I was raised in and brainwashed by hustle culture and external definitions of success—but I had to be, as the child of immigrants, as part of a generation that internalized the "work hard, play hard" ethic and the belief that women are as good as, if not better than, the men around them. This conflict between wanting (or needing) to succeed on society's impossible terms and wanting a broken system to get better is at the heart of some of the intergenerational battles around work ethic, failure, and hustle culture happening today.

As a Gen X woman, I was fed strong myths about the benefits of working hard, which then made me feel like shit if I wasn't always working. It helped me beast my career, but it also meant that when I hit forty, I was exhausted, which I now recognize as seismic burnout.

And then the pandemic hit.

The Year Everything Changed

A week before New York City went into lockdown, I woke up one morning too afraid to go into the office to get my laptop. By then, I'd been executive editor at *Teen Vogue* for two years. Half my colleagues at Condé Nast had just returned from Milan Fashion Week, and Milan, over the past few weeks, had become the first major epicenter of the COVID-19 pandemic outside of China. Two people at our company had been diagnosed with COVID; one worked on my floor. The office hadn't shut down yet, and we were told to continue coming in, but I'd read enough. It was March 11, 2020, and, in an anxious haze, I concluded it was too risky to return for my things.

The following week, it became clear that we wouldn't be able to go back to the office for a while—but we were still planning photoshoots and events for the end of the month. Around this time, I wrote in my journal, "Everyone thinks we're going back to the office by the end of this month. They don't realize this, but we are *probably* not going to be going back in until the end of April." I must have been very proud of myself at the time for my no-nonsense assessment of the situation at hand. (My former team didn't return to the office until the fall of 2021, and then only on a part-time basis.)

At the time, I was living in a tiny, overpriced studio apartment in Brooklyn, which meant I was also suddenly living and working in one room and a bathroom. Signing the lease in the fall of 2019 was a be-lated fortieth birthday gift to myself that I felt I deserved; the rent was slightly above my means, but I'd convinced myself that getting older meant getting more comfortable with living in debt. Plus, I said to myself, I'd spent the last few years taking care of everyone else, and it was time to take care of me.

The year before the pandemic had been a difficult one. In 2019, my father passed away after years of health problems. Two months after he died, my mother was diagnosed with breast cancer. I was managing my grief for my father, the care of my mother, and work—almost as though I was competing with myself over how much I could take on without falling apart. I was finding out, even before the pandemic: My hair was falling out in patches, my ankles were swollen, and there was not enough concealer in the world to make me look less tired.

So, by the time the pandemic officially arrived in New York, I had already been in panic mode for months. As the city and then the entire country shut down, the only sounds—day and night—wafting into my twelfth-floor Brooklyn windows from outside were those of ambulance sirens, most likely rushing people to hospitals and, eventually for some, ventilators. Those of us who didn't have to work as frontline responders or essential workers prepared to work from home indefinitely; those with kids grappled with childcare needs or homeschooling or both.

My job as the editor of a digital magazine transitioned easily to the land of Zoom and Slack, but my lifestyle as a single woman in charge changed overnight. Before the pandemic, I'd spent a lot of time shuttling around NYC in cabs—feet pinched in uncomfortable shoes, body stuffed into Spanx, jumping between the office, events, bars, restaurants, and let's not forget Fashion Week. Then, a typical day started at eight A.M.—even though it really should have started at seven A.M.—when I'd roll over to grab my phone while Alexa yelled at me to get up. I'd open Slack and the Google News app to see what fresh hell the day had in store. I'd crawl out of bed to make coffee and often end up back in it to answer emails (and to blunt the anxiety that came at the start of each day with the coziness of my bed).

Those days usually ended well after eight P.M., either because I worked late or because I had an event or was seeing friends, or sometimes just because I wasn't even sure what I'd do at home in my studio apartment. (I didn't have time to date—I was *busy*.) The lifestyle was exhausting me, but I wasn't conscious of that—I was doing important work, which was what mattered. *This is the price of success,* I told myself. *You feel like shit all the time!*

Working from a home that I couldn't leave during a pandemic gave me space to reassess my "girlboss" life. My overpriced studio started to feel like a grown lady's dorm room—upgraded from Ikea to West Elm. It had really only ever served as a place for me to sleep and microwave leftovers. And, as we learned more about the virus, what was an indulgent treat for grown-up me started to feel like a death trap: hundreds of other people lived in my building, and we had to share the same hallways and elevators. In my most paranoid moments, I worried that the vents—connecting my apartment and everyone else's to the heating and cooling systems—could pump air from infected people's apartments into my own. (Listen, I'm not an HVAC specialist, and in those scary weeks of isolation, anything seemed possible.)

Meanwhile, I was aware even then that I was one of the lucky Americans: I'd kept my job and got to work from home during the pandemic. At the height of the pandemic, only 35 percent of American workers were able to work from home (a number that surprised me, considering how much airtime our WFH experience got), while the rest had to leave their houses and be at constant risk of exposure. Americans who pivoted to working from home were mostly office workers. A Pew study found that eight months after the pandemic started, in December 2020, 71 percent of this work-from-home pool was still working remotely. By early 2023, the same Pew study reported that 35 percent of workers who were able to work from home still do.

And who were those workers getting to work from home? Generally, they were college-educated Americans who were more likely to have a job that they could do from home—middle- and upper-income workers. The pandemic, then, further widened the divide between the service sector and office workers. Though we live interdependent lives, employees who could work from home during this time were safer, less likely to lose their jobs, and more able to save extra money as their expenses decreased than those who continued to have to go to a separate workplace, furthering the wealth gap.

Beyond those who got to work from home and those who still had to commute are the twenty million people whose jobs were lost in the first few months of the pandemic. That shot our unemployment rate to 14 percent, a number not seen since the Great Depression. Many of those people were in the service sector. In one study, 25 percent of U.S. adults reported that they or someone in their household had lost their job because of COVID-19, and 15 percent said they themselves lost their jobs. The majority of this job loss was among younger adults and lower-income workers. (By late 2022, it was reported that most of the jobs lost had been recovered.)

The pandemic was a wake-up call on a lot of fronts, but perhaps one of the most crucial was our awakening (however briefly) to labor conditions—our own and those of others, especially hospital workers, frontline responders, and other essential workers. What was already true became clear to those who had been able to ignore it before: Many middle- and upper-middle-class lives are propped up by an underclass of support workers, including home health aides, nannies, babysitters, house cleaners, drivers, and other workers I am not rich enough to really know about. And the most undervalued members of our society were also finally seen (however briefly) as the most important: nurses, teachers, grocery store workers, and home care workers.

For working mothers, the ability to work had long been supported by access to childcare, be it from nannies, daycare, or school. Without those supports or the money for those supports, 15.7 percent of working mothers experienced unemployment by April 2020, and not all returned to the workforce in the following two years.

The "age of inequality" was laid bare in front of us; the pandemic erased any pretenses we may have had that there isn't a stark line between the privileged and the not-so-privileged, and an even starker one between the rich and the middle- and working-class. According to

Forbes, as of April 2021, "U.S. billionaires have gotten about $1.2 trillion richer during the pandemic."

The pandemic was simply the tipping point, as many people were already sick of working all the time. Enough was enough; American workers were fed up.

Meanwhile, scared as I was in that first pandemic month, isolated in my apartment, I started to notice some other data points. My joints hurt less. The bags under my eyes had started to fade, as did the constant feeling of dread I'd had every night before going to bed. I noticed that in the Zoom window my face looked brighter. My body was communicating that it liked the forced break from hustling. I began to wonder if there was more to life than this career I had fought to build, this job I had killed myself to get.

And I was far from the only one who was experiencing this shift.

The Great Realizations to the Great Resignations

"I just don't want to work this hard anymore," my friend Anjali texted me in late August 2021. At the time, she was a senior director for a tech company and regularly worked sixteen-hour days for a women-led start-up. She wasn't someone who ever shied away from a long workday; it was practically part of her identity. Pre-pandemic, whenever we had dinner plans, I padded in extra time because I knew she'd get caught up leaving the office. She knew that, to be really successful in her male-dominated field (where she was used to people underestimating her intelligence because she was a pretty young woman), she would have to work twice as hard as the men around her.

But during the pandemic, that excitement for work was slowly replaced with a recognition that she hadn't been spending enough time on her personal life. A chronically single NYC lady, she started dating someone seriously, and they were spending a lot of time together. She was happier than she had been in a long time and started to realize there was more to life than her hustle. Her love of getting ahead transitioned to a consideration of what work could look like if it was a little less demanding.

Her pandemic epiphanies came one after the other. "If you are miserable at your job, most people now know everything else will also suck," she told me.

It wasn't just Anjali who felt the need to shift the role that work took in her life. My group chats were full of friends and colleagues voicing frustration that they were working so much. They wanted to focus more on other parts of their lives—work on their relationships, get healthier, and all the other things that we were taught, especially as women, that we'd have to sacrifice to get ahead in our careers (or even just to survive in them).

Another friend and former colleague, Asia—a twenty-five-year-old Black woman from Queens who works as a beauty writer and influencer—regularly worked from morning until night pre-COVID, heading to breakfast events, then lunches, and finally soirées at night, all while writing her articles. One of the most motivated young women I've ever met, she told me that since the pandemic, she worries she is "behind in her career" but asks herself if what she is doing is really of benefit to both her personal and her career growth, a question she probably wouldn't have asked before. A few years later, she's mostly back to regularly scheduled programming but makes sure to find enough time to rest, exercise, and spend time with her boyfriend.

Another friend and colleague, Kelly, a white woman in her midthirties who put in long hours for her executive media job, told me she was less depressed and less anxious after not having to go to the office anymore; she ended up giving up her NYC life and moving to Austin, Texas. Now she's living in L.A. with a big job and is balancing working from home with going to the office, while taking better care of her mental and physical health.

A college senior at UCLA, Mona, an Asian American woman, grew up putting school first, with the belief that working toward the future should be at the front and center of her life. Now she was rethinking what life after graduation might look like. Even though she has a job in management consulting lined up after college, the downtime during quarantine had given her space to realize "There was more to life than just getting a job and making money."

This was the theme of late 2020 and 2021: Friend after friend told me they were rethinking how much they work and why they work, reflecting on what makes a meaningful life outside the milestones we subject ourselves to. And these were not necessarily people who had cushy savings accounts or family money on which to fall back.

I, too, had been actively rethinking how I wanted to change my life. After my father died, our family shifted in irrevocable ways, and that made me see life differently, too. So, in April 2020, I decided to ditch the expensive apartment in Brooklyn and move in with my mother an hour and a half away in upstate New York. We owned the house she lived in together, and I had regularly struggled to keep up with my apartment rent *and* my share of the mortgage. She was also going through her final round of chemo all alone amid a pandemic. After quarantining for more weeks than was recommended (since people who were immunocompromised were the most vulnerable), I jumped in our Nissan Rogue with my few bags and one grumpy cat. I began the drive upstate windows down, masked, and with the cold April air making my eyes tear up.

What I thought would be a few weeks turned into five months of living in the woods of Putnam County. As NYC, and then the country, were hit with tragedy after tragedy—the endless loss of human life, our lives disrupted, our politics altered—I was going for walks in the woods and working at my job with a view of trees instead of skyscrapers. It took a cataclysmic, life-changing event to pull myself out of my environment and bring into stark focus how, despite how it looked on the outside, I was deeply unhappy and unhealthy in my "successful" career.

In the beginning, you see, working from home had the energy of a snow day, but the work quickly started to feel more intense: from endless Zoom meetings to new tasks and check-ins. There was a lot of anxiety about layoffs, and many of us were feeling the pull to overperform even while the world was falling apart. Days would go by when it'd be dark outside, and I'd realize I hadn't eaten that day or even brushed my teeth. I was severely burned out and crumbling under the pressure of being a leader in a moment of such trauma and transition.

My friend Syreeta, who had been working as an English professor at a community college, told me that her days got longer as she moved from a more flexible work schedule of a few days a week to teaching online. "My teaching load went twenty to thirty percent more work, and that was completely tied to helping students transition, or at least feel secure while things started to fall apart around us," she told me.

My friend Daphne, who is a maternity nurse in a busy NYC hospital, didn't have the ability to work at home. To call her job "extremely stressful" during the pandemic doesn't even begin to describe what she went through—a now well-documented experience, as we learned just how stretched thin and struggling from burnout health professionals were and continue to be.

Nurses and other healthcare workers were among the many workers who decided to call it quits during and after the pandemic. According to the Bureau of Labor Statistics, 2.9 percent of all employees—or 4.3 million Americans—had said goodbye to their jobs as of the summer of 2021, a trend that has carried through to today. These resignations were not clustered in what you might consider safer industries where people have backup plans: the highest number of resignations was in the hospitality industry and retail. Those losses in healthcare have led to continued labor shortages.

According to a 2022 Pew study, workers left their jobs because of low pay, not enough opportunities for promotion, and feeling disrespected at work. But of the many theories of why this might be—from government relief efforts supposedly making it easier not to work to a lack of childcare workers to low wages—the explanation that seemed to resonate was that Americans' relationship to work is changing. What has economists and social scientists marveling, though it is perhaps hardest to measure, is what Dr. Anthony Klotz, the organizational psychologist who coined the expression *the great resignation,* calls "pandemic epiphanies." He argues that one reason for the high number of resignations was the backlog of people waiting for the pandemic to ease before they quit. (I did!)

But that alone doesn't account for these statistically high numbers of job ditchers. The reality was that many jobs became dangerous and untenable, employees suffered burnout, and many people began to feel like their only option for their health and well-being was to quit. Middle-class Americans also had a little more savings than before, after spending a year at home forgoing family vacations and other living expenses that come with going outside.

The pandemic was a life-changing event, and here's the thing about such events: They make you more reflective. That's certainly what happened to me as I began to rethink what I was doing with my life. It can be easy to forget a few years later, but most Americans' lives changed profoundly during the pandemic in one way or another, which led to people reflecting on what makes for a meaningful life, especially outside of work. People were asking themselves why they were working so hard and leaving little time for their families, their friends, hobbies, or even a good meal. Maybe we didn't need as much as we thought we did. Yes, most American families need two incomes, but maybe there were some pieces of our budget that weren't as necessary as we thought.

Less fortunate families were asking the same questions: Was risking their life for poor treatment and low wages worth it? Many decided, no; others made the calculation that it was more affordable to have one parent stay home to do the care work than to spend money on childcare. Single mothers had to make impossible choices.

In a survey two years after the pandemic, most American women said their lives were disrupted in some way by the pandemic—either their relationships, their future, their mental health, or their work.

People who lost their jobs reconsidered their priorities, changed careers, or figured out how to make ends meet in other ways. People who quit their jobs reconsidered what kind of worker they wanted to be. And people who stayed in their jobs started to agitate for change: There was a rise in workplace organizing, with people demanding better pay and working conditions. In early 2022, the National Labor Relations Board reported a 60 percent jump in workers petitioning for union elections. Workplace agitation was at an all-time high, with everyone from fast-food workers, Starbucks employees, Amazon workers, Hollywood employees, and farm equipment makers to hospital workers pushing unionization efforts and going on strike. Despite all this, the Bureau of Labor Statistics reported in late 2022 that overall union membership was on the decline, despite the increase in petitions for representation. (According to NPR, this was due to the increase in nonunion jobs.)

But, despite all the headlines and the anxiety about the great resignation, most people didn't actually quit their jobs; they just really wanted to, or they "quiet quit"—as in, they stopped working above and beyond and all the time. Rent, student loan payments, and inflated prices on goods did not allow for most people to stop working. The great resignation was less about leaving your job and more about resigning yourself to it.

In March 2021, I quit my *Teen Vogue* job. I had already spent most of the year on Zoom, leaving the shiny twenty-fifth floor of the World Trade Center behind to work from the safety of home. With that came the loss of all the perks that make a job like that fun: eating at restaurants, in-person events, and wearing cool clothes sent to you by designers. Instead, I was facing long days in virtual meetings, and an increasingly agitated staff that I had to push through experiencing the trauma of a pandemic so they could write and report on it.

I had also long wanted to write more and edit less but could never figure out how to make the numbers work. Plus, I had been overlooked for promotion and was given no real options for advancement at the company. But leaving a stable job with a solid salary and benefits takes planning and often a secondary income, which I didn't have. The freedom to work from anywhere, however, had given me the space to leave the hustle-bustle of New York City for a little while, reduced my cost of living, and allowed me time to write a book proposal. And I was able to take on a series of side hustles to cover any financial gaps and the exorbitant cost of health insurance.

I was lucky to get space during the pandemic to reflect on what would make me happy—and it turned out it wasn't a fancy, big-shot full-time job. Despite the glossy exterior of working at a magazine, I was frustrated with the rat race and wanted to spend more time being creative and less managing an increasingly unhappy staff in the face of budget cuts, constant turnover, and living life during a time of endless turbulence.

A lot of people have asked me why I'd leave such a dream job ("What actually happened?" many well-intentioned but extremely nosy friends and family members have asked), and I've told them that I knew it was a dream job . . . for someone other than me. My prior work experiences had been focused on social-justice causes and working for the independent press; *Teen Vogue* was my first foray into mainstream media. And I knew that despite the glitz and glamour and fun of working at a magazine, I'd probably never realize my full potential there—and the idea of really making an impact felt impossible.

Looking back, I also realize that I had worked so hard for so long that I had never had the space to be anything but absolutely and completely grateful for any institution that was willing to pay me for the skill set of a professional feminist. But times had changed, and even *Teen Vogue* had become politically focused. So I bought in, and the next thing I knew, I was posting gratitude selfies from professional-quality fashion shoots about fate, luck, and hard work. I was fixing my fake fur to the loud thumping music of New York Fashion Week.

And it wasn't just that I worked hard but that I had come to believe that I was the lucky one, not the other way around.

A Scarcity Mindset

We are not hustling in a vacuum: We're hustling for money, power, or to beat out the supposed competition. Women are exhausted from hustling because it is assumed we will work twice as hard as our male counterparts. There's no time to look up at who is setting the terms of the hustle, but only at other would-be hustlers. I have felt this personally: I'm a woman in her midforties. I didn't get my first "big" job until I was thirty-three. It paid $65,000 a year, and that felt like a lot of money at the time. For my family, it was a good, stable salary, and no sooner did I start earning it than my father fell ill, and I had to take on quite a bit of family financial responsibility.

I felt pretty good about myself for making $65,000 in that job, considering how little I had been making up until that point. Since then, though, I've been routinely surrounded by people, often younger than me, who make so much more than that (and ask for even more). I think they should! And all the same, even though I know it's foolish, I sometimes feel flashes of bitterness that I didn't get paid as much at their age. I'll forget how happy I was to earn what I did and only regret the security I might have built up if I had earned more.

But of course, money is not fair, and earning it is not fair, and the fact that someone makes a little more than me, and at a younger age, is not why I didn't make more. Yes, perhaps there were cultural barriers and generational barriers; I didn't have the right networks until much later, and people weren't really interested in hiring mouthy feminists when I embarked on my career (the way they may be today). But that's not the fault of a new generation of workers who demand better. That's the fault of managers, CEOs, and people who don't pay enough taxes (the rich), as well as systems that have historically stopped people like me from advancing in the workplace.

But it's easier to blame the people directly in front of us, to focus on them instead of the bigger picture, to be jealous and fight amongst ourselves so that we forget to consider how the bosses—the people who determine our salaries, the HR people—are usually the ones who are nickel-and-diming us. It's much easier to believe we are special, and that our inherent contributions are valuable, and that this value is reflected in what we make.

At *Teen Vogue*, I made $153,000—a miniscule salary compared to what most people make in an executive-level job (and people regularly assume I made much, much more), especially at a big company, but it was the most money I'd ever made. I thought I was pretty much rich, and by certain standards, I was: It put me well within the upper-middle-class income bracket. It was *a lot* of money, and I was grateful for it, but given the nature of who I was around, I still wanted more. I felt like I contributed more than I was being paid for, that people around me made more for doing less—even though I made so much more than the people who worked for me. All I could see was up, where I thought I needed to go.

All that navel-gazing, and then I woke up one day and realized it was bullshit to think that anyone around me had anything to do with how I was valued. I was just a number on a spreadsheet, and how much I earned had less to do with what I brought to the table than with what they could afford to pay, and what they could get away with paying me. I could have said no or asked for more (and I did), but I also made a personal assessment that, at the end of the day, the money was enough for me because it was more than I had ever made, and I was getting paid for something I loved to do. Baby Samhita never thought that was going to be possible.

But the fact I believed that it was enough, or that I had earned it, was a trap. I did earn it! But that doesn't necessarily mean I was treated equally or that the salary was either plenty or not enough—each of these things might be true, depending on how I looked at it. The push and pull about where to put the blame for our own fortunes in the workplace can be hard to make sense of. Of course we should ask for more money, but relying on ourselves and our fallible managers to determine our worth is inherently flawed. Believing the myth about money being tied to our worth only perpetuates the lie that compensation is somehow fair.

And what better way to remove the threat of workers considering the collective than by making everybody focus obsessively on themselves?

To keep us complacent at work, there are myths that we have to believe about our own success: that we earned it, that working hard is a good and noble thing to do, that we are special and deserving because we sacrifice everything to get ahead. But when it becomes apparent that it is more than just hard work that puts certain people in different class strata, people start to question the belief that, in order to live a good life, you have to dedicate that life to your vocation.

The idea of working yourself to the bone is unraveling because people—especially young people—are asking themselves why they are doing it. Research suggests that Gen Z (which will make up one third of the workforce by 2025), while still factoring in salary when choosing a job, tends to show as much if not more interest in jobs that match their values, whether that be their views on social and cultural issues or their views on work-life balance. (Having managed young teams, I've also found this to be true—though I have also found that it varies based on employees' socioeconomic and racial backgrounds.)

Yes, we all have to work enough to make ends meet, but do we need to be clawing our way to the top? Does that have to be how our lives and our successes are defined? And why are so many of us working full-time-plus, yet barely able to cover the basic things in life?

What if work was structured to support employees rather than squeezing every little bit out of us? In a job posting that went viral, the astrology app Chani, founded by the astrologer Chani Nicholas, was hiring for positions on their newly expanding team. In it, the benefits for employees at the company were listed:

- A salary floor of $80k (meaning, no one is paid less than that) #LivingWagesForAll;
- Fully covered health, dental, and vision insurance;
- A 401(k) with a 5% match;
- A flexible work-from-home policy;
- A 4-day workweek;
- 7 weeks of paid office closure a year;
- 4 months paid parental leave;
- Unlimited, flexible paid vacation, plus a vacation stipend;

- Gender-based violence paid and protected leave;
- Unlimited menstrual leave for people with uteruses;
- An annual tech stipend;
- A personal and professional growth stipend; and
- A stipend to help you build wealth.

The job posting ended up being a conversation starter, as it was clearly created to counter some of the thinking that undergirds hustle culture and start-ups: Rather than paying people the least you can get away with, pay them a living wage. Rather than making people work all year round, recognize that they need and deserve downtime (in fact, research suggests it makes them more productive). And rather than keeping your employees dependent on checks month to month, help them build wealth. Plus, be explicit about offering these benefits to historically disenfranchised communities.

And it turns out it's been great for business at the company. The CEO of Chani, Sonya Passi, told *Forbes* that investing in their staff has paid off, and that since they launched, their revenue has grown. "Living in a capitalist world, we are so indoctrinated with a scarcity mindset, and I refuse to invest in a scarcity mindset. I believe that abundance begets abundance, and my experience . . . is showing this to be true," she says.

Imagine a culture where abundance is at the core of how people think about building their business: putting the needs, values, and desires of employees first and focusing on creating an environment that sustains great work.

But achieving all that is not so simple, and companies like Chani are few and far between. Since I left *Teen Vogue*, I've struggled to figure out how to live life on my own terms while sustaining myself. I'm still trying to navigate challenging questions about work/life balance, how to find work that fulfills me that I want to actually do, and how to figure out what "impact" ultimately is and what it looks like at work.

Meanwhile, workplaces are scrambling to figure out what to do with employees who are uninterested in working all the time, regardless of how much they get paid. The pandemic pushed people over the brink, but skepticism among workers toward their workplaces—along with a desire for a better work/life balance—had already been growing. And now that we're a few years out from the pandemic, we have a new set of circumstances to consider: Life has largely gone back to normal, but people still want the flexibility that pandemic life afforded them. Many are not interested in going back into the office five days a week, nor are they interested in resuming their extra work commitments at pre-pandemic levels. This cultural shift is a profound one that we have yet to see the effects of. And there is probably no group of people that is forcing us to reckon with these truths and demanding change more than mothers.

5

HAVING TOO MUCH

To destroy the institution is not to abolish motherhood.
It is to release the creation and sustenance of life into the same
realm of decision, struggle, surprise, imagination, and conscious
intelligence, as any other difficult, but freely chosen work.

—Adrienne Rich, *Of Woman Born:*
Motherhood as Experience and Institution

Recently, I have spent a lot of time thinking about why I haven't had children—mostly because, until I turned forty, I had thought that I would. But one day I looked up from a Zoom meeting, and I was single and in my midforties. Having children had become for me what economist Sylvia Ann Hewlett dubbed a "creeping nonchoice." And if I wanted to have children, it would likely take a medical intervention I was not prepared to have.

I'd never previously imagined I wouldn't have children, but the more I thought about why I hadn't, the more I realized that I *had* made a choice, even if it didn't feel like one. I had subconsciously assessed that I wasn't ready to make the financial, physical, emotional, and spiritual sacrifices I saw my friends making to be parents.

This doesn't mean my life is free of care labor: I take care of my mother, and while we are not yet at the point where I have to do so, I'm already planning to manage her physical care—hopefully by hiring someone. When she was recovering from breast cancer and going through chemo treatments, I would spend half the week in the city and half the week upstate, taking calls in hospital rooms, to be by her side—something I had done while my father was sick. After my father's long illness, I learned what it takes to truly care for someone who is helpless by watching my mother as she would administer his home dialysis. Providing physical care is really hard, and even if I can do it and *will* do it for the people I love, I don't necessarily want to do it.

On the other hand, my brother is a better physical caretaker—he has an actual aptitude for it—but he isn't involved in my mother's care now, and there are no plans for him to be in the future. That's because care work is fused with women's identity. Women are expected to have a natural inclination for care work; women are considered nurturers, a maternal instinct is seen as innate, etc. Care work—whether for our children or our aging parents—sits squarely on our shoulders. There is an assumption that care work is a woman's burden to manage: It is not just her duty; it is her *nature* as an all-sacrificing mother (even if, like me, she is not).

Socialization plays a part in this. Cisgender men learn to do less work at home; they may have grown up simply not thinking about all the details that go into making a household function. Even my most feminist-minded friends lament that their husbands and partners forget basic things, like a much-needed pack-and-play for a family vacation, or require continual reminders of what's next on the daily to-do lists for their household. Almost all these women told me their husbands' seeming ineptitude was not for lack of trying on both sides— there just wasn't enough time in a day to do everything *and* ensure that labor was appropriately divided. Some mothers resigned themselves to doing the bulk of the care work because they simply could not fight with their husbands or partners anymore. "It's like, I can't take care of a third child," one friend told me. As Reshma Saujani writes in her book *Pay Up,* "No matter how much women earn, where they live, or what political party they vote for, they still end up doing about twice as much housework and child-rearing as their male partners. And although it's killing us, we're supposed to act like that's okay."

When I looked around, it seemed like this was mostly true of my friends in male-female relationships, but less so for my friends in same-sex ones. Two female friends of mine from college, Catrin and Amy, married each other, and their relationship struck me as in line with what I'd seen with other same-sex couples I knew. I asked them how care work happened between them, especially after they decided to have a child together more than a decade ago. Catrin took on the labor of pregnancy—and ultimately gave birth to twins—but Amy fully shared in all the work of raising them. "Knowing Catrin and myself, I know this was something we'd fully give to together," Amy said.

Shortly after the twins were born, it became clear to them that childcare for two children cost nearly what Amy earned at her job caring for developmentally disabled adults. So she switched up her schedule and started working weekends while Catrin worked during the week. They both believed that continuity of care for their children was that important. And, as their professional lives progressed, so have their sacrifices to maintain that continuity for their kids. "We've done a pretty good job, and the sacrifices we've made have been worth it," Amy said, even with lower salaries. While they were raising their children, Catrin put herself through nursing school, and now that their children are older, Amy works at Trader Joe's, where she has some scheduling flexibility, while Catrin works in a hospital.

Now, ask yourself, How many cisgender men in heterosexual relationships do you know who have made those kinds of choices to ensure continuity of care for their children? And have the ones you do know faced discrimination or judgment for not being "real men" or "not really working"? The idea of simply demanding that care work be considered real work is an easy one to get behind—we all mostly know and believe it is—but how that can or should play out in policy (especially in policies from which husbands and fathers may still disproportionately benefit without doing more care work) is one of the fundamental questions to tackle when thinking about the barriers to women's equality in the workplace.

The question of "having it all" is not, as Gurley Brown presented it, about sex, money, and career; instead, it is about the real "problem that has no name." Care work is hardwired as the domain of women, it is under resourced, it is not seen as real work, and it is positioned in opposition to progress in the workplace. It's also something women are expected to navigate in isolation if they want to successfully pursue anything else in life—a reality that continues to stymie women's progress.

. . .

When my friend and former colleague Amanda decided to have children, she never imagined that she'd end up at home with them 24/7 in 2020—without childcare, school, or the ability to leave the house and go to the office. In fact, for a long time, she hadn't even been sure when she'd have children, but the election of Donald Trump pushed her timeline for doing so. "I felt really powerless and out of control and was like, 'The one thing I can control is making other good people,'" she says.

Despite working for progressive organizations, Amanda had to fight for sufficient paid parental leave when she decided to have children. And she still felt like she had to assure her employer that her becoming a parent wouldn't be a burden on them. "I felt pressure to not take the time off, like I needed to assure people I would be available to them during that time and be back to work quickly," she told me. Meanwhile, her husband, she noted, was "being celebrated" at his job for taking paternity leave. His doing so was a sign that he was a good dad, while her taking leave was a sign that she was failing people.

I frequently hear similar stories from other women in my circle and, if you're of an age where your friends are having children, you likely have too. My friend Sadye, who had a high-pressure job working for the New York City mayor's office at the beginning of the pandemic, told me, "It's adorable to see everyone else's kid on Zooms. But it's not adorable when you are trying to lead a team or stand in your womanhood, power, and prowess, and you have your kid behind you, hopping around, nagging at you, maybe exposing your bra. It's not cute."

Mothers often face discrimination and suffer material consequences at work because of their family-care responsibilities, in ways that fathers and people without children do not. Sociologists call this "the motherhood penalty": the repercussions that women face at work after having children, whether that means lower wages or being overlooked for promotions. The implicit bias here is the belief that women who have children are less committed to their job or are less capable of doing that job because their motherhood responsibilities get in the way. Every mother I talk to has stories about feeling guilty if childcare needs come up during the workday, being judged by colleagues for leaving the office early to pick up their children, or firmly believing they have lost opportunities because they have children. The long-held assumption for ambitious women in the workplace is that if you want to have children, you will have to sacrifice your career for it. As Sheryl Sandberg laments in *Lean In*, women often remove themselves from the workplace because they know that if they want to have children, there will be limits on how far they can advance there.

Women with care responsibilities at home are more likely to be overlooked for promotions and kept out of C-suites. It is, on some level, acceptable to be biased against mothers at work. Maybe nobody says anything, but the vibe is there—eye rolls, not being invited to meetings, snide remarks about workload. The assumption is that women who have care responsibilities are dropping the ball at work, and that they are less reliable than childless people or fathers (who apparently do not have children?), who can allegedly work uninterrupted.

There are two myths about motherhood at play here. The first is that once you have children, your priorities shift, so you can no longer focus on your career the way you could pre-childbirth. (The reality is, this is sometimes true and sometimes not true.) And the second is that motherhood *should* be the main focus in the life of any woman who has a child. Jessica Valenti writes in *Why Have Kids*, "We *must* believe that parenting is the most rewarding, the hardest, the most important thing we will ever do. Because if we don't believe it, then the diaper changing, the mind-numbing *Dora* watching, the puke cleaning, and the 'complete self-sacrifice' that we're 'locked in for life to' is all for nothing."

The question of whether caretaking is rewarding or not is almost secondary to the bigger issue, which is that, whether it is or is not rewarding, most mothers have to do it. The irony, of course, of mothers getting short shrift at work is that much of society is structured around the maintenance of the nuclear family. Our economic system is only possible because of the unpaid labor of mothers and caretakers. Angela Garbes writes in *Essential Labor*, "If mothers and care workers were to withhold their labor, whole countries and economies would grind to a halt." Consider the cooking, cleaning, diaper changing, clothes washing, homework helping, doctor's appointments, elder feeding, and schedule maintaining that a woman does for her family. What would happen if she stopped all of it? And why is that work considered less valuable? Garbes writes that moving "reproductive labor" to the domain of the home, making it a private matter and not part of the economy, inherently devalues that work, making it low-wage or free labor. "If those who do 'professional' work had to commensurately pay the care workers who made their work possible, there would be less profit to be made. Without us, the system falls apart," she writes.

This free labor is ultimately unsustainable.

Our treatment of mothers is indicative of a society that devalues motherhood, caretaking, and the contribution of mothers to the workforce. Caretaking is core to a healthy, just, and balanced society, and we are nothing without the work of mothering. So, why do we treat women with care responsibilities like an afterthought when we talk about the workplace and what it takes for women to succeed?

When the pandemic arrived, the imbalanced treatment of women who decide to have children revealed itself even more, even as the assumption that middle-class or slightly more privileged women would somehow be protected from this gender-based divergence in attitudes was also exposed as a myth. A generation that was fed a tall tale about "having it all" realized, en masse, that having it all meant literally *doing* it all. They had it all and then some, but not enough time to manage it.

Working mothers—who'd likely already suffered job losses as they gave birth to and raised young children—were more likely than fathers to leave their jobs at the beginning of the pandemic in order to focus on childcare. Nearly two million women had dropped out of the workforce by 2021—many of them mothers, and many of them in low-paying service-sector or retail jobs. As of late 2022 there were still about one million women missing from the workforce compared to the pre-pandemic years, but it's worth noting that the majority of mothers kept working—often under untenable circumstances. The dividing line between mothers who were pushed out and mothers who kept their jobs was educational status. Mothers were pushed out of the workforce for a variety of reasons, but among those reasons was the need to provide childcare or homeschool their children or both—either because their male partners made more money or didn't do as much caretaking or simply because they were single moms and there wasn't anyone else to help them.

And if you were to think that transgender mothers faced a different fate, you would be wrong. According to one study, 25 to 56 percent of trans people have children. In interviews with fifty trans parents in the United States, it was found that those families were also hit by the difficulties of parenting during COVID, but for them, the difficulties were compounded by the spate of anti-trans legislation that forced many parents—and trans mothers in particular—to face additional discrimination and be questioned about their competency as parents.

And single mothers, of course, have different considerations: They are responsible for not just all the care work in the house but also all the financial responsibilities of raising the child. The burden on single mothers is tenfold; they are among the most financially vulnerable groups.

It is perhaps for these reasons that the United States is facing declining fertility (despite a pandemic baby bump). Women are delaying

having children because of how untenable it has become to be a working mother. But the majority of women will have children or have to
provide care for someone at some point in their lives, so we can't talk
about women advancing in the workplace if we don't also talk about
the caretaking role that women are expected to play in their families
and society, as the people who take care of *everyone*.

The Fallacy of Choice

Motherhood is sold to us as a personal choice—even after the Supreme
Court overturned *Roe v. Wade*, leading to the loss of abortion rights in
several American states and fundamentally limiting the choice to *not*
be a mother. But the idea of motherhood as a personal decision is a
relatively new phenomenon: For most of humanity, it was just expected that if you could have children, you would often have them by
force or pressure, being tasked with producing the good people of a
given nation.

As journalist Jessica Grose details in *Screaming on the Inside,* "The
expectation that a woman should be a perfect, moral vessel began at
conception. In colonial times, the understanding of reproduction was
that men provided all the material to make the baby—it was their seed
and their seed alone that grew into a person." Those who did not fulfill
this supposedly divine purpose were often judged, chastised, and—
depending on culture and geography—shunned, even though there
were few, if any, ways for women to control their fertility (or treat a
lack thereof) until modern times. (The few exceptions to the judgment
of childless women across history tended to be women who opted or
were forced to serve their society's divinities in lieu of marriage and
children.)

And then there were the women whose reproduction was coerced or
enjoined by state-enforced control. In the United States—both before
and after its founding—enslaved women were forced, often via rape by
their enslavers, to have children and then often violently separated

from those children. In the twentieth century, at least seventy thousand women were forcibly sterilized because they were considered "feebleminded" based on their race, lack of wealth, or alleged disability. This includes the more than three thousand Indigenous women sterilized by federal government health services in the 1970s. Undocumented teen migrants in the United States were being denied abortions as recently as 2019, ostensibly with an eye to forcing them to give birth and adopt out their children, three years before the fall of *Roe v. Wade*.

But controlling our own reproductive rights is fundamental to our ability to decide when, how, and on what terms we enter the workplace. It also plays a role in whether mothers end up in poverty, drop out of college, are forced to take lower-wage jobs to provide for their newly expanding family, or are ultimately pushed out of the workforce for having children.

And what kind of choice is motherhood if you are forced to bear children or are forcibly prevented from doing so? What feminists and other activists have long argued is that "choice" is more than just abortion: It's a full range of reproductive options that give those of us who can bear children the ability to decide when, if ever, is the right time to do so, without shame or judgment. The ability to control when, how, and if they have children is fundamental to women's ability to determine their career and work trajectory, and to ensure their financial well-being.

. . .

But motherhood, and the gendered care work that goes into parenting after you've exercised your options, is in some ways feminism's unfinished business, because it's (for lack of a better word) complicated. There is an unfair division of labor in parenting—driven as much, if not more, by assumptions about how different genders parent than by the biological functions of motherhood like pregnancy, birth, and breastfeeding.

After Friedan's 1963 manifesto, feminists jumped into decades of debate about the oppression that they saw at the root of the institution of motherhood, and the ways women's bodies had been used to uphold it. The physical elements of biological motherhood manifested in the nuclear family with a male "breadwinner" and a stay-at-home mom, which was most popular in the mid-1950s. This led some feminists to be very critical of the social and biological reality of motherhood, arguing that as long as women could physically have children, they would always be under the thumb of the patriarchy.

This was a radical notion that led people outside the feminist movement to assume (in some cases correctly) that said feminists were against motherhood itself. For instance, controversial radical second-wave feminist Andrea Dworkin argued that motherhood fell into the farming model (a cringeworthy description) of womanhood: "women as a class planted with the male seed and harvested; women used for the fruit they bear, like trees; women who run the gamut from prized cows to mangy dogs, from highbred horses to sad beasts of burden."

Shulamith Firestone wrote in *The Dialectic of Sex,* "The heart of woman's oppression is her child-bearing and child-rearing role." She argued that the only way for women to be free was to abolish the nuclear family and pregnancy, calling for the development of fake wombs (honestly, iconic). Her views were as radical then as they sound today, but while these views were not widely shared, her views on children's liberation were. Many feminists believed at the time that without children's liberation—the idea that children should be granted more rights and freedoms, along with protections—there could be no women's liberation.

These feminist thinkers and others are rightfully and readily criticized for their often simplistic and essentialist views on gender as well as their untenable so-called solutions—more thought experiments than actual policy ideas that might help mothers. But they weren't wrong in noticing that the biology of human reproduction is used to justify gender oppression in both public and private spheres.

Obviously, not all second-wave feminists were so skeptical of motherhood. Many, in fact, had children and were deeply interested in the institution of motherhood and how care work was feminized and therefore minimized, not regarded as real, serious work. Poet, writer, and feminist essayist Adrienne Rich, for instance, had three children from her first marriage to Alfred H. Conrad, an economics professor at Harvard University. In 1976, thirteen years after Friedan's *The Feminine Mystique,* Rich wrote her treatise on the institution of motherhood, *Of Woman Born.* Reflecting on her own role as a wife and a mother, she writes that, in their family, it was understood that her husband's job was the more important one, and Rich's burgeoning career as a poet was secondary to supporting him and their children.

After her husband's death, she came out as a lesbian and began a lifelong partnership with the Jamaican American writer Michelle Cliff. As her own politics radicalized and her lived sexuality changed, she reflected more on the role of motherhood—both her own and that of mothers from less privileged backgrounds—and considered how the institution of motherhood held women back from true freedom.

Ultimately, she came to a rather optimistic, holistic view on how society needed to change to support mothers and mothering. "We need to imagine a world in which every woman is the presiding genius of her own body," she writes in *Of Woman Born.* "In such a world, women will truly create new life, bringing forth not only children (if and as we choose) but the visions and the thinking necessary to sustain, console, and alter human existence—a new relationship to the universe."

Black mothers had different concerns at stake—around economic stability and institutional violence. Audre Lorde, who had two children from her first marriage, introduced herself as a "black, lesbian, mother, warrior, poet" and wrote of the differences between Black motherhood and white motherhood. "Some problems we share as women, some we do not," she said in her 1980 essay "Age, Race, Class, and Sex: Women Redefining Difference." "You fear your children will grow up to join the patriarchy and testify against you; we fear our children will be dragged from a car and shot down in the street, and you will turn your backs on the reasons they are dying."

The feminists of the 1970s were fighting for women's equal participation in the labor force; for equal pay; for universal childcare and for care work to be recognized; and for women to be able to control if, when, and how they had children. One of the most definitive moments in American women's lives and their ability to enter the workforce was 1973's *Roe v. Wade* decision, the Supreme Court ruling that constitutionally protected access to abortion.

Roe was arguably one of the causes of women's changed participation in education and the workforce: After *Roe,* the average age of marriage increased (from twenty-one years old to twenty-seven), the number of women that entered the workforce increased (from 43 percent in 1970 to 57 percent in 2019), the likelihood of women going to college increased (in fact, surpassing men in the thirty years since).

· · ·

In the decades since *Roe,* we have gone back and forth on the role personal fortitude and ambition play in women's ability to achieve at work and also at home. In the late nineties, talk of the "opt-out revolution"— the idea that women were choosing to leave the workforce in droves to focus on child-rearing—flooded the media, and a new round of pearl clutching about working motherhood took over. The journalist Lisa Belkin wrote about this phenomenon for *The New York Times* in 2003, and the piece suggests many parallels to what we're seeing now in terms of women leaving the workforce.

In her piece, Belkin explored why so many women around her— many with graduate degrees from Ivy institutions—were voluntarily leaving the workforce. While Belkin acknowledged that the women with whom she was speaking were privileged, she pointed to the systemic issues that shaped their "choice" to leave their jobs—which often had to do with how untenable it had become to have a career while taking care of their families. The women leaving were simply reacting to a no-win situation. As Belkin put it, "It's not just that the workplace has failed women. It is also that women are rejecting the workplace."

Twenty years later, mothers are once again rejecting the workplace in droves. (And we have yet to see what long-term consequences the 2022 overturning of *Roe v. Wade* will have in terms of women's participation in the workforce.) As was true for the women Belkin was writing about in 2003, the choice to leave sometimes isn't a true choice at all.

While much has changed since 1973, it is in many ways worse to be a working mother these days than it was twenty-five years ago. In a 2017 piece for *The New York Times,* Bryce Covert wrote that the 2001 recession pushed many working mothers out of the workforce, and that the numbers never quite recovered. The United States, she noted, ranked sixth globally in women's labor-force participation in 1990, but by 2010 it had fallen to seventeenth. "About a third of that drop . . . could be explained by the fact that other developed countries instituted and expanded policies like paid family leave, subsidized childcare and flexible work arrangements while the United States did barely anything at all," she explains. The experience of motherhood has always differed according to race and class. But whether things are better for some groups of mothers or not, Americans believe things are harder for mothers today than they were twenty-plus years ago.

This trend continued through and after the pandemic, when millions of women were pushed out of the workforce—often after being faced with impossible choices around childcare and work. And while the number of women in the workforce has recovered to pre-pandemic levels, according to one study, the pay gap for women has held steady, and women are still five to eight times more likely to have their careers impacted by their caregiving responsibilities.

The consequences of pushing mothers out of the workforce or straining their participation are far more dire than what you'd gather from a few trend pieces about mothers making impossible choices or dealing with unrealized personal ambitions (though those are also terrible). Mothers make up an important segment of the workforce and our economy. And 41 percent of mothers are sole or primary breadwinners in their families, and that strain puts the financial stability of them and their families at risk. While the debate is often framed in terms of women's ambitions and women's choices, it's not really about that. In reality, mothers' workplace participation is influenced by a lack of infrastructure at work and at home to support them working.

If that trend continues—and all indications suggest it will—being a working mother will become increasingly untenable. And rather than recognizing this as a colossal social failure, ambitious women who want to have children generally feel like they are failing at both. Meanwhile, women who don't have children will still likely have care-work duties and are often expected to stay late and work more, because "you don't have kids"; even more, they're encouraged to emotionally center work in their lives as if it were a real family—another pernicious trend of our time.

Shifting to a Culture of Care

That domestic labor became so closely associated with "mothering" might seem natural—even inevitable—but the idea that women would bear children, cook, clean, and nothing else is a relatively recent development. Sarah Jaffe writes in *Work Won't Love You Back* that domestic labor became a commodity because that was the most convenient structure for enabling capitalism to thrive. She writes that in precapitalist, medieval times, women worked both in and outside the home "as doctors, butchers, teachers, retailers, and smiths." It was through the violent rollout of capitalism that this "dichotomy between 'home' and 'work'" was created, Jaffe writes. As she further notes, the socialist feminist scholar Silvia Federici has also written that women's labor became a "natural resource."

We can hardly argue that women in preindustrial societies had it easy, but with the rise of capitalism—by definition, an economic system in which owners enrich themselves by minimally paying others for their labor—someone had to engage in in-home care work that freed laborers up to toil for others. And that, it seems, is when the idea came into fashion that home-centered care work is both women's natural calling and their personal responsibility, not actual work.

This reconfiguration of domestic labor and parenting into what Jaffe calls "the labor of love"—the idea that care work is something women do naturally, not an actual skill that requires development and expertise—led to the devaluation of both women's labor as wives and mothers and that of domestic workers. In later capitalism, a key component of middle-class women's ability to enter the workforce was the hiring of care workers—disproportionately, women of color—to caretake and raise their children. By then, care work was already denigrated, regarded as less critical, paid poverty wages, and considered necessary for relatively privileged working women.

But some people imagined a better world.

Back in the 1970s, while feminists were debating the social and political constraints of the institution of motherhood, working-class women and women of color were organizing around care work. The imbalanced division of labor when it came to care work was the impetus for the Wages for Housework movement in the 1970s. Led by Italian feminists Mariarosa Dalla Costa and the aforementioned Silvia Federici—and joined by an international crew including American feminist Selma James—the International Wages for Housework Campaign's demands included the simple but controversial idea that housework should be paid as the labor that it is. Historian Louise Toupin writes that the purpose of this international movement was to "change their situation of dependency, reverse the relations of power, and redistribute the wealth that they produced."

The idea of paying "parents" for housework was and remains controversial, even among feminists. Demanding pay for home-based, family-based care work, often performed in lieu of traditional work, can be seen as undercutting efforts to make both homes and workplaces more equitable for women and men—and it indeed runs afoul of efforts to get women out of exclusively serving in the domain of the domestic.

There has, however, been a renewed interest in wages for care work—especially after the pandemic pulled back any pretenses about how much invisible labor parents (and primarily mothers) do. Matt Bruenig argues in *The New York Times*, "It would be possible to give parents with young children a choice between heavily subsidized child-care services or a cash benefit to compensate them for care at home. Finland and Norway already do it."

As writer Jill Filipovic points out, however, his use of the word *parents* is dubious when the majority of parenting still falls on the shoulders of women, and men don't opt into parental leave at equal rates as it is. She writes, "What Bruenig is really advocating for is pushing women out of the labor force, which leaves women financially vulnerable and much more likely to wind up impoverished in the long run; incentivizing more women to opt into the most isolating version of parenthood, which is tied to serious mental-health consequences; and doubling down on the gender-divided earner/carer model that has left so many women miserable and accorded men unearned benefits, status, and resources."

Filipovic is right to be wary: Incentivizing and paying for gendered care labor runs the risk of furthering pay inequality. But it's also true that giving lower-income families money does help them. In a 2018 editorial, Selma James, one of the founders of Wages for Housework, reflected on the 2000 women's strike. One of their core demands was "payment for all caring work—in wages, pensions, land and other resources."

During the pandemic, the child tax credit helped many families stay afloat—and, when it ended, those same families began slipping back into poverty. Rebekah Barber writes in *The 19th,* "Between 2020 and 2021, the credit—which gave monthly payments of up to $300 per child—helped reduce child poverty by more than 40 percent. More than 36 million families received the credit in 2021, and the money helped push the child poverty rate below that of adults for the first time."

But the more significant point about who does care work and who goes to work stands: Women should have the ability to engage in and fulfill their creative and professional desires without social and financial pressure at our throats. *All* people deserve that and are happier when they have it. People who have to prioritize care work for others miss considerable opportunities to be fully invested in their own lives and careers because they have to take care of their families. And people who prioritize outside work often miss opportunities to be as invested as they'd like in their home lives and families.

So, what if care work was accepted as the dignified, skilled labor it actually is, and was compensated as such? What if care work, in general, was accepted in workplaces rather than perceived as a burden on employers? These are big questions that Angela Garbes tries to answer in *Essential Labor,* building on the work of the National Welfare Rights Organization and the Wages for Housework movement. She writes, "Mothering can no longer be considered supplementary or inferior to wage labor. If we reframe domestic work as essential labor and insist upon its centrality in the global labor movement, we create opportunities for solidarity among caregivers, mothers, and all workers."

This is one reason women without children aren't really on the opposite side of the motherhood wars. The gendered expectations that lead employers to subtly discriminate against mothers also lead to the expectation that, if you don't have those specific responsibilities, you are married to your job—because what the hell else is a woman going to do with her free time? And while parental leave in the United States is not long enough even when parents are offered it (it is not federally mandated, but generally, when offered, it's anywhere from eight to twelve weeks), anyone should be able to go on leave for the many events that life throws our way.

And bucking the gendered expectation that women should be partnered and bearing children comes with its own set of prejudices. For instance, one study published in *Organization Studies* found that both men and women felt "single analytically-talented women [are] least suitable for a leadership promotion compared to identically-described single men, married men, and married women." The study also surveyed the success rates of six hundred single women MBA graduates and found that "single analytically-talented women prove the least likely to advance post-graduation compared to all other genders, marital status, and talent groupings."

This "damned if you do, damned if you don't" attitude toward women naturally has disproportionate effects on the most vulnerable among us—trans women, women of color, Black women, Indigenous women, and single mothers. Many such women may "have it all" and then have to do it all without pay, support, or dignity.

We need to move on from a feminism that only prioritizes getting women into the workplace to compete with men (while still doing everything at home) to one that recognizes all the ways in which women contribute their labor to society. So, what would a feminism in the workplace that recognizes care work as essential and legitimate look like? What paths could we take, singly and collectively, to play to our strengths? And how do we define a movement not based just on "girlbosses" but on a reconnection to the very feminine qualities we have been taught to diminish in order to get ahead in the workplace?

This constant tension between following your ambitions and grappling with the reality of your life or your care responsibilities is something Black mothers have had to long navigate. Writer Dani McClain writes in her book *We Live for the We* that there are lessons for this in Black motherhood, which—contrary to tropes around single Black mothers—was never considered a solo mission. Black mothers, she says, didn't just have to parent their own children, but—drawing from sociologist Patricia Hill Collins—they also had to "other-mother" and take care of any child that needed parenting in their families and their communities. McClain writes, "In addition to serving as other-mothers, we had to fight for our right to be mothers." According to McClain, Black mothers have had a different relationship with motherhood—a much more communal one.

McClain has reason to know. When she was living and working as an organizer and activist in Oakland, California, she started traveling back to her hometown in Ohio to care for an aunt who had taken ill. During that time, she met someone in Ohio and ultimately decided to move back to pursue the relationship. Eventually they had a baby, and after having the child, she decided it made the most sense to continue staying in Ohio. She said it was an obvious choice: "How do you raise a kid when you're away from your family? It never occurred to me to move back to New York or to Oakland."

When I asked her if she felt like she'd sacrificed her career advancement to remain close to her family, she said she hadn't considered that, because "part of it is just accepting that life is hard and life is not always what you expect it's going to be [or] what you plan for." Before her move back to Ohio, she'd owned a home in Oakland and had been able to fully realize her career ambitions. But having all those successes "doesn't just automatically make you happy," she said.

Notably, after her move, her mother suffered a paralyzing stroke, and had Dani not been living in Ohio, she likely would not have been the one to find her—let alone been so instrumental in her recovery and care. She helped rehabilitate her mother, who is now walking, talking, and eating on her own again. There is no career accomplishment that could replace that, Dani said.

To be sure, Dani's career accomplishments have still been impactful and tremendously valuable: She is a thought leader, a published author, and has an impressive editing and reporting career. But as much as I love the idea of redefining what ambition and success look like, we both agreed that our decisions to choose care work over career ambitions came with financial consequences. And when she's stressed about the day-to-day, Dani told me she has "no expectation that anything on a structural level is going to help me."

None of us can do this alone. What McClain, Garbes, and many other thinkers and journalists reenvisioning motherhood have written spurs us to ask a much bigger question: What does it mean to have a caring society that supports and centralizes the people who do what Ai-jen Poo, the founder of Caring Across Generations, has called "the work that makes other work possible"? Poo's work has focused not just on organizing domestic and care workers but also on prioritizing their ambitions, their families, and their desires for personal and professional success. Working motherhood is still seen as the realm of privileged white women who rely on the self-sacrificing support of women of color, whether it be online assistants from India or the Philippines, nannies, or elder-care providers.

How do we create workplaces that embrace care, that incorporate our families, that normalize family leave—even when it is not urgent or legally mandated by the state? And consider that the care of others is a societal good and should not be solely an individual responsibility. Poo says, "It's not that it isn't the responsibility of women and families and individuals, but it is about what is our responsibility collectively to each other as a society to ensure that we have real choices and real agency when it comes to the people we love."

What would it look like to consider a workplace and a culture where children and the elderly are our collective responsibility—and thus, supporting people who care for them is, too?

6

THE DIVERSITY-
INDUSTRIAL COMPLEX

It is certain, in any case, that ignorance, allied with power,
is the most ferocious enemy justice can have.

—James Baldwin, *No Name in the Street*

At the end of 2015, I was (still) working for Carla Harris at the
National Women's Business Council. But, after being mentored
by her for a year and listening to her talk about authenticity and
the role it should play in how you show up at work, I knew I had to
follow my gut and change jobs. It turns out my most authentic self was
not the head of comms for a federal advisory council; I wanted to pursue my dreams to work in media and become a full-time writer. I had
been publishing more freelance pieces and was ready to pursue a career
in journalism, but I just didn't know what that career could be.

My longtime friend Jamilah King was working as a journalist at a
self-described millennial news start-up called Mic. They were hiring
someone to manage a section of their website that had been the first of
its kind with an explicit focus on race, gender, and sexuality. She (being
the supportive friend that she is) strongly encouraged me to apply.

I thought perhaps the job was too senior, but I went for it anyway. What I lacked in newsroom management credentials I thought I might be able to make up for with my experience in senior roles that demonstrated an ability to handle most things thrown my way. But still, I knew media companies tend to give preference to those with Ivy League degrees and traditional journalism experience, neither of which I had, so I didn't really think I'd get the job.

Turns out, I was the front-runner. I was plucked from my D.C. career detour to become an editorial director by a South Asian woman, Madhulika Sikka, who was the editor in chief at the time; she said my "pedigree" was exactly what they were looking for.

Ooh, pedigree—no one ever said that about me! (Well, minus the one boss who once said I mostly lacked it.)

The job was a turning point—in my eyes and heart, I had "made it." After years of struggling to find my way, freelancing, and mostly editing for free, I'd been hired for *exactly* what I was passionate about— telling stories from a social-justice perspective and working with a young, diverse team in doing so. The publication was then at the forefront of covering racial politics and the emerging Black Lives Matter movement, Indigenous issues, gender justice, and sexual politics. *And* I was making six figures. The team I was tasked with managing was supremely talented, and the company was invested in making this content as impactful and viral as possible.

It felt like a tiny window had cracked open, and an organization wanted to invest in the work I had long been willing to do for free. Surely, only good could come from this. Baby Samhita never thought it would be possible to find a place where she could use her voice and have access to a platform to exercise it while also making real money. I felt *so cool* and so rooted in purpose. What a time!

In the first few months, I shined, and was quickly promoted to a bigger role covering more of the newsroom, expanding my coverage area to pop culture, gender, and LGBTQ issues. It was exhilarating. I was adept at managing big personalities and facilitating grand ideas, which is exactly what a job like that requires. I was feeling myself—

putting together fresh outfits, getting to work on time, and marching through the halls with a lanyard around my neck. We were making *news,* baby!

My outlook at this time was straight-up idealistic: It was incredibly exciting to work in an environment where the growing societal concern with racial and gender justice would be taken seriously and would be core to our remit. All the same, it was also a job. It wasn't enough that a story be *good*—it had to have an impact, it had to also go viral, and ultimately, we'd have to figure out how to repeat and sustain our successes. That's the conundrum of trying to do work aligned with your values: They may not always align with how to make actual money.

I was in a unique position in the industry, because I had the support to continue to hire diverse teams—not just because it was the right thing to do but because it was necessary for the job. The organization was trying to do something different from what newsrooms had done in the past, and they understood that objectivity wasn't a real thing, because who you are always impacts how you see the world. The goal, instead, was fairness. So, if we wanted to tell diverse stories, we needed diverse voices. I learned firsthand why hiring and cultivating diverse talent is important, and also why it's challenging to do it effectively.

What is our "margin of maneuverability" as people of color, especially women, trying to navigate all the land mines and realities of diversity in the workplace? Women, especially women of color, are in a unique position: We are the ones who are hired when no one else wants the job; we are the fastest-growing segment of business owners; and we have become symbolic of a type of change on which corporations can rely. But the question of what actual diversity and inclusion means is elusive: How does diversity truly benefit us? Is change even possible in environments that are so deeply stratified?

Many of the strategies we had hoped would help us overcome gender inequality in the workplace—from leaning in to hustling to girlbossing—have thus far fallen short. It's clear that focusing solely on our personal ambitions doesn't shift the power dynamics that undergird inequity; instead, we need strategies that elevate and center our collective well-being. And while we may know this to be true, most of us have to figure out how to exist in these environments in which the narratives around our own success compete with broader calls for equality.

What I explore in the second half of this book is what I've learned working as a middle manager and a woman of color about how hard it is to truly live your values in the workplace while taking care of your team and yourself.

In the past few years, we've seen meteoric growth in diversity and inclusion (DNI) or diversity, equity, and inclusion (DEI) programs at work, in schools, in universities, in entertainment, and more. This includes a cottage industry of training and coursework, books, consultants, and coaches. In fact, spending on DNI or DEI was estimated at $7.5 billion in 2020, with projections of reaching $15.4 billion by 2026. Ostensibly, this should be great for people of color in the workplace! But the reality of how these programs function and the beliefs that undergird them are much more complicated.

Is Diversity Good for Business?

The conventional wisdom has long been that diversity helps businesses thrive. Consulting firms like McKinsey have published breathless reports advising businesses on diversity and why it's good for a company's bottom line, workers' creativity, a workplace's overall culture, an organization's cultural relevance, or creating a better connection to a business's customers. The long-standing belief sounds reasonable: Be more relevant, make more money.

Statistically, increased diversity at the top does have an impact on the diversity of the rest of your staff: When there are more women (and/or people of color) at the top of an organization, there are more women (and/or people of color) hired across the company. Research on this goes back a long way: A 2001 paper from sociologists at UCLA analyzed employment data from five different American cities in the early 1990s, concluding that "firms where blacks are in charge of hiring (or black employers) are considerably more likely to employ blacks than are firms where whites are in charge of hiring (or white employers)." More recently, the World Economic Forum found similar data about women in leadership positions: The key to hiring more women is to hire more women.

Anecdotally, before I started working at *Teen Vogue*, almost every person that hired or promoted me was either South Asian or Black. The one time I was hired into a professional job by a white HR person, she hired me at entry level when I was already a decade into my career. Within my first two months on the job, management realized they had made a mistake, and I was swiftly promoted and given a raise.

But the research that claims increased diversity helps a company's bottom line is less compelling when pressure tested. In a *Harvard Business Review* piece titled "Getting Serious About Diversity: Enough Already with the Business Case," authors Robin J. Ely and David A. Thomas write that when they delved into diversity-is-good-for-business research, it didn't fully hold up. "We know of no evidence to suggest that replacing, say, two or three white male directors with people from underrepresented groups is likely to enhance the profits of a *Fortune* 500 company," they write.

They did find that diversity supported "higher-quality work, better decision-making, greater team satisfaction, and more equality," but those rarely impacted the bottom line. The skepticism about these corporate policies isn't an argument against DEI programs, but it underscores the fact that when you reduce diversity initiatives to a money-making enterprise, you run the risk of creating an environment where people from underrepresented backgrounds feel like token hires—and, should those diversity initiatives fail, you lose support from management. Saying "Diversity is good for business" is not a holistic or equitable solution.

And last, and perhaps most surprising—though unsurprising to those of us who have tried to manage teams these past few years—

without proper infrastructure and support, increased diversity can hurt team dynamics. Ely and Thomas write, "Having people from various identity groups 'at the table' is no guarantee that anything will get better; in fact, research shows that things often get worse, because increasing diversity can increase tensions and conflict."

Erica Lovett—who I met when she was the head of diversity and inclusion at Condé Nast—echoes this sentiment. In a 2019 report from the Council of Fashion Designers of America, she is quoted as saying that, while fashion has become interested in the visibility of diversity, "visibility alone is not the solution to advancing diversity and inclusion."

Now holding a similar job at Cartier, she told me that one of the reasons she advocates so hard for diverse leaders is that they are more likely to have empathy for their staff. "The more managers you have that come from just a plethora of backgrounds, of all different socioeconomic statuses and classes and religions and backgrounds, then [the more] those experiences become normalized," she says. This means employees have more potential advocates. "They themselves have had these experiences, and they're in a position of power, so they're not afraid to say something about it," she says.

Still, Angela Davis was right when she said, "I have a hard time accepting diversity as a synonym for justice. Diversity is a corporate strategy. It's a strategy designed to ensure that the institution functions in the same way that it functioned before, except now you have some Black faces and brown faces." Davis and Lovett are drawing for us the lines within which we can color: A diverse staff is a good thing, but at the end of the day, we are often working within corporations and organizations that are fundamentally unequal. If DNI programs are an estimated $7–$8 billion industry, it's fair to say that is a lot of investment for questionable progress.

Perhaps that's because, regardless of the race or gender of your boss or the training programs in which your colleagues are enrolled, everyone is still working within unforgiving systems that largely remain unchanged. For instance, my experience of being a woman of color in middle management positions was that it felt like my bosses, who were often white, relied too much on me to "manage down" certain aspects of their directives to a diverse staff who might view those asks differently coming from a white person than from a woman of color. The role of a manager is to serve as a go-between, someone who can absorb directives from *their* managers and implement them on their behalf. I was OK with that, but in these contexts, I often felt like human padding for conversations my bosses felt uncomfortable having themselves; even when I had not bought fully into their vision, I had to execute and hold my team accountable to it anyway.

In 2019, sociologist Victor Ray published a provocative paper titled "A Theory of Racialized Organizations," in which he combined theories of racial justice and organizational theory to analyze how institutions themselves create and sustain racial stratification. Ray found that organizations reproduce racial inequality through invisible hierarchies that impact everything from hiring bias to resource distribution, concluding that, despite the best intentions of staffers who might want to eradicate racism in the workplace, the structures of the organizations themselves are rooted in racial hierarchies, from who gets what salary to who is expected to do what tasks. He writes, "Racial inequality is not merely 'in' organizations but 'of' them, as racial processes are foundational to organizational formation and continuity." Instead of casting organizations as race-neutral and then having to deal with racial hierarchies once they become apparent, he writes, "we should begin with the assumption that discrimination, racial sorting, and an unequal distribution of resources are not anomalous but rather foundational organizational norms."

Or, as Lovett told me, "organizations can hire people of color into these very high-level positions, but if they themselves are not reporting into a CEO or a board who just wants them there because of what they represent, but not what they're actually able to do, then there's not going to be any change." Conflating diversity and inclusion with representation is similarly dubious. An overemphasis on leaders of color within institutions that are nebulous in their values or harmful to the very communities the leaders may represent is not exactly effective change. Sure, it is a type of progress, but what does it do to change actual systems?

Uprisings from the Street to the C-Suite

In the summer of 2020—after people had been in lockdown for months and thousands of Americans had already died from COVID-19—a public reckoning about racial injustice began. The anti–police brutality movement that had started with Michael Brown's death in Ferguson in 2014, then somehow petered out despite ongoing police violence, broke through again after a Minneapolis police officer killed George Floyd during his arrest for allegedly using fake currency. A video of the killing taken by a young woman went viral, and Americans of all races took to the streets in record numbers to protest his death and the unjust killings of Black Americans—including, shortly before Floyd's death, the murders of Ahmaud Arbery in rural eastern Georgia and Breonna Taylor in Louisville, Kentucky.

Workplaces, including *Teen Vogue,* participated in this "new" awareness of Black lives mattering. On social media, companies and brands posted messages affirming their solidarity with the protesters who were on the streets demanding accountability. But, in trying to avert what would've been the public relations disaster of not declaring their support for Black lives in that political moment, corporations unwittingly created a different communications nightmare with their hollow social-media posts.

Onlookers, employees, and ex-employees reversed the gaze and began to try to hold these companies accountable beyond their expressions of solidarity, with users chiming in with some version of "Appreciate the Black Lives Matter post. Now follow that up with a picture of your senior management team." For example, several travel companies that posted messages about Black Lives Matter on social media—including luggage company Away, which, as mentioned in Chapter 3, would later come under scrutiny for how they handled that moment internally—came under much criticism because those brands rarely catered to Black audiences in their actual marketing. One Black travel writer told *The New York Times* that Away's social media post, like much of what was posted at that time, felt "performative."

Due to the social pressures, conversations about diversity and racial equality started up across industries, including in tech, publishing, media, and entertainment. For years, companies in such visible industries (now visibly supportive of racial equity) had continually promoted white men into the upper ranks of their organizations while ignoring the lack of Black and brown employees in leadership roles. Executive teams scrambled to figure out what to do when it became obvious to outsiders that the diversity and inclusion numbers were ghastly and pay disparities were running amok.

Then there were several high-profile exoduses, some of which were driven by public altruism and others by bad behavior. Reddit cofounder Alexis Ohanian stepped down from the board, vowing that his seat would go to a Black executive (it did). The CEO of CrossFit stepped down after saying he wasn't "mourning" the loss of George Floyd. As I talk about in Chapter 3, there was also the girlboss reckoning, with Audrey Gelman stepping down as CEO of the Wing after women of color came forward with stories about pay inequality. Yael Aflalo, the founder and CEO of clothing brand Reformation, stepped down after an employee claimed she was not given a promotion due to racial discrimination.

The mainstream—and often white-led—media fared no better. James Bennet, head of *The New York Times* opinion section, departed after running a controversial and barely edited piece by Republican senator Tom Cotton of Arkansas, which suggested that military intervention should be used to stop the Floyd protests. Adam Rapoport of Condé Nast's *Bon Appétit* stepped down after a photograph of him in brownface circulated online, prompting employees of color to break their silence about pay disparities and microaggressions at the legacy magazine.

Condé Nast vowed to do better, but in an open letter published just one month after Rapoport's ousting, one of *Bon Appétit*'s treasured cooks, Priya Krishna, wrote that she was leaving because the new leadership had failed to come up with a contract that would compensate her fairly. Despite the "very public reckoning," she wrote on Twitter, the commitment to diversity was largely "lip service," and the contract she received was "nowhere near equitable" with her white colleagues.

This wasn't the first time that pay and hiring disparities in major corporations had been highlighted. Everyone knew those disparities likely existed, but they had rarely been addressed and never with the fervor required to change conditions for brown and Black employees.

But something felt different in 2020. Whether because of the inequities laid bare by the pandemic or the horrifying, broadly shared video of George Floyd's final breaths, it did feel like we'd hit a tipping point in how we talked not only about race but also about injustice more broadly. People started to have conversations in earnest. Families were talking about racism at the dinner table; white influencers and celebrities were sharing their platforms with Black voices to elevate important stories. We started to talk about what we wanted society to look like. And, against all the odds, the analysis and the accountability from the movement was also trickling up in the workplace—the executive suites, the boardrooms, and the offices of CEOs.

Shining a light on the inequalities at work reinforced the fact that people of color—especially Black people, and *especially* Black women— had been systematically excluded from advancement in the workplace. Most corporate board seats were overwhelmingly filled by white men (and continue to be), and the pay gap, especially for Black women, has held steady. As of 2020, Black women earned 58 percent of what white men were paid.

A number of corporations stepped forward with pledges of commitment to change, announcing monumental outlays of money for programs that would increase investment in Black-owned businesses and work with existing companies to recruit, hire, and retain more Black talent. By the end of 2021, corporations had pledged approximately $50 billion to the cause of racial justice. And in August 2020, Reuters found that recruitment calls to the National Society of Black Engineers, the National Black MBA Association, and Blacks in Technology had "tripled" since the George Floyd protests. In December 2020, the OneTen Coalition was announced—a group of major corporations committing to hire one million Black employees in the next decade, including major companies like General Motors, Delta, Comcast, AT&T, Verizon, Merck, Walmart, and Bank of America.

But how many organizations were hoping to create lasting change, and how many were waiting for the dust to settle? And for the organizations that were truly committed to diversity and equality in the workplace, where were they to look for a model of success?

In an investigation into the $50 billion pledge, a reporting team at *The Washington Post* found that 90 percent of the money went to "loans or investments they could stand to profit from, more than half in the form of mortgages"—mostly from JPMorgan Chase and Bank of America. And the rest went to grants "promoting upward economic mobility for Black people, through increased opportunities for homeownership, entrepreneurship and education." As Mehrsa Baradaran, a law professor at the University of California at Irvine who studies the racial wealth gap, told the *Post,* "We don't want just benevolent billionaires and nicer, softer, more-woke monopolies. We want an economic structure that allows for more mobility, and we don't have that." The *Post* found what had already been fairly well documented: Despite efforts being made to close the racial wealth gap, from home ownership to investing in Black banks or education, the long-standing structural barriers like employment discrimination, generations of redlining, tax codes, and crumbling schools had hardly shifted at all.

And even with all the heavy hitters involved in the OneTen Coalition, the organizations that made up the group had hired only seventeen thousand Black employees by December 2021. To meet their goals, they would have to create one hundred thousand new jobs per year. Meanwhile, a Pew study found that 67 percent of Americans supported Black Lives Matter in June 2020. By the end of 2021, that number had gone down to 55 percent, and down to 51 percent by 2023.

What Bias Does to Us

Perhaps the most frequently addressed topic in DEI training is unconscious bias—the idea that people make assumptions about other people without even realizing they are doing so. Our personal experiences shape both what we know of the world and our biases, conscious and unconscious. Unconscious bias (also known as implicit bias) includes the stereotypes and assumptions we hold about people based on their race, gender, sexuality, age, ethnicity, religious background, geographical background, and more, without truly realizing we think like that. Unlike with conscious or active biases, we often act on unconscious biases without being aware that they impact our decision-making.

Scientists have found that one of the ways unconscious bias works is that we are subconsciously drawn to people who are of the same racial, economic, or educational background as ourselves. In the workplace, this often means that people hire people they recognize, feel comfortable around, or can relate to—which can come down to people who are very much like them. This is likely why more racial, gender, and socioeconomic diversity at the top does, in some way, lead to more diversity throughout an organization.

That's also why, when hiring managers say things about rejected candidates like "it wasn't a culture fit," these phrases should be interrogated. It can often mean the candidate didn't go to a specific type of school, didn't come from a specific socioeconomic background, or even just that the candidate didn't match the race or gender that the hiring manager imagined in the position. Or it could mean that the candidate didn't understand certain unspoken rules and social codes of the in-group—rules and codes based on things like class, gender, race, and sexuality.

This is also why most current diversity and inclusion training starts with unconscious bias training: to highlight the assumptions and blind spots we all have when interacting with people we don't know or who come from backgrounds and experiences that are different from ours.

But the sad truth is that there is very little evidence that unconscious bias training works long-term. In a 2018 paper for the journal *Anthropology Now*, researchers Frank Dobbin and Alexandra Kalev found, after doing a review of strategies used to "reduce discrimination and promote diversity," that the tactics had largely backfired. They write, "Companies that establish formal hiring and promotion criteria—through job tests and performance rating systems—to limit managerial discrimination see reductions in managerial diversity." The reasons for this are varied and include the reality that short-term interventions may not work on mindsets, behaviors, and habits that have developed over a lifetime. Or, as Zulekha Nathoo writes at the BBC, elevating and naming stereotypes can sometimes put them front and center in an employee's mind rather than being useful in defusing their power.

Ultimately, sustained change has to come from workplace and hiring practices that ensure the long-term prioritization of the needs of historically excluded groups. Relying on the goodwill of one or two people doesn't create lasting systemic change. Lovett, a DEI expert, says that's partially because, even if you give everyone the same access to opportunities, you may not have the same outcomes, especially among people who have different backgrounds. "Companies need to be very clear about the difference between equality and equity," she told me—which is that equality gives everyone access to the same thing, while equity recognizes that different people need different things to achieve similar outcomes, and that strategies to help should be tailored appropriately. She said that effective DNI programs need to take into consideration "all the different factors that impact the experiences of underrepresented groups, whether that is just their culture, how they identify, the systemic issues tied to an organization, or bias that we know all of us have but that we know people of color and people of underrepresented groups face at a much higher rate."

The only way to have a truly equitable workplace and a truly diverse staff is to have multipronged strategies that include ensuring employees will either succeed in the job or receive the mentorship and support they need to succeed. And Lovett says you also need support from the CEO and the company's board. "They set the culture; they lead by example," she explained. In other words, as Ray's work similarly says, simply hiring a diverse pool of employees and managers is, in and of itself, not enough to shift power dynamics in the workplace.

A study from the management-consulting firm Deloitte found that successful workplaces weren't just diverse; they were also inclusive and had leaders that prioritized inclusion. It appeared to be less important if someone looks like you and more important that they can understand and be empathetic to your experience. The researchers identified four main factors in employees feeling seen, heard, and included: being treated equitably and with respect; feeling valued and like they belong; feeling safe, especially in expressing themselves; and feeling empowered in their work and decision-making.

These practices help all employees, not just underrepresented ones. But they are often ignored during pushes to hire more diverse candidates. Take Google, for example. In 2020, the company announced that they'd be making a concerted effort to hire more Black talent at senior levels. And they had some success there. The company's annual report, released in July 2021, showed that almost 9 percent of Google's U.S. 2020 hires were Black, up from 5.5 percent the previous year. But a year into these efforts, the company identified another problem: retention. The report found that attrition was a major issue, especially with Black and Indigenous female employees.

Still, focusing on hiring the best candidates with an eye to diversity is a welcome change from how diversity at work had historically been talked about and understood. The racist idea of a "diversity hire"—someone who is presumably hired only because of their race—had become shorthand for how diversity was talked about (often secretly) in the workplace. Often, a nonwhite person in a given role might appear so out of the ordinary that the idea that they procured the position on their own merits appeared to baffle people. So people of color routinely felt like they were on the outside looking in, reduced to their ethnic or racial identity, navigating bias, looks, comments, and the seeming belief that the only reason they were hired was because they filled a diversity quota.

As someone who has now spent many years hiring and managing diverse teams, I have found two things to be true. The first is that, if we demand that every employee be able to do all of the job and be a perfect cultural match on day one—which is impossible—we will continue to reproduce inequities at work. Another is that a new hire with raw talent but less experience may need additional support navigating specific office cultures, including an introduction to the norms of their roles or clarity around expectations (something that is helpful for any new hire, to some degree). I know this as someone who hasn't always fit in where I was hired, due to either my work experiences or my socioeconomic or educational background. I was often considered "raw talent," but was ultimately a fish out of water when it came to culture. When I was finally able to hire for roles myself, I was committed to giving additional support should an employee need it—because I wanted our teams to have the best players, not just the easiest people to manage. I made plenty of mistakes. Still, not every leader is willing to take that on. And not every boss who is willing will have the ability, skills, time, or commitment to do that. (I barely did.)

But when you hire someone from a historically excluded background, and that person does not have the support needed to succeed and thus flounders, it is damaging for that employee and for the company. Successful diversity initiatives can't really be printed in a to-do list or handy one-size-fits-all binder. They need to involve more than just hiring diverse candidates. These initiatives need to consider what those candidates need from managers and the company or organization to succeed. Inclusion goes deeper than just giving someone a seat at the table. If a workplace is truly invested in equity, diversity, and fairness, it needs to consider how its organization is structured to reproduce exclusion, from hiring practices to retention strategies, from raise structures to promotion ladders, and from the energy in the cafeteria to the unspoken dress codes. Every step of the way, there is a wall, a structure, a tradition, or a barrier that has kept women, poor people, queer people, and people of color out.

Representation to Solidarity

To say representation matters feels obvious. Of course it matters, even if it's imperfect and even if it doesn't immediately reflect broad, sweeping systemic change. As the award-winning actress Viola Davis said on *The View,* "You need to see a physical representation of your dreams."

The first of anything can serve as an inspiration or a model for success. For historically disenfranchised communities, it is a necessary corrective to always and only seeing one type of person in a given role—be that an astronaut, an award-winning actress, or the president of the United States. Also, sometimes, the people who are heralded for breaking barriers have, in fact, broken those barriers, and those successes are worthy of our respect and admiration.

But our desire for representation can be messy when mapped onto real people in the real world. It's hard for one person in a group to be everything we need them to be. And, when the quest for representation becomes little more than tokenism, it is an easy strategy to give people a distraction, prioritizing a flattened sense of identity over substance. Celebrating someone who has overcome all the obstacles feeds into a type of American exceptionalism that says, if you can dream it and you work hard enough, you can also be it. It eschews any kind of systemic analysis.

As race scholar Kim Tran writes about her research on DNI programs in *Harper's Bazaar:* "I found that DEI asked incomplete questions like 'How to increase representation of people of color,' without ever mentioning that they would be working in companies and industries that deepen inequality." Consider the military-industrial complex, which is very good at diversity and inclusion *and* also good at maintaining the American empire and the worst savagery of Western imperialism. Representation for the sake of representation is not in and of itself enough of a meaningful political ambition, even if it is *something.* We have a tendency to focus on representation as the final destination rather than as a strategy to reach a just, more equitable place. As Davis says, most DNI programs exist to keep business functioning as usual, not to radically rethink those institutions.

Sometimes the push to make workplaces more diverse is viewed as an extension of identity politics, with *identity politics* used as a pejorative (similar to *political correctness*). It's interesting, though, to look at the origin of the term: The Combahee River Collective—a group of Black lesbian socialists, founded in 1974—are credited with coming up with the term *identity politics*. Founded by feminist author and activist Barbara Smith, the collective was a response to what they felt was the inability of the mainstream feminist movement to deal with the issues that faced women of color, and the Civil Rights Movement's failure to truly incorporate gender justice in their broader platform.

The term *identity politics* was first used in the Combahee River Collective's statement, published in 1977. They write,

> We believe that the most profound and potentially most radical politics come directly out of our own identity, as opposed to working to end somebody else's oppression. In the case of Black women, this is a particularly repugnant, dangerous, threatening, and therefore revolutionary concept because it is obvious from looking at all the political movements that have preceded us that anyone is more worthy of liberation than ourselves. We reject pedestals, queenhood, and walking ten paces behind. To be recognized as human, levelly human, is enough.

For them, identity politics was not a superficial exercise or a diversity initiative but a concept that rigorously examined power. They were asking questions that got to the heart of social injustice: How does your access to power change if you are Black, Indigenous, working-class, lesbian, etc.? Those are inquiries that might feel front and center in any social-justice activism today, but they were not centered then, when people were building broad-based movements for racial and gender equality.

Despite these radical roots, identity politics has become little more than a nod to diversity and inclusion—an additive to an existing power structure—rather than a radical position that questions power itself. In response to this dulling down and deradicalization of the terms set by the Combahee River Collective, leftist writer Asad Haider writes in *Mistaken Identity* that we have to move to "reject 'identity' as a foundation for thinking about identity politics." He writes, "If it is not questioned, people of color, along with other oppressed groups, have no choice but to articulate their political demands in terms of inclusion in the bourgeois masculine ideal." In response to this, philosopher Olúfẹ́mi O. Táíwò writes in *Elite Capture* that while identity politics hasn't "stopped police murders or emptied prisons," it has "equipped people, organizations, and institutions with a new vocabulary to describe their politics and aesthetic—even if the substance of those political decisions are irrelevant or even counter to the interests of the marginalized people whose identities are being deployed." This "elite capture" has less to do with the veracity of identity politics than with how they are being used, he writes.

Similarly, other theorists such as Judith Butler, Angela Davis, Wendy Brown, and bell hooks have regularly criticized a type of neoliberal co-optation of identity politics that makes them less about justice and freedom than about a photo op. Representational politics have been interrogated rigorously on the left (and either decried or manipulated on the right), partially due to the frustration that politicians have relied on them too heavily and at the cost of a narrative about the broader betterment of American lives. Why were we spending so much time on Hillary Clinton being a woman in 2016 when we had Trump to beat, and an opportunity for messaging that resonated across a greater swath of voters? Why should we celebrate Kamala Harris as a win for diversity when she may not be able to execute a progressive vision for the future?

When running for president, Harris was criticized on the left as an imperfect candidate, but her election as vice president in 2020 was also historic. In an analysis for *Time,* the professor and writer Brittney Cooper writes, "Black women leaders are so important to this democracy precisely because they dare to keep dreaming, even after the immediacy of a perpetual nightmare like Donald Trump. Representation is not everything. But it is absolutely something."

Novelist and editor Kaitlyn Greenidge also wrote about the difficulty of firsts at *Harper's Bazaar* after Harris's election: "To think that the first happened just because the right person finally managed to emerge and break through, and not because there was a whole system put in place to make sure no one who looks a certain way or comes from a particular background ever has a chance to do so in the first place." Since then, Harris's tenure has left all of us wanting more from her politically, partially because she was sold to us as a once-in-a-lifetime candidate who would make things measurably better, not just for women of color but also in terms of the issues about which we care.

Our obsession with firsts—with crowning them as super-heroic achievements based on hard work that overcomes harrowing circumstances—papers over the fact that these milestones are more a result of the surrounding circumstances than personal achievements. These examples convince us that if we work hard enough, we, too, can run the country one day.

We are not wrong to believe we can succeed; sometimes the alchemy of hard work and being in the right place at the right time does help you secure a seat at the table. But, as Greenidge notes, there are many who deserve success or could have achieved similar feats had they been given the tools, the education, the circumstances, or the access to get there. Or if those in charge, she observed, had decided it was "their time."

These anxieties about the meaning or accomplishments of a "first" are, of course, dwarfed by the gross and systemic inequalities that continue to plague most industries; business leadership is dominated by white men. All the same, the sociologist Victor Ray says there is still reason to be optimistic about changes—including singular representations, even if they feel like a drop in the bucket—and there is a reason the right is so offended by small diversity accomplishments. "I don't think we should dismiss symbolic change. Conservatives feel that the symbolic push that Black Lives Matter represented, these promises from corporations, the interest in Critical Race Theory, and books about racial inequality . . . they realize that those symbolic pushes, given enough time and given cultural change, could be a threat," he told me.

Adding a handful of people to the roster within an inherently unjust structure still adds that person—and allows other people like them to be hired. A structure is, after all, a constellation of individual actors. And it's still better to have imperfect diversity and inclusion initiatives working toward parity than not to have any at all. It's still better to push for leaders of color within institutions that have a long way to go than to let business continue as usual. And it's still worth doing the difficult work of holding those leaders accountable.

My friend Sadye has long worked on the issue of equity and diversity and, in January 2022, became the chief equity officer for the New York City comptroller. She knew the challenges going into the job and told me that the influx of chief diversity officers in both the public and private sectors is "very much a symptom and a response to a nation that has not had honest conversations about race and racism." But she is optimistic about the growth of DEI programs. "Being a lone chief equity officer is not the perfect solution . . . we will not reform our way out of racism, but not putting someone in or not acknowledging that we need to explicitly and intentionally examine systems that have caused harm and oppressed people isn't the answer, either," she says.

We expend a lot of energy examining how to (and if it's even worth it to) navigate systems that we know are fundamentally unfair and unbalanced. Most people can't avoid them—we have to go to work, and we have to go to work in places that rely on a type of racial caste system. But it's hard even with raw data to fully understand both how effective diversity efforts are and what true, heterogeneous leadership looks like. As Ray notes, we don't have much evidence to make our point about the beneficial effects of diversity and inclusion over the long term, because so few organizations—if any—have true diversity at the top. We simply have no way of yet knowing how successful a truly diverse company (or industry) could be at tipping the scales of injustice at work. The urge to move beyond the conversation about diversity and inclusion starts to feel premature when you consider how little progress we have actually made.

My experience working with the team at Mic was life-changing for me. We never took for granted the opportunity to work on a team that was all people of color. Having each other made work slightly less miserable—I mean, it was still *work,* but at least we were doing it together and with purpose. We've all stayed close (the group text is still popping), and we understand that it's rare that you get to work on a team of people who share similar worldviews and experiences and have a sense of solidarity. My friend and former colleague Aaron Morrison told me that the experience was special to him for many reasons. As a Black journalist, he had never worked on a team where the leadership was all women of color who "affirmed the value of my perspective as a Black cisgender man." This made it easier, he said, for him to pitch stories he cared about, to ask for what he needed to effectively do his work, and to find support in telling his stories.

I carried these lessons with me in the years ahead and brought them along when I went to *Teen Vogue.* Increased diversity isn't a cure-all for what plagues the workplace, and we should be wary of an overemphasis on diversity and inclusion strategies, especially when they obscure the opportunity for more substantive and rigorous changes. But it's worth considering how these strategies can be and are beneficial for people of color in the workplace, and what conditions need to be created for them to help us attain the longer-term outcomes of equity and justice.

NOT-SO-MODEL
MINORITY

When a woman you work with calls you by the name
of another woman you work with, it is too much of a cliché
not to laugh out loud with the friend beside you who says,
oh no she didn't. Still, in the end, so what, who cares?
She had a fifty-fifty chance to get it right.

—Claudia Rankine, *Citizen*

"It's another rejection!" my mother shouted at me from upstairs as I got home from school. There it was: a torn-open envelope with the University of Michigan logo on it, perfectly centered on the coffee table, laid out like I had received word from the queen.

"You couldn't wait for me to open it?" I yelled back, the tears welling up.

It was my eighth rejection letter, and that time it had come from my top choice. Attending Michigan was a long-standing dream, but I'd known my chances of getting in were minimal. I had lied to myself and then to my parents, puffing up the idea that I had a good shot because I'd spent three high school summers at a debate camp on the campus in Ann Arbor. But my grades were terrible, my SATs middling, and—looking back now—the confidence with which I'd sent off my application was near delusional. (I've always wondered if admissions officers chuckle when faced with applications from students who have woefully overestimated their chances.)

I don't remember a time when getting educated wasn't a complete disaster for me. For a little brown girl in the early 1980s, elementary school in the New York City suburbs wasn't the most welcoming place. I was mercilessly teased for my brown skin, accused of smelling like curry, and mocked for having a funny name. I hated going and would come up with any excuse to stay home. None of it helped me get good grades.

Eventually, when the five elementary schools in our district were dumped into one middle school, I did find my tribe of misfit suburban brown girls who helped me form a sense of self, taught me how to give myself a red lip lined with black eyeliner, and showed me how to style my wavy, thick black hair. In high school, I found a social home in extracurricular activities like the debate team and hanging with the cool older kids—the metalheads and riot grrrls—who taught me how to smoke cigarettes, and the language of feminism. *This town is for losers,* they explained to me. We were dead set on leaving it.

But my grades never got better; I was mostly earning Cs but got a few Ds and Fs, too. And I spent more than a hundred days in detention my senior year—usually for talking in class or some other such disruption. The school threatened to bar me from graduation (which would have been a serious wrench in my "goodbye to all of this" plan) because I had missed first period so many times. I had somehow squirmed my way into AP English (the word *potential* was used a lot), only for the teacher to point out that English was clearly my second language (it wasn't), which was probably why I was struggling so much.

Conversely, my math teacher once told my parents he'd never met an Indian who was so bad at calculus, a heartbreaking observation for my mom and dad. "Hardworking and good at math" was seen as the path to middle-class American life—and it was a way for them to push onto me what they couldn't do for themselves, as well as a seductive myth about acceptance when their own experiences were deeply rooted in alienation from both India and America.

Given my grades, the idea that I would go to college at all was optimistic. According to the guidance counselor, a proper university was not in the cards for me. He suggested I apply to a community college. There is absolutely nothing wrong with community college, but my mom was not having it; incensed, she marched into school demanding a list of other institutions I could apply to. They gave us a list of State University of New York schools that might consider me. I decided to add a few of my own volition, including the University of Michigan. Of the ten schools I applied to, I was accepted to just two: SUNY Albany and SUNY Plattsburgh. I chose Albany.

I graduated from high school by the skin of my teeth—and I didn't fare much better in college, at least not in the beginning. I didn't show up to classes, choosing instead to get high with my new friends from Brooklyn, Queens, and Buffalo, who taught me about hardcore music and the Wu-Tang Clan. After two semesters, I was on terminal probation: If I didn't turn things around, I was going to get kicked out. (This might sound like Gen-X slacker bragging, but it is all true.)

As a last-ditch effort to turn things around, I took some summer classes, landing in a sociology class that had some women's studies readings in it. I was hooked. I somehow finagled a B in the class, which was enough to buy me another semester. I filled it with women's studies and sociology classes and found mentors within the department—a motley crew of activists and feminists, people invested in me, people who thought I was smart, people who gave a shit, people who would wake me up to make it to class and make sure I got my papers in on time. It took me three summers and an extra year, but I graduated from college in 2000 . . . with a 2.8 GPA.

That I managed that turnaround might sound like a success story—the very "pull yourself up by your bootstraps" BS I'm spending much of this book decrying—but that's not why I'm sharing it. Yes, I worked hard to turn things around for myself and had enough proximity to resources and enough privilege to do so. But, starting in elementary school, I had also internalized a deep sense that I did not belong at school or anywhere else, making it hard to see myself succeeding. I carried a tremendous amount of shame for my performance, and because of the amount of pressure my parents put on me to be a good student despite being a middling one, I literally never thought I could grow up to be the sort of person who would make a great salary, manage teams, and have a robust, creative life.

But by being bad at school, I had also rejected the myth of the model minority—that hot mess of a stereotype that ruins the lives of wayward Asian teens around the world. My parents were so disappointed in me: They could never really get over my bad grades, in part because they saw them as a failure on their part. We can comfortably say the model minority construct is racist, that it sets up a dichotomy between "good" and "bad" minority groups, and that it erases the complexity and diversity of the Asian and Asian American experience. But that same myth provides an entry point for Asian immigrants into the American imagination—a place, however narrow, to be a part of the lie of pulling yourself up by your, uh, chappal straps. It's not surprising that many people embrace it.

Being considered a bad student, a nuisance, a troublemaker, is a shame that I've carried with me into adulthood. It's had implications for how I behave in the workplace, how I receive critical feedback, and how poorly I deal with rejection—to a degree that is almost embarrassing. And despite how hard I've worked and how much success I've had, the limitations that were set forth for me, in my childhood and education, continue to plague my sense of belonging.

• • •

People's sense of belonging (or lack thereof), and how it impacts their understanding of self, have been studied by philosophers, social scientists, writers, poets, songwriters, etc., throughout history. Karl Marx in particular applied the existing concept of alienation to his economic philosophy of work, describing the "estrangement" a worker may experience when they participate in labor without owning the means of production, disconnected from both the ownership of and fruits of their labor.

The broader idea of alienation is also a concept used in modern philosophy when describing how people experience race and gender. In a lecture about the technological revolution, Martin Luther King, Jr., said that "alienation is a form of living death. It is the acid of despair that dissolves society." Writers such as James Baldwin and feminist theorists Simone de Beauvoir and Sandra Bartky also considered the implications of alienation for a person's psyche, recognizing that race, class, gender, and sexuality have a unique impact on our sense of self in the context of a society that dictates membership based on who you are. In *The Second Sex,* de Beauvoir writes, "We are shown woman solicited by two kinds of alienations; it is very clear that to play at being a man will be a recipe for failure; but to play at being a woman is also a trap: being a woman would mean being an object, the Other; and at the heart of its abdication, the Other remains a subject."

Feminist theory and ethnic studies often involve explorations of what happens to the mind and the body when society casts you as an outsider and denies your humanity or the legitimacy of your experiences. It turns out that navigating a society that does not want you—that violates you, that wants to incarcerate or deport you—is not the stuff of healthy self-esteem. (Who would have guessed?)

There is a plethora of research that indicates the roles that institutions and our relationship to them—schools, universities, workplaces, prisons, government, and even popular culture—play in shaping our identities. This research is about more than inclusion and identity—it's about the analysis of interactions that are defined by state and sometimes coercive power: Black/white, nuclear family/broken family, insured/uninsured, incarcerated/free, citizen/undocumented, employed/unemployed. These relationships to institutions and social structures don't just define our sense of self; they dictate how our lives are lived, what rights we have, and what we believe or know is possible for ourselves.

Elementary and secondary schools are often some of our earliest formative experiences outside of the home. When history is inaccurately represented in the books, when our teachers are not reflective of the worlds from which we come, or when we are ostracized by our peers as "different" in some way, our bodies remember, even if our minds do not, that we do not belong. Schools in particular—places where we are supposed to go to learn without a focus on our differences—often highlight our differences in stark and challenging ways.

In a 2015 TED talk, Dr. Dena Simmons, a professor at Yale who specializes in social and emotional learning for students of color, shares the story of her mother moving her from the Bronx to Connecticut, where she attended boarding school. Because of the lack of safety that she and her family had often felt in the Bronx, the new environment initially gave her a new sense of stability. But that lasted only so long.

"Very quickly, I felt like I didn't belong. I learned that I didn't speak the right way, and to demonstrate the proper ways of speaking, my teachers gave me frequent lessons, in public, on the appropriate way to enunciate certain words," she says.

Many of us have the experience of being reminded that we are different and of the ways that institutions, especially schools—and the people in them—repeatedly underlined those differences: The AP English teacher who asked if English was my second language when it wasn't, the professor who thought there was no way I'd be able to pass their class, the guidance counselor who suggested I consider alternatives to four-year colleges, and so on.

This injury is universal: Many people, regardless of their race or gender, have stories of feeling alienated for all kinds of reasons, whether it be their body size, the texture of their hair, the home they live in, the clothes they are wearing, or something else. But when that alienation reflects larger stereotypes, it has a different impact.

When women aren't called on in class, they are taught that they shouldn't speak up and that they have nothing worth saying. When Black children are repeatedly kicked out of class, they are taught they do not belong in the classroom. When Latine students are kicked out of school for bad behavior, they internalize the idea that school is not a place for them. When trans students are denied the ability to use the bathrooms corresponding with their genders, they are taught—in the most intimate way—that their genders are wrong and that they do not deserve the dignity of using a bathroom in which they feel safe. These are lessons we bring with us into adulthood, into the workplace, or into higher education, and they play out in what we believe we are entitled to, how we expect to be treated, and our feelings of belonging.

Affirmative action and diversity and inclusion efforts—while necessary and important stepping stones—don't go far enough to address the covert cultural scripts and stereotypes that perpetuate and keep in place policies that exclude or sideline marginalized people in certain environments. And even when those stereotypes and expectations are thought of as positive, they can still have deleterious effects on people who don't (or don't want to) live up to them.

Mythical Minorities

My father came to the United States in 1970 as part of the wave of Asian immigration that followed the passing of the Immigration and Nationality Act (also known as the Hart-Celler Act), signed in 1965 by Lyndon B. Johnson. While it removed nationality quotas based on nineteenth-century immigration patterns that favored Western Europeans, people pursuing professional degrees were also given preferential treatment and the ability to bring their families. This type of "brain drain" policy prioritized visas for promising young students and highly skilled workers from other countries.

Given that immigrants from countries in Asia had often previously been barred from entry or denied citizenship, and Asian Americans had been subjected to racist violence (including from the U.S. government), Johnson's immigration reform represented a real turning point. Jay Caspian Kang writes in *The New York Times* that "no single piece of legislation has shaped the demographic and economic history of this country in quite the same way," as the passage of this bill brought "tens of millions of immigrants from Asia, southern and Eastern Europe, and Africa."

In her book *The Making of Asian America,* Erika Lee writes that, despite the law's intent to prioritize immigration from southern and Eastern Europe, "it can be argued that no group benefited more from the act than Asian Americans." The preference for educated and education-seeking immigrants—who often skewed Asian—meant that Asians who immigrated after 1965 were predisposed to take or get higher-earning jobs, which ultimately changed how those groups were perceived in the larger American society.

Cathy Park Hong writes in *Minor Feelings,*

> This screening process, by the way, is how the whole model minority quackery began: the U.S. government only allowed the most educated and highly trained Asians in and then took all the credit for their success. *See! Anyone can live the American Dream!* they'd say about a doctor who came into the country already a doctor.

The term *model minority* entered the lexicon by way of sociologist William Petersen in a 1966 *New York Times Magazine* piece titled "Success Story, Japanese-American Style"—less than a year after Johnson's immigration reform was enacted and twenty years after the World War II internment camps for Japanese Americans were shuttered. Petersen asks why, of all the ethnic and racial groups in the United States, had Japanese Americans been able to overcome the harm done to their communities from discrimination and internment. His answer was that they had a better work ethic and stronger family values than what he dubbed "problem minorities," who he claimed were defined by "a number of interrelated factors—poor health, poor education, low income, high crime rate, unstable family pattern, and so on and on."

Reading this today, it's pretty obvious why Petersen's was a dubious proposition. It also specifically pushed Asian Americans to live up to untenable and unrealistic standards of success and homogenized an experience—being Asian American—that is incredibly diverse. Erika Lee writes in *The Making of Asian America* that "highlighting only the successful characteristics" of Asian Americans obscures how many "struggle to survive, live in poverty, are unemployed or underemployed, and have low rates of education." Asian Americans, she writes, are a "community of contrasts," not of homogeneity.

The idea that Asians and Asian Americans are somehow a model for other races also obscures the ways we directly benefited from the work of Black American activists in the Civil Rights Movement. Johnson's immigration reforms were part and parcel of the laws that he signed after pressure from that movement. But because those immigrants came here after the laws were passed, many were not aware of the shoulders they were standing on. As scholar Vijay Prashad writes in his 2012 book *Uncle Swami,* on what he calls a "doubly privileged population"—individuals with enough resources both to come to the United States and to gain entry into top U.S. institutions—"At least two generations of people sacrificed their lives and longings to overturn the injustice of Jim Crow. Because of them, the new migrants who entered the universities and laboratories, hospitals and research centers could live with the formal promise of equality."

The tension between communities of color around scarcity and success has been a hallmark of how Asian American identity has formed. Take for example the 2022 Supreme Court case that determined the fate of affirmative action in college admissions at Harvard University (and beyond). Brought by the conservative group Students for Fair Admissions, the suit claimed that affirmative action programs were discriminating against Asian and white students while giving preferential treatment to Black and Latine students. In a review of admissions at Harvard, the plaintiffs alleged that Asian students, while often stronger than white students in terms of academic grades, were consistently rated lower in terms of "leadership" and "likeability" and were held to a higher standard for test scores than white, Black, and Latine students. Their claim was that Asian students were being denied admission at a disproportionately high rate, given their grades and test scores, while other minority students were getting preferential treatment. The lower courts initially found that Harvard did not intentionally discriminate against Asian or Asian American students, though the Supreme Court ultimately ruled against the university in 2023.

Nonetheless, the Supreme Court gutted all race-conscious decision-making in college admissions by ruling against Harvard and against the University of North Carolina in a similar case. The decision effectively rendered all affirmative action in the college admissions process illegal.

Affirmative action was never a perfect solution; it was a drop in the bucket of what would truly be needed to achieve racial equity in college admissions—for instance, it failed to consider students' economic background. Bertrand Cooper writes in *The Atlantic,* "Most Americans seem to think affirmative action sits at the foundation of some beneficent suite of education policies that do something significant for poor Black kids, and that would disappear without the sanction of affirmative action. But the reality is that for the Black poor, a world without affirmative action is just the world as it is—no different than before."

In looking at the evidence in the case, Jay Caspian Kang writes, "When you apply the normative definition of discrimination. . . . the evidence against Harvard on that front is, frankly, overwhelming." He goes on to say, "Their flimsy approach to 'diversity' and their desire to stay as academically exclusive as possible have created an indefensible system of racial nonsense that demeans not only its Asian and Black applicants, but everyone else who has to play this absurd game."

Still, many have argued that it was better to have affirmative action than not. Professor Anne A. Cheng at Princeton said of the decision, "Affirmative action is an imperfect and yet still necessary solution to a very broken social system in America."

Given how complex college-admissions decision-making is, it's hard to be concrete about how these policies impact different groups of people, though we do know that the universities believed these policies actively increased the number of Black and Latine students. But suggesting that Asian students aren't accepted into elite universities because Black students are is missing a bigger point. Asian and Asian American students have experienced discrimination in the college-admissions process, but suggesting that affirmative action—one of the most important wins of the Civil Rights Movement—is the cause of that discrimination is inaccurate. Consider how the Ivies are filled with legacy students and children of families who have made sizable donations, or how the majority of students at elite universities are affluent white people. The solution should be to *expand* affirmative action, not strike it down. It is hard to believe that less attention to race or its role in college admissions will ultimately *help* Asian and Asian American students.

The crooked and complex ways these policies and opposing narratives play out impact how we navigate institutions, how they define us, and what success looks like—or what is even possible given who we are.

On Belonging or Not

Feeling like you belong is also important in the workplace, where our feelings of alienation can be triggered easily (not to mention that if you feel alienated, you're likely not going to do your best work). Workplaces often replay our worst high school tendencies: They can be cliquey or rely on a sense of exclusion, not to mention the gossiping or how some colleagues may socialize outside of work without including everyone.

According to a study by the leadership development organization BetterUp, the consequences of feeling like you do not belong in the workplace include financial loss, decreases in productivity, and ineffective collaboration on teams. And according to a 2019 study reported in the *Harvard Business Review,* 40 percent of office workers felt "physically and emotionally isolated" in the workplace—a feeling that likely only intensified during the pandemic.

These dynamics are exacerbated for underrepresented groups in the workplace.

In a study on loneliness by health insurance company Cigna (which is truly sad across the board), they found Black and Latine employees were the loneliest at work, saying they felt "abandoned by coworkers when under pressure at work," "more alienated from coworkers," and "more emotionally distant." The study also found that lonely workers considered quitting their jobs twice as often as workers who didn't report feelings of loneliness. So, in addition to making you feel frustrated, overlooked, or alienated, loneliness can contribute to a sense of not belonging at work.

In 2012, Ellen K. Pao was working at the Silicon Valley venture capital firm Kleiner Perkins when she filed a suit against the company claiming gender discrimination. A few months later, she was let go. In the 2015 trial—when she was the CEO of Reddit—her testimony revealed a culture at Kleiner Perkins that excluded women: She was left out of lucrative deals, was subjected to hostile attitudes in meetings, and couldn't attend a men's-only ski trip, on which women weren't invited because the company didn't know how they'd house the women. A jury found the firm not guilty of gender discrimination, but the trial started a conversation about sexism in Silicon Valley and venture capital more broadly, and the ways that culture reinforced a "boys' club" mentality.

Among the hardest workplace customs to enforce are the ones that involve interpersonal relationships: being invited to networking dinners and parties, being considered a friend or peer, etc. And one of the visible but inappropriate side effects of the increased awareness of #MeToo accusations in the workplace was male bosses openly deciding not to have social outings with women employees—a crucial way that business deals are facilitated, promotions negotiated, and relationships built. Cultural assumptions by bosses about what women and people of color should be allowed to have access to, the types of roles they should be considered for, and the kind of money they should be making are biases—implicit and explicit—that keep us from being truly equal players in the workplace.

And then there are the microaggressions—to use a term that is often misrepresented but at its root is meant to indicate a small nastiness, often even unintentional, based on someone's race, gender, nationality, disability, sexuality, or gender identity. As defined by the psychology professor Kevin Nadal, microaggressions are "the everyday, subtle, intentional—and oftentimes unintentional—interactions or behaviors that communicate some sort of bias toward historically marginalized groups." Examples of microaggressions include subtle comments about where someone lives or comes from or what they are wearing, making assumptions about someone's thoughts and feelings because of their identity, and using inappropriate language about a group.

Because microaggressions often live in gray areas, they can be hard to tackle in the workplace. Confusing two employees of the same race, expecting the woman in the meeting to take the notes, talking over a Black employee, asking an Asian person an offensive question about their lunch, making assumptions about someone's education status based on where they are from—these are all things that happen at work. Generally, workers are not always sure when and if they should be reporting them because, as has happened to me, they think maybe they imagined it, or they are being overly sensitive, or it's too minor to warrant a discussion with the higher-ups.

Microaggressions in the workplace, however, are very common. According to a SurveyMonkey and *Fortune* magazine study, 26 percent of American workers have experienced microaggressions at work and another 22 percent think they may have, while 36 percent said they had witnessed one. And a Gallup study found that microaggressions in the workplace disproportionately impact Black employees. They're called "aggressions" because they're hurtful to the people who have to deal with them: Like pinpricks, even if one isn't a big deal, the accumulation of a lot of pinpricks draws a lot of blood. And they contribute to marginalized people's already keen sense that maybe we don't belong.

You Shouldn't Be Here

Some years ago, I was asked to sit in on a high-level meeting with some senior executives at my company because my boss couldn't make it. I was already anxious about being in the meeting at all, so I intended to sit quietly, take notes, and hope no one would call on me.

So, when the person running the meeting called me by the wrong name, I didn't know what to do. They didn't just call me the wrong name, but they called me by the name of another South Asian American executive who was supposed to be there but had missed the meeting.

At first, I felt like I had done something wrong—and I almost wasn't sure it had happened at all until the person next to me leaned over and said, "Did what I think happened just happen?" I nodded, feeling my face turn red-hot with humiliation. The missing woman was a friend, so I texted her shortly after the meeting to tell her what had happened and that "it was awful." She just replied, "Oh my god." Then I brushed it off as an awkward encounter that I hoped never to speak of again—more embarrassed for the person that did it than angry for myself.

My friend was upset by the incident. "[That person] knows exactly who I am; this is absolutely outrageous. And we look nothing alike!" she said to me later, over the phone. (The person also knew who I was, but that wasn't the point.)

The science of why people sometimes confuse people of other races with one another is complicated. Social scientists have named the difficulty in differentiating members of a different race as the *cross-race effect* or *own-race bias*. The first study on the cross-race effect was published in 1914, stating that part of what causes people to misidentify is a lack of exposure to a diversity of faces. Since then, studies in multiple disciplines have come to similar conclusions: We are better at differentiating between people of the types we are used to seeing.

In a more recent investigation by Zulekha Nathoo for the BBC, she found that there are racial and power disparities within the cross-race effect—in other words, some groups are better at recognizing the faces of other groups. It perhaps shouldn't come as a surprise that when someone is in a position of power over you, you recognize their face more easily than they recognize yours. Susan Fiske, a psychology professor at Princeton University, tells Nathoo, "People pay attention up the hierarchy . . . people categorize other people by gender, age, race, social class, frequently—in less than a second."

This makes what happened to me perhaps more damning: Ostensibly, part of why this executive confused me with someone else was because I didn't belong in this group of people (race-, power-, or hierarchy-wise), which made me consciously or subconsciously less important enough to them or not worth remembering. (And it was symptomatic of a deeper issue at the company, which had little diversity in the upper ranks.)

Misrecognition in the workplace can be harmful—especially for junior employees. It can impact how people feel about themselves; it is disrespectful and dehumanizing. It makes you feel as though the you who exists in your colleague's brain is the single characteristic of your race or gender; it can make you feel disposable.

I personally wanted the entire incident to go away, but of course, it turned into a *thing*. Someone from the company's HR department paid me a visit to "check in"; apparently, the incident was so awkward for other people in the room that someone *else* had gone to HR asking what they could have done better in the moment. News of the incident, it turned out, had also made it to my boss and my boss's boss— and the Accused wanted to meet and explain their side of the story.

I didn't want to sit through some milquetoast apology; I would have done fine with a card and a bottle of vodka. Besides, how could my (required) acceptance of their apology ever be genuine, given the unequal power dynamics? This person sat several rungs above me on the corporate ladder, so I'd never be able to tell them how I really felt. The attention being paid to something so minor felt like a giant waste of time and resources, especially when the people involved could have done something—literally anything—about the larger structural imbalances across the company.

The "apology" was even more appalling: The events—which I hadn't even reported—were denied, and I was reassured that something like that could never happen, as I am well known by all senior management, including said senior executive. The person was committed to diversity! What a terrible mix-up for me to think what had happened had actually happened when it clearly didn't happen.

I was dizzy, and I felt like it was my job to make them feel like it was

OK. I said it was fine and behind us and tried to sneak in an ask to be promoted. (I was ignored.)

My friend for whom I was mistaken had already made an important point to me: "How do we expect to be taken seriously as diverse and necessary leaders if executives can't even tell us apart?"

On some level, I realized my standards were far too low for how I felt I should be treated in the workplace. "I never really thought they could tell us apart," I'd said to her. But in reality, I felt I'd never mattered enough to be worth telling apart from someone else. I told myself that I hadn't even belonged in the meeting in the first place.

I did not think this person intended to cause me harm; I do think that people make mistakes. But these mistakes can also be connected to deeper subconscious thought patterns that create blind spots. How many people in positions like that make similarly innocent mistakes and then also overlook a person of color for a promotion? Or don't call on them in a meeting? Or don't bother learning their name and thus exclude them from participating in most meetings?

All these little moments at work matter—not just for your efficacy at work, but because being seen and heard gives employees a sense of belonging. We should all want that kind of workplace.

If you are managing people at work, there are easy steps that you can take to ensure your employees feel like they belong, rather than triggering their lifelong feelings of constant alienation. If that executive had simply said in the moment—or even shortly thereafter—"Oh my God, I'm so sorry for making that mistake. I was expecting [the friend] to be sitting there. Of course I know you are Samhita!" that would have de-escalated the incident, acknowledged a simple (albeit embarrassing) mistake on their part, and signaled a commitment to not do it again.

Accountability and apologies shouldn't be so fraught. If we were just a little more comfortable acknowledging when we say things by mistake—things that might or might not reveal our own blind spots— maybe those mistakes wouldn't carry so much weight or get so blown out of proportion.

We are human; we make mistakes.

I'll start.

A former colleague of mine is nonbinary; I know this, I honor it and respect it, and I care about this person! But for whatever reason—probably related to my age and the blind spots that come with that—there was a period of time in which I could not get their gender pronoun right all the time: I'd regularly mess up and forget to use their they/them pronouns. I'd apologize if I noticed—they never corrected me—and publicly commit to remembering. They were always super gracious about it. I eventually got it right but, for whatever reason, I couldn't in the beginning.

But my misgendering of them was also a microaggression: What might feel like a harmless or understandable mistake to you (though it did not feel like either to me; I usually felt terrible about it and would inwardly wince for the rest of the day) can be quite damaging to the other person. Microaggressions can impact someone's self-esteem, they can feel invalidating, they can make you feel invisible. It is tiring to have to correct people constantly (especially if they are senior to you), and it can riddle you with guilt even if it was *their* mistake.

There is, of course, a way to interrupt this pattern: You can stop, you can slow down, you can be more intentional and commit to doing better. So I stopped, and I reminded myself, and I tried not to do it anymore. And that was a very small thing for me to do for someone to feel seen at work and in our friendship. And they were able to—though they did not have to—acknowledge that some people's brains can take time to catch up to the changing culture, that we are all prone to make mistakes, and that those mistakes are not always nefarious. How we deal with them afterward says much more about us than the initial mistake.

Most people who are fighting for inclusive language get that—no matter how much money certain pundits make inveighing about so-called woke culture. Most of us just want to be addressed respectfully, whether we're the ones asking for the change or the ones making the mistake. The words we use to address each other are symbolic: connected to ideas about power, permission, acceptance, and the ability for each of us to exist as individuals on our own terms—something we can all agree is a fundamental right in a free democracy.

It's hard to fully comprehend the role our workplaces play in re-inforcing our sense of belonging. I don't know that we can fairly expect every workplace to address the needs and sensitivities of every staff member, and I don't think that's a particularly useful standard to set. But I do think there are more comprehensive steps we can take in the workplace to help people feel seen and respected that have less to do with the language we use and more to do with paying them fairly for their work, including their perspectives on the work and giving them more ownership over that work, giving employees real opportunities for growth, and treating them as equals.

Workplaces are not structured for that type of inclusion; if any-thing, they benefit from us feeling alone, isolated, and like we must prove that we belong. What better way to convince people that they have to sell themselves to you—the boss—even when it is on your shoulders to create an inclusive environment.

But it doesn't have to be that way. As leaders, we can be better and we can do better. And in the next chapter I explore how.

IMPOSSIBLE COMPROMISES

Every moment is an organizing opportunity, every person a
potential activist, every minute a chance to change the world.

—Dolores Huerta

My main claim to having enough experience to qualify for a management position by my midthirties was a dubious one: I had been the executive editor at the popular early-aughts feminist blog *Feministing,* a volunteer gig that was less heavy on management duties than on being a public face and a cheerleader for the brand and the writers. I had led teams within grassroots organizations when I worked in consulting, and I'd had an early-in-my-career foray as a public school teacher . . . but my on-paper experience in senior management positions was sorely lacking.

So when I actually started getting hired for management jobs, I was thrilled. I had finally outgrown my Bad Student Energy™! Important people wanted other people to listen to me? Um, yeah, I'd take it. Over the previous ten years, I'd become the tap-dancing poster child for the maxim "fake it till you make it"—a piece of advice I both followed and was quick to dole out to friends, mentees, and colleagues. Add to this that I was never good with boundaries at work: If someone was willing to pay me to work, and especially for something for which I had a passion, I felt like I had to work twice as hard to prove myself. In other words, as a rehabilitated Bad Student, I was ready and willing to overcompensate when it came to proving myself in the workplace.

Need me to work late all week to make that unreasonable deadline? No problem, chief! Did another employee drop the ball on something they should have handled? I'll cover for them and then maybe do their task myself. Was the boss asking me to take on a workstream that was most definitely not in my job description? I was on it. I could not say no if I *tried*.

Like most managers, I didn't have much training, and in my first management job, I learned quickly that some of the things that made me seem like a good manager were ultimately not great skills for the job. I'd envisioned a manager's role as someone who is primarily dedicated to the development of their employees; that part was no problem. The piece I hadn't fathomed was how much of middle management had to do with acting as a go-between between your employees and your senior managers as an enforcer of the latter's edicts. That part was less fun. As a middle manager, you're held accountable for the outcomes of your employees but unable to determine the standards for those outcomes (or even the outcomes themselves). You wield just enough power to keep you feeling invested (plus you earn slightly higher pay), but you ultimately lack any real power or authority within the organization.

I tried hard to appease everyone, which didn't work. I was regularly told by bosses that I was too sensitive to the needs of my teams, too invested in making sure they didn't fail, and too obsessed with trying to save them when they "could not be saved." Maybe that feedback was fair on some level; sometimes, the handholding I did was too much work for me and probably didn't help the employee much, either. But I also felt that my bosses were misguided: Leadership could and really should be about giving solid feedback and helping people succeed, not just a constant quest to figure out what they can do for you, and if they can't do it, deciding that they need to be replaced.

When it came time for promotions, raises, or layoffs, I could always make recommendations but ultimately had little say in the final decision—despite often having to be the face of whatever had been mandated from above. And the people who worked for me usually knew that, which I imagine made it harder to take me seriously. Why worry what I think if, ultimately, someone else has the final say?

This all came to a head for me when a company I was working at decided it was time for layoffs. The bosses had decided both that the head count had to be reduced and that some strategic shifts in the business needed to happen. But one of the people on my team who was on their layoff list was pregnant, and while I could see the business and management reasons for the change, the decision to take someone's job when they were about to expand their family didn't sit right with me. So I pushed back, advocating for finding another role for this employee or at least delaying their layoff. After making my plea, I was told that I was a good person for advocating for this employee, but the decision wouldn't be reversed. Instead, I was recused from the process; they said I was too emotionally invested and unable to make objective decisions. I was *relieved*.

Not that anyone likes them much, but I really hate layoffs. They often feel unnecessary—or at least based on faulty strategy—and make clear a company's inability to prioritize their most important resource: people. I had to sit with this conflict: If I wanted to be a manager, and if I wanted to advance in my career, I'd have to make tough choices along the way. There were parts of my humanity I'd have to cut myself off from. Facing the reality that you are going to take someone's job away is awful—even when the person is not working out on the team or for the company. It's traumatic for them, it leaves them in an uncertain predicament, and it could be career-ending.

The pressure suffocated me. This is, once again, not a sob story: Managers are not victims (any more than we are all victims of workplaces we can't control), and I'm aware that I had some power and a six-figure salary. But I was also a cog in the machine; rather than being a site for change, I was—I had to be—a site for compliance.

The higher you go up the job ladder, the further you get from the very thing that put you on the ladder in the first place—and the more your days get filled with internal politics, management concerns, and fixing things for other people. For me, rather than being an opportunity to make a real difference at organizations with missions I believed in and people I could mentor, management became a thankless task filled with the stress of getting people to perform to my boss's specifications (or do their jobs at all), as well as trying to balance doing what I felt was the right thing with what needed to get done.

The Glass Fortress

A friend of mine—let's call her Rachel—who was a longtime journalist decided in her midthirties that she needed a bit of a career change. She decided to pursue a senior-level management job at a well-known media company. "It had been really hard for me to see myself in leadership positions," she told me. "Everybody who does that type of work has a certain sort of pedigree." But she had been encouraged to apply for the job by her colleagues. She knew the job was a reach but also asked herself the question a lot of us do: *Why not me?*

Management agreed, and she got the job. She became the first Black woman in the position—something that was widely celebrated.

A few months into the job, she texted me, frustrated: "I feel like I've been thrown into the deep end and there's no one here to help me. And I feel like I'm a token." I jumped on the phone with her, ready to offer support, and heard a story I've heard before, especially from women of color and especially from young Black women. While the people who had hired her had expressed a lot of excitement when she'd accepted their offer, that excitement hadn't translated into any concrete support once she was in the role. It was all "so happy you're here!" followed by crickets and then open disappointment. Everyone was ready to point out what she didn't do right or well, but few had any words of wisdom or mentorship to help her in the position. As she struggled on alone, the situation had an all too familiar feeling. "Being a Black woman, being a woman of color, I don't get help when I ask for it—in the world, in life," she said. So why, she acknowledged, would this job be any different?

When you are thrust into a position that you might not be ready for, you end up being anxious about asking questions, afraid to ask the fatal question that reveals that you're not prepared. As Rachel told me, "What I underestimated was, I didn't know what I didn't know. So I didn't know which questions to ask, I didn't know what to look out for, I didn't know that it's OK to ask someone."

Rachel was set up for failure: The job for which she had been hired was a new one, and there was no clear sense of what success would be in an environment that could change quickly based on *her* success. And the organization wasn't doing particularly well—in hindsight, they had needed a miracle to turn things around. (She later told me she did eventually get the support she needed but only after the situation had become dire.) What my friend was experiencing is something the few women and people of color who are promoted to senior management roles experience. It's called the *glass cliff*. Everyone knows the concept of the glass ceiling—the place near the top where no woman has broken through, where success in your field is visible but just out of reach because of your gender (and race). But the challenges women, including women of color, face while *in* leadership have been dubbed "the glass cliff."

The term was originally coined by Michelle K. Ryan and S. Alexander Haslam, professors at the University of Exeter, in a 2007 paper, "The Glass Cliff: Evidence that Women are Over-Represented in Precarious Leadership Positions." In it, they look at the propensity for organizations to hire and promote women and people of color in times of crisis when leadership roles are most challenging. In a study of the FTSE 100 (the top companies listed on the London Stock Exchange) they found that "during a period of overall stock-market decline, those companies who appointed women to their boards were more likely to have experienced consistently bad performance in the preceding five months than those who appointed men."

In other words, rather than considering women or people of color for executive roles at the height of an organization's power and influence, we instead collectively look for them to lead when it's time for the clean-up job—including the dirty work of layoffs, budget cuts, dealing with misconduct issues, and facing staff grievances, often in the face of decreasing revenue, profit, and investment.

Building on that concept of the glass ceiling, the glass cliff is a metaphor for being pushed to the top, unaware of the coming invisible ledge; one misstep or shove can send you barreling down the side. The view might be nice from the top, but it's not pretty when you fall.

It's a useful framework for thinking about the types of management that might be needed when things aren't going well at a company, as well as the pressures that are put on women to perform more gendered tasks, such as collaboration, mentorship, and providing support, in ways men are rarely expected to do. Add to this the double pressure that is often put on women and people of color leaders to "fix" the representational problems in their office by either hiring more people like them or tackling the issues. Rachel told me, "I'm the only Black person on the leadership team—one person cannot fix a structural issue."

And, for midcareer professionals, a "glass cliff" position can be hard to turn down. After years of fighting to get recognition in the workplace and internalizing the ethos of hustling to the top, it can feel fair and ameliorative to finally be offered a leadership position. That promotion usually comes with a pay bump, long-sought-after recognition, and a chance to call the shots instead of always having to follow them.

It also feeds the mythology that it is possible to win at this system if you work hard and follow the rules (or, in some cases, "break the rules," an idea businesspeople love to tout but that is not really rewarded). We're often told that our hiring is a "new day," an opportunity to change the system from within, and that we will be empowered to really make that change.

There has been lots of research into (and opinions about) both how women are effective leaders and how, when women end up in positions of unmitigated power, they can end up adopting the behavior of male leaders. Conversely, the suggestion that women are better leaders only because they're more nurturing or supportive, communicative, or collaborative could do with some examination. They're not always, nor should they be expected to be.

But data suggests that many women, more often than not, exhibit qualities in the workplace that are historically considered soft. This could be a result of socialization, of expectation, or of the fact that there are professional consequences for women who "act like men" at work: We all know that pushy women are considered bitchy, bossy, or aggressive if they unapologetically assert themselves.

I internalized these expectations throughout my life and found the path of least resistance was where I felt most comfortable. I excelled at a more nurturing management style, partly because it's what most young people need these days (and I'm not oblivious) but also because it came more naturally to me. But a more "feminine" management style didn't make the job of managing and having tough conversations any easier—if anything, it made the job harder, because I had set the tone that I was "nice." The boss can't really be *that* nice, at the end of the day.

Then there was a further complication: I wasn't just a woman in a leadership role, I was an Asian American woman in a leadership role. With that came an implicit expectation that I would be a certain type of corporate soldier—yes, a person of color in a senior role, but one who is perhaps less threatening to the establishment. Maybe this expectation was undergirded by an assumption that I'd keep my head down and work hard and never disobey my bosses.

The myth of the model minority suggests a rather imbalanced idea of how much Asian Americans advance in their careers. Despite being one of the largest minority groups in professional fields, Asian Americans are held back from leadership in a variety of ways, including through microaggressions, being confused for one another, and because we are perceived as good workers but not necessarily good leaders.

The phenomenon of Asians and Asian Americans not advancing in the workplace has been referred to, rather unfortunately, as the *bamboo ceiling*. The phrase originally appeared in a 2006 book by leadership coach Jane Hyun titled *Breaking the Bamboo Ceiling: Career Strategies for Asians*. The term may now be a wincer, but Hyun was describing a real phenomenon: the "combination of individual, cultural, and organizational factors that impede their career progress."

And data has borne this out. In a study commissioned by McKinsey on the experiences of Asians in the workplace, they found that Asian and Asian American workers "are overrepresented in low-paying occupations such as manicurists and skin care specialists, cooks, and sewing-machine operators," while simultaneously being "overrepresented in higher-wage technical fields such as software development and computer programming." Due to this diversity of fields, they report that the group has "the highest income inequality among races in the United States."

According to Project Include founders Tracy Chou and Ellen K. Pao (the famous sexism-in-tech lawsuit plantiff), Asians and Asian Americans are overrepresented in tech compared to other industries. "Asians in tech are now frequently considered so white-adjacent that we are no longer identified as people of color," they write on Medium.

But despite our proximity to whiteness—perceived and real—Asian Americans continue to face obstacles in the workplace. The assumption is that Asian Americans are less challenging to hire and promote, and despite coming from a wild diversity of backgrounds, economic classes, countries, castes, families, and communities, we are perceived as being more passive, or as peacemakers. No one ever explicitly told me that I was a "model minority," or that I was expected to smooth things over with other employees of color and women because the bosses didn't want to do it themselves. It was never explicit, but it didn't need to be. I was willing to perform the function all the same—and the people managing me benefited from these quiet narratives.

It is worth noting that, when it comes to occupying leadership roles, the rate of promotion is growing more slowly for women, and particularly women of color, than for any other group, continuing a decades-long leadership gap in most industries. According to a sweeping 2023 study of 276 organizations and 27,000 employees along with 270 HR leaders, performed by McKinsey in collaboration with LeanIn.org, "Women face their biggest hurdle at the first critical step up to manager . . . for every 100 men promoted from entry level to manager, 87 women were promoted."

This number is even lower when accounting for race: "73 women of color were promoted to manager for every 100 men, down from 82 women of color last year." They conclude, "As a result of this 'broken rung,' women fall behind and can't catch up."

Because of this, only 4 percent of leaders in the C-suite are women of color—a number that has held steady for the three years prior to the survey. This is especially true for Black women: According to the study, "more than a quarter of Black women say their race has led to them missing out on an opportunity to advance."

Despite the endless barriers women of color, and particularly Black women, face in getting promoted into leadership roles, research suggests that employees *like* working for women. In a study surveying the impacts of women's job losses during the pandemic, one reported implication was the loss of effective managers. Potential Project surveyed five thousand companies about how leaders function under immense pressure (like during a pandemic), looking at two characteristics: wisdom and compassion. They write in the *Harvard Business Review*, "55% of the women in our study were ranked by their followers as being wise and compassionate compared to only 27% of the men. Conversely, 56% of the men in our study ranked poorly on wisdom and compassion." Additionally, women are shown to be better at implementing diversity and inclusion initiatives—across the board.

One of the toughest things that I've struggled with in leadership roles is toggling between what is expected of me and what I ultimately care about, which is having diverse, effective teams. It's a bit of a "damned if you do, damned if you don't": I always tell myself it's better that I'm the one making these calls about handling race issues, interviewing more women, mentoring the only queer person on the team, etc., than someone who doesn't have the experience to do it. But it's also a trap, and a standard to which my white, straight, male colleagues are rarely held.

Chou and Pao write, "It is [our] mix of privilege *and* exclusion that also gives us a unique position from which to advocate for anti-racism and the dismantling of structural and systemic racism." Despite all the pressures, invisible narratives, and even my own skepticism, this is also how I saw my own position: If I was in the club, I was going to take all my friends with me.

Can We Save the Management?

When I first became a manager, I thought I had a real opportunity to make a difference. I also thought it was something I'd get better at, well, managing as time went on. But what I've come to see is that the role of middle manager itself—and most roles that women and people of color are put into—is inherently fraught. Historically, any management role is in direct opposition to the worker, and a middle manager is a person who must ensure worker compliance for the benefit of their own boss(es) and the company's bottom line. In a corporate structure, middle managers are the glue that holds the hierarchy of the workplace together: They are the people who implement their bosses' agendas; they are the faces of upper-management decisions to their employees; and they are the ones with direct contact to the people doing the work.

In leftist thinking, criticism of management falls into two camps. In Marxist thought, they are described as the "petite bourgeoisie"—the lower rung of the middle-class and aspiring capitalists who do not own the means of production but are hired by those who do to control the workers (the proletariat). Another way they have been described is as a contained political group of their own, the Professional-Managerial Class (PMC), a term coined by Barbara and John Ehrenreich. In a 1977 essay in *Radical America,* they write, "We define the Professional-Managerial Class as consisting of salaried mental workers who do not own the means of production and whose major function in the social division of labor may be described broadly as the reproduction of capitalist culture and capitalist class relations."

Some argue the PMC sits in opposition to the working class; others suggest that it is a porous and persuadable group that has more in common with the working class than the capitalist class. Arguments continue as to whether the PMC is an important group with which to build solidarity as workers, or whether solidarity is impossible because this class exists to maintain the status quo.

If we buy the idea of a PMC at all, it is worth noting that it is a fairly diverse group that can include anyone from schoolteachers to nurses, from college adjuncts to journalists, and from police officers to tech workers. As such, this hypothetical band encompasses huge variations in terms of financial standing and education. Some of us are on the lower end of the band, while others are on the higher; some of us worked our way into it, and others were born into it. Some of us went to state schools, and some of us went to Yale.

Historian Gabriel Winant argues that because conditions have gotten so tenuous financially even for the educated classes, "for the precarious academic, the overworked nurse, or the underpaid teacher, the contradictions between official ideologies of professionalism and the material reality of existence have become so vivid as to create a chasm." This chasm makes an opening where it may be "possible for a member of the PMC to glimpse broader solidarity with the working class, even to imagine self-redefinition as one with it," he writes.

Barbara Ehrenreich spoke in support of this view. In an interview in *Dissent* in 2019, she clarifies that she's surprised to hear that PMC is used as a pejorative, saying that she hated to see it "turned into an ultraleft slur. We're going to have to work together!"

And she's right: Middle managers (or that particular sector of white-collar workers) are, as Noreen Malone wrote in *The New York Times Magazine,* coming into "class consciousness." Unionization efforts are not just happening among the lowest rung of workers, but also in the professional or managerial classes that include teachers, journalists, engineers, architects, actors, TV writers, tech workers, and more.

Middle managers are usually left out of unionization efforts, because they often have to sit on the other side of the bargaining table, and it's a conflict of interest—not to mention that they are regularly disincentivized from advocating for or being in solidarity with their employees. This is also due to the Taft-Hartley Act of 1947, which grossly limited the power and influence of unions, though one of its key provisions barred supervisors from joining union efforts. Today, since managers often do not have a ton of power or say over their own roles or their teams, they are starting to join efforts to organize and agitate for change at work.

There is a lot of skepticism about managers and why we choose to take these roles. For some people, it's just the inevitable next step in your career as you get older; others enter the work world hoping to get to management; and yet others are invested in what they are working on and want to tackle it from a new angle. When I entered the corporate world, the raise I got as a middle manager was both consequential (who doesn't need more cash?) and not nearly enough to buy my loyalty to my bosses over my employees—an allegiance that often felt expected of me. Our loyalties as managers should theoretically lie with our employees, but often we ourselves fear being laid off and end up having to make impossible choices, because we are not protected in our jobs, either. And for women of color, missing out on a promotion could mean getting pushed back down into a cycle of debt and financial insecurity from which you worked so hard to emerge.

Managers are going to remain necessary for quite a while longer, and I don't think the solution for marginalized people is to reject these positions out of fear or because of ideology. Even in an imperfect system, it's better to have diverse and interesting people in management roles, especially if you are trying to make them better. For those of us marginalized people who take management roles, look: Work decisions are really hard, and I don't think we need another thing to beat ourselves up about. Focusing on our individual choices in a broken system isn't on its own ultimately going to be what leads to sustained change.

But, as the sociologist Victor Ray said to me, our individual choices matter to the extent that we have to live with them—and because institutions are made up of people making individual choices that impact other people. Management is one of the places where that happens. As managers, we have to toggle between fighting for the bigger picture and trying not to be shit bosses in the short term. We can have all the great politics in the world and still be shit coworkers, shit managers, and shit bosses, so those personal politics aren't inherently going to make the biggest difference.

What if, instead of pointing fingers at ourselves, one another, and the system we often deem unchangeable, we started to consider what ethical leadership might look like? I'm not talking about simply embracing the cottage industry of leadership advice; much of that stems from a neoliberal idea that the more we personalize the office—the more bosses make it a "family," give out snacks, and pretend they're emotionally invested in their employees—the more productive workers will be, and the better the current system will be for the company's bottom line.

And, as workers, it behooves us to recognize that our position vis-à-vis the bottom line isn't exactly neutral, either: On some level, under capitalism, we all must be invested in our employers' profit, or we will face layoffs and job insecurity. But that doesn't mean middle managers have no power. There is a difference between a manager and a leader, and we need more leaders who are invested in equity, see their employees as part of their rise, support worker-led initiatives and organizing, and are driven by values of justice and fairness.

I'm not saying it's going to be easy—we are usually disincentivized from being this kind of manager—but taking the time to think about why you want to get ahead at work and why you want to manage

people will go a long way in determining how you lead. As Brené
Brown writes in *Dare to Lead*, "More often than not, our values are
what lead us to the arena door—we're willing to do something uncomfortable and daring because of our beliefs."

If I had not been so insecure and wide-eyed about having the chance
to be a leader, I probably would have fared better, because I would have
had a clear sense of what I believed in and how I would execute that in
my leadership. When I was at *Teen Vogue* and at prior jobs, I was deeply
anxious about supporting my staffers in their labor-action efforts, even
though, intellectually, I agreed with them, because their actions made
me feel vulnerable, and I didn't know how to maneuver. And, just because I was (or tried to be) fair-minded did not mean that I didn't
make mistakes or that I wouldn't be disliked by my staff. (People often
don't like their bosses, and trying to earn your employees' affection is a
wrongheaded thing to do, because being the boss isn't actually cool!)
But there is a better chance your employees will respect you if you
stand for something and aren't afraid to speak up about it, even if it is
not always what they want to hear.

So, what are areas we might concentrate on when thinking about
the kinds of leaders we want to be? Vulnerability, offering feedback,
and taking accountability are all important parts of being a good leader
and a better colleague. Often, even the most well-meaning managers
will deliver feedback in a way that shuts down the conversation. Rather
than giving examples of how someone can improve, they voice disappointment without giving a clear sense of what success might look like.
Part of this is because most of us are, in general, shitty communicators.
We are conflict averse and, as such, may deliver feedback with haste
because we don't even want to do it in the first place. Or we ourselves
don't have a clear sense of success, so we're often just going off "vibes"—
a recipe for disaster when trying to get a team to accomplish something.

So, here's a simple play we can use to start trying to be better. What
if, instead of feedback being one-sided, it was a two-way conversation?
What if you asked your team for feedback on what you could do better
along with giving them feedback on what they can do better?

Having difficult conversations is something we all need to get better at—and not just at work. In her groundbreaking book *Conflict Is Not Abuse,* Sarah Schulman says we live in "a culture of underreaction to abuse and overreaction to conflict." By that she means that our culture allows some unfettered abuses—from the criminal justice system to rape culture to the military-industrial complex—but we struggle to talk to people with whom we have disagreements.

We have tremendous language to express our rage and our anger, and we are starting to truly be able to express the extent of harm done to us and others. But conflict resolution language often eludes us.

Schulman offers a simple solution: "Nothing disrupts dehumanization more quickly than inviting someone over, looking into their eyes, hearing their voice, and listening." Imagine applying that to the workplace: Getting comfortable having vulnerable, honest conversations with your staff could probably go a long way toward disrupting the never-ending cycle of tension and exploitation in which management and employees seem endlessly locked.

For instance, when I was working for a consulting firm focused on social responsibility, a senior colleague saw me struggle through a presentation with a client. I was new to that type of work, and having largely worked with scrappy grassroots organizations, I was a little rough around the edges. What started as a friendly conversation in a client meeting descended into chaos when the client didn't understand what I was saying. Rather than explaining it in different terms, I got impatient and continued to explain it again in the terms with which I was most familiar. It was a disaster—the presentational equivalent of trying to say something in English to someone who doesn't understand the language, so you simply repeat yourself more loudly in English.

My colleague watched the interaction and decided to give me some feedback. He put a document together about what he observed in that meeting and what he thought I could have done better, while also recognizing the things I did well. This might sound like a heavy-handed response from someone who was not my direct manager, and I could easily have been deeply offended—but I also knew that something had gone wrong and didn't know what it was. And it was a life-changing interaction: He took the time out of his own schedule and took me out for a drink to give me feedback. As he delivered the feedback, I felt seen, empowered, and held accountable—but in a way that gave me a path forward, with clear examples of what I could do next time something like that happened.

It is a tactic that I have now replicated in my own management— I have come to call this strategy "glows and grows," and it has served me well. And when I've used it with employees, I've been told it's very helpful.

Don't get it twisted: The structures that we rely on at work are failing, and they are often unfair. What our workplaces need most are effective unions, equal pay, and real and legitimate ways for employees to file grievances and have them heard, not just more pep talks. But that's not everyone's life. Most of us still have to get up and go to work every day, and some of us are going to end up in management roles. It matters that we aren't total assholes in those roles, particularly to the people who have to work with us.

So if you want to take a promotion and lead a team, do it, while keeping your heart and mind focused on these theoretical concerns. One of the ways I tried to manage that constant tension between what I believed philosophically and how the organizations I worked for were not ideal was to realize that (a) I am only one person and can't change the trajectory of an entire organization, and I must stop thinking I can; and (b) my focus is and will always be the people who are working for me, and especially the people who have historically been left out of these spaces—no matter how challenging that may be, and despite what my bosses want.

To genuinely be a better leader is an easy commitment to make if you are truly looking to have more impact in your work and be more in solidarity with your employees, as we all reconsider what work is and what ambition is. As organizational psychologist Adam Grant said in his book *Give and Take*, "Focus attention and energy on making a difference in the lives of others, and success might follow as a by-product."

If what you want is just more power and more money, be honest with yourself that that is what you want and what you are buying into and realize it probably won't lead to the liberation of everyone like you. We should stop conflating the language of social justice with our personal ambitions; they are not always going to be one and the same. But I see tremendous potential in rethinking personal ambition for all of us. What would it look like if we started considering our advancement as a class of people, not just as individuals?

REVENGE BODY

You won't break my soul.

—Beyoncé

I t started with a bad performance review.

My boss sat across from me in a glass conference room, with me facing the hallway, and he said, "You're not going to be happy with this."

My chest tightened, and I realized I had forgotten my tissues.

I'd got a two out of five—an adult D—on my performance. He said I hadn't met the mark in my management; I hadn't executed ideas the way he thought I should have; and I was overall disappointing, especially for someone who had come in with so much buzz (or something to that effect).

It was my first time getting anything but glowing feedback from a manager. I started sobbing hysterically, tears and snot pouring out of me. It was so embarrassing: Anyone who walked by could see me. I couldn't get myself out of there fast enough.

I was so upset that I couldn't go back to my desk. Instead, I went to the bathroom and texted a colleague to bring my sweater and purse to a stall so I could leave the building quietly. I then sat outside in a newly built miniature park for a few hours, convulsing with sobs—the kind of cry that is about much more than the one thing you say you are crying about.

As I sat on this bench in the middle of this weirdly paved, try-too-hard nonpark in downtown NYC, a nice man asked me in a comforting New York accent, "You OK, sweethawt? Can I get you anything? Don't cry!" He then ran to a nearby pretzel cart, bought me a bottle of water, put his hand on my shoulder, and said, "Whatever it is, it'll get better." I felt so stupid, crying in public like I had lost someone.

I mean, I guess I had: I had lost myself.

I somehow went back into the office and got through the rest of the day after that but called in sick for the rest of the week. It wasn't just that I couldn't get out of bed; I started to have intense chest pains, and when I wasn't feeling those, I was imagining myself jumping in front of one of the buses that ran up First Avenue next to my fourth-floor walk-up, or wondering what would happen if I took a whole handful of my Xanax prescription.

That's when I knew things were *bad* bad, so I called my best friend, who said we could talk about what happened later but that I needed to hang up and call my doctor right away and tell her everything, too.

I emailed my doctor instead, and she told me to come in right away.

I had struggled with bouts of depression, but it had never been this bad, I told her. She switched my medication to something to manage the anxiety and the depression without the risks of suicidal ideation and suggested I take off as much time as possible—one month at the minimum, but I should consider much longer. I said, "There is literally no way," so we agreed to three weeks.

She wrote me a note, and I was in the clear for a little while: I didn't have to go in to work and face the reality that the people who were then in charge of me didn't think I was very good at what I do. I had hit my breaking point, but I wasn't even aware of it yet; I was still focused on getting better to get back to work.

I went to stay with my parents for a week, but our cozy upstate home had essentially transformed into a medical facility to deal with my father's end-stage renal disease. My mother suggested I check into a retreat center I'd visited in the past and liked, and so I did, spending the rest of my medical leave lying on the floor in yoga class.

After I returned to the office, things were—not surprisingly—awkward. My job duties were slowly given to a new hire with a stronger background in organizational management. I see now that the writing was already on the wall (and had been even before the performance review). But at the time I didn't get it. I was on good terms with everyone, including my bosses. I was still working on projects and collaborating with colleagues. I thought that I would just continue on in my job. I'm "the person everyone likes"—that's my whole thing, my survival skill.

I kept thinking that it was all going to be relatively OK till one day, a few weeks after I returned, the inevitable happened: I was fired.

I mean, technically, I was laid off. Everyone told me it was not about my talent but about a "strategic redirect," and I was one of several employees whose positions were being eliminated. I was told my departure could be framed to everyone as a "transition," and I had the option to continue to work for the company on a freelance basis. Then my bosses asked me if I could come in the next day for the rest of the layoffs. I could have said no, but I decided to party all night and showed up on no sleep, fully numb and disassociated from the day's activities.

Management had tried their best to help me save face, but the damage was done. I was enraged, devastated, and destabilized; I felt gaslit and betrayed. I was also fucked financially because I had just helped my parents relocate to that cozy upstate home and was footing a good bit of the bill. When I got back to my apartment that night after a terrible day, I looked around at my couch, my window—it all looked different.

It was never officially diagnosed as such, but after my bad review I suffered what I now know are the symptoms of a nervous breakdown. I was taking a few different types of medication, drinking too much alcohol, and turning to late-night eating to keep my feelings of abject failure at bay. In the middle of this, I had a book coming out. Instead of spending some time working through whatever was happening (and it was clear to me even then that it wasn't entirely about losing my job), there was a book tour to go on. Flights around the country. Media appearances. The need for big smiles and polished hair and being "on" in interviews.

And then, four months later, I got an email inviting me to interview for the executive editor job at *Teen Vogue*. I took the job but hadn't fully recovered from the layoff. I still had bad work-life boundaries; I was emotionally unstable and hadn't processed anything that had happened. Most people didn't see this part of it—they saw me coming off a successful book tour and starting a fabulous new job. I was commended for my grit, hard work, and ability to build myself up from being an indie blogger to a major player in New York media.

I was on a short-term high: One place didn't want me, but another much more desirable, cool, and successful place did. I started the job like you start a rebound relationship when you aren't over your ex: I hit the ground running, posting nonstop selfies with my Drybar blowout and gifted plus-size fashion outfits, bragging about all the exciting and awesome things that were happening around me. I was the girl who had made it, sitting front row at New York Fashion Week.

I never acknowledged how much the failure at my previous job still rankled me or that I was deeply tired and depressed. But even though I didn't acknowledge my feelings, my body tried to make them visible to me: I gained weight, I was chronically tired, and I had huge dark circles under my eyes.

Imagine, if you can, that as I stepped into the most body-conscious, thin-centric place on earth (or at least, at which I had ever worked)— the halls of *Vogue*—my body was the largest it has ever been. I had never been a thin woman, but the gain was enough of a difference that people noticed and made comments. I was less upset by the comments than by the lack of control I felt over the way my body kept changing. It added to my stress; I had failed at work, and now my body would derail my career.

I'd love to tell you a story about how I embraced this new body and was excited to smash the barriers holding fat women back in fashion. Instead I was suffocated by shame. How could I let this happen? And yet, when fashion brands started to knock down my door in earnest to take pictures of me in their clothes and ask what it was like to be a fat editor at a major fashion magazine, I was still wondering, *Am I really fat?*

Weight gain is often judged, pathologized, ignored, and hated—and fat people are discriminated against in the workplace, which has more consequences than simply making us feel bad or insecure. As the writer and brilliant podcaster Aubrey Gordon writes in her book *What We Don't Talk About When We Talk About Fat,* "After all, thinner women simply aren't subjected to the same levels of societal prejudice, harassment, bullying, and overt discrimination as fatter people."

But fat empowerment also somehow became something *else* I had to girlboss through. I knew my weight gain was a response to trauma—that I'd started overeating because feeling my feelings was too scary, that the medication I was taking was having a side effect, that my hormones were out of whack, and that I was in a constant state of panic. Yet, suddenly, I had to embrace my fatness like it was the best thing that had ever happened to me.

I did embrace it, and I'm eternally grateful to all the people who helped me welcome it, cherish it, dress it, and build community with women who refused to judge themselves in any way for the size of their bodies. But my weight gain wasn't really about my body; it was about what was happening inside my mind. I was engaging in self-harming behaviors—disordered eating, compulsive drinking, bad stress management—that partially caused the weight gain, and then being celebrated for it (though not nearly as much as I would've been celebrated for losing it).

My body was telling me a story about myself that I couldn't handle yet.

Then, the pandemic hit, and I moved to upstate New York to live with my mother. I got the time and space to become more present in my day-to-day life and more aware of how I was treating my body to avoid treating my mind. I'm still not great at stress management, but whether it means practicing good boundaries, leaving New York City life (which I did for a little while), disappointing friends, or being picky about the work I take on, I'm slowly learning how to handle my actual needs.

I want to emphasize this again: My concern about my weight gain wasn't about being fat. People gain weight, they lose weight, and they chastise themselves for absolutely normal fluctuations. It's also OK to be fat: It's your fucking body, you make the rules. (It's also physically OK to be fat; the idea that being fat inherently means you are un-healthy is not backed by real science.)

But *thinness* is part of the "having it all"–industrial complex (if you recall, Helen Gurley Brown's bible on the topic had diet recipes) that I grew up swimming in. The life I wanted and should yearn for was contingent on the size of my body. I had internalized the idea that gaining weight would have material consequences, and I wasn't wrong. Successful businesswomen girlboss types are not fat: They go to the gym, usually *multiple* times per week. Being or getting thin is part of the work we as women take on to "succeed," and it's part of the emo-tional weight that many of us carry until we drop.

My weight gain was from an eating disorder I wasn't addressing, and the stress about my weight gain and having to appear OK about my weight gain was adding to the emotional load that was already too heavy for me to carry . . . and I had no idea how to set it down.

I was eventually forced to reckon with what a true path to a better life could be. I realized how much I had been aiming for other people's goalposts—regularly overexerting myself to meet obligations to my job, my friends, and my family. I had to accept that the shortcuts I thought were making my life better—eating takeout at my desk, tak-ing cars all the time—were making things worse. My path to better health would have to be less about what I did and more about what I wasn't going to do anymore.

It was time to stop trying so hard at *everything*—to slow down, to listen to my body, to go for walks, and to let myself get hungry instead of eating out of anxiety. I was lucky. The pandemic gave me the space to realize that it was the lifestyle of success at any cost that was hurting my body and not what I was eating or my exercise schedule, no matter what society was telling me.

I hadn't ever really given myself the space I needed to adjust to high-powered, high-stress jobs. I'd started practicing "fake it till you make it" back in my twenties, and on some level, I was still faking it twenty years later. And I didn't even realize it, because I was pushing myself so hard all the time. I had no mentors at work, no one who was able to give me constructive feedback on my performance (companies benefit from this dissociated obsession with work over self), so I just kept barreling ahead—making mistakes left and right.

I don't think giving feedback or mentoring is easy, but I also don't think my bosses really knew how to, any more than I did. Years after I'd sat weeping by the hot dog cart, I kept obsessively going over the day when I got fired, again and again. In therapy, I'd be raging, blaming everyone for what happened—and then I gradually started to see the complexity of the situation. I started to see what I couldn't see then: I had also not been thriving in the position. And that was OK.

Still, that rage was important. It uncovered something much deeper that I'd been tap-dancing around for years, which was that, at my core, I doubted that I even had a right to a job like that in the first place. My rage was actually shame: I had failed, and admitting it broke me for a long time. But it also helped me face the fact that I had to stop faking. I took being fired as a referendum on my right to be where I was at all—my right to have a job like that. I was deeply ashamed. I had failed.

And I let it break me.

The Trauma of Capitalism

In May 2021, four-time champion and the world's second-ranked women's tennis player Naomi Osaka decided to forgo the mandatory post-match press conference at the French Open. In a message posted to her social media accounts, she cited her mental health and the treatment of athletes, in general, for why she'd be sitting it out. "We're often sat there and asked questions that we've been asked multiple times before or asked questions that bring doubt into our minds, and I'm just not going to subject myself to people that doubt me," she wrote.

The French Open fined her for skipping the press event after she won her match and threatened to increase sanctions and potentially suspend her from the tournament for violating their code of conduct. The next day, Osaka beat them to the punch and dropped out of the competition. She has since reduced her playing schedule to focus more on her mental health and happiness. In 2022, she said, "For me, I just want to feel like every time I step on the court . . . I'm having fun. I can walk off the court knowing that, even if I lost, I tried as hard as I could."

A few months after Osaka's French Open, the greatest gymnast of all time, Simone Biles, withdrew from the team, individual all-around, and three other Olympics gymnastics events where she was expected to win gold, citing mental-health concerns after she got a case of the "twisties." She wrote on social media, "It's the craziest feeling ever. Not having an inch of control over your body. What's even scarier is since I have *no* idea where I am in the air, I also have no idea how I'm going to land. Or what I'm going to land on." Competing would have been too dangerous at that point, so Biles chose herself and her safety instead of pushing through. (And her team and the world cheered her on, while the U.S. team still went on to win the silver; she competed in one solo event and took home a bronze medal.)

Both athletes were widely supported and even celebrated for coming forward with their mental-health struggles and prioritizing their health over their professional duties. And they started a much-needed and long-overdue global conversation on the inordinate pressure that is put on athletes to perform at all costs, often neglecting their own mental and physical health.

Of course, it wasn't all support and roses: Osaka was lambasted for not understanding the rules and expectations of tennis. Conservative British pundit Piers Morgan called her an "arrogant spoiled brat" and a "petulant little madam," and a sportswriter at the *Telegraph* called her behavior "diva-like." Conservative gadfly Charlie Kirk called Biles a "selfish sociopath" and a "shame to the country." *How dare they behave like they have control over their own lives?*

Biles and Osaka said no, pushing back against tidal waves of pressure and expectation—the same pressures and expectations that imperiled their mental health in the first place. They were well aware of the stakes, and they knew they were running the risk of disappointing their fans and perhaps wasting all the hard work they had put in to get there. But they still found the courage to prioritize their health. They refused to follow the cultural script given to all of us to push our way through the pain—to do as we are told, to hustle harder, and to get the job done.

Biles and Osaka put famous faces on a confluence of pressures that women—and especially women of color, and *especially* Black women—face daily: the expectation to be great at what you do, do it while often living up to Western beauty ideals, and also be super likable. Most of us are not world-class athletes, but we are often saddled with the expectation of being "superwomen," as though we aren't human beings with limits to our physical, mental, and spiritual resources.

Call it sweat equity, the nurture tax, passion points, or whatever you want, but this invisible and unpaid emotional labor from women comes at a cost. We believe women are inherently nurturing and that they will do the work of being likable and exceptional without complaint, while we universally dismiss the value of women's likability and pay them less for their work (if they are paid at all).

But Americans are currently more anxious than ever: The inordinate pressure that work puts on the average person is causing a mental-health crisis that transcends gender. A year into the pandemic, one in five Americans were still reportedly experiencing "high levels of psychological distress," according to a study from Pew. People who'd had their lives impacted by the pandemic in some way—lower-income people whose livelihoods were threatened by the crisis, young people ages eighteen to twenty-nine, and people with disabilities or other types of health issues—were most likely to report that distress. As of 2023, these numbers were largely unchanged, as more than 40 percent of Americans had "experienced high levels of psychological distress at some point during the pandemic."

This level of anxiety is a pandemic in and of itself.

Still, the pandemic only pressure-tested a conclusion we were already coming to: Work itself had become untenable. And that's had a profound impact on our stress levels as well. According to the American Institute of Stress, 83 percent of American workers experience some form of daily stress, and 25 percent of them say it's directly related to work. Approximately one million Americans miss work every day because of depression. Work as it is currently structured has led to a mental-health crisis.

But women are especially burned out—and, as I talked about in Chapter 5, especially mothers. A similar 2021 study from McKinsey and LeanIn.org, about the state of women and work, found that women were more burned out than they had been in 2020, and one in three women "have considered downshifting their careers or leaving the workforce this year." Four in ten women had "considered leaving their company or switching jobs." A 2023 study from Future Forum found that 46 percent of women say they are burned out (compared to 37 percent of men).

We're *all* fucking burned out.

The term *burnout* was first used in this context by German-born American psychologist Herbert Freudenberger in a 1974 paper titled "Staff Burn-Out." In the paper, he defines burnout as "to fail, wear out, or become exhausted by making excessive demands on energy, strength, or resources." Some observable symptoms he lists include "exhaustion and fatigue" and "irritation and frustration." It took forty-five years, but burnout is now understood by the medical profession as a serious health concern. The World Health Organization added burnout to the

International Classification of Diseases in 2019, and although it is not a medical condition, it is an "occupational phenomenon."

Many psychologists and social scientists built on Freudenberger's work to explore burnout and its relationship to work, productivity, and happiness. In their book *Burnout: The Secret to Unlocking the Stress Cycle*, Amelia and Emily Nagoski condense the psychologist's findings further and identify three categories of burnout specific to women: "1. emotional exhaustion—the fatigue that comes from caring too much, for too long; 2. depersonalization—the depletion of empathy, caring, and compassion; 3. decreased sense of accomplishment—an unconquerable sense of futility: feeling that nothing you do makes any difference."

And burnout isn't just about being *tired*. It's also linked to various health issues: chronic fatigue, excessive alcohol consumption, hypertension, and so on. Burnout has become so commonplace that it's a word that we all immediately understand when it gets tossed into a conversation. We tell one another we are burned out, and we understand immediately and have empathy for one another, but we are often unable to even support one another because each of us is suffering from it. It's taken for granted that, if you have a certain amount of responsibility or success, burnout is part of the package.

In fact, if we are all burned out, is that even burnout, or is the inability of the general public to keep up in the fast-paced late-stage capitalist system a societal failure? "Burnout isn't special anymore," Eve Ettinger writes at *Bustle*. "A term suggesting a rock bottom stops meaning rock bottom when we're all there and, somehow, still going despite the struggle."

Somehow, burnout is not broadly thought about as a systemic issue; it's become another thing we are responsible for managing ourselves. Rarely do we as a society address the confluence of factors that are at the root of burnout: the unreal expectations that are put on workers; the lack of support for working mothers and families; the lack of access to good and natural foods; many people's mounting student loan debt; social pressures; the high speed of modern communication in which we are expected to be available and responsive; and job instability or general unhappiness at work—to name a few.

And what about the things we truly can't control: global catastrophes, wars being fought without our consent, climate change and its impending doom, school shootings, and an ongoing pandemic?

It's practically easier to be burned out than it is to be rested, healthy, and thriving.

. . .

I grew up Gen X—the generation that takes a lot of pleasure in working through pain. So, even though I knew better, once I got in management positions I'd secretly scoff when younger colleagues would take "mental-health days." That attitude was probably how I ended up having a nervous breakdown—I was so busy faking it till I made it that I wasn't able to track what I needed, nor did I feel deep down that I was "safe" enough to take time off. *It's not an ER,* I'd regularly say to myself about my job, both as a way to calm my feelings of urgency and to suggest that we were not doctors performing lifesaving work. (Nor were we working in fast food or other industries that so obviously harm, exploit, and underpay workers—the jobs that, along with medical professions, social work, and teaching, statistically lead to the highest levels of burnout.) It also didn't help that the very nature of working in media means that you may be exposed to stressful and triggering events every day, and your job may require the ability to work through that.

But most people—across industries—report feelings of burnout in their jobs. We are all privy to the harm created by unstable environments where our expectation to work without limit is connected to our ability to provide for ourselves.

Employers today are more and more often providing mental-health days, now sometimes called "wellness days," to employees, offering paid time off that's not just because they are physically ill or have some kind of personal or family emergency. But as Jonathan Malesic writes in *The Atlantic,* wellness days are often a Band-Aid on the root cause of burnout, which could be anything from a mismatch between what you want to be doing and what you *are* doing at work, your workload, or working in a stressful and challenging environment. What difference does a day off make, knowing your workload hasn't changed and you'll probably have to work doubly hard the next day?

"We might think of a mental-health day, then, as a form of work-place avoidance dressed in the language of self-care," writes Malesic. "If we want to improve workers' mental health and address widespread burnout, we need to make much bigger changes to the American way of work."

Even now, I very rarely take a day off. For me, even a vacation is a time to think of more ideas (something a lot of creative people will say). But work is *by far* the most stressful thing in my life—ask anyone who knows me. I'm always stressed about how to balance whatever project I'm working on with finding time to write, regularly daydream-ing about what it'd be like to be independently wealthy (or at least from a family with the resources to fund me as I focused on my writ-ing). In fact, in the months before this book was due to my editor, I started to feel tightness in my chest, and my arms were going numb. Around the same time, I was managing a huge project and event, going on a trip to India to take care of some family business, had lost a dear friend to suicide, had my therapist disappear due to a health problem, and was managing a job that wanted more from me. When I went to the doctor, my blood pressure had gone up again—as it had when I'd gotten my bad performance review.

Work, for me, is directly connected to my ability to provide for myself; I have to do it and do it well, whether I like it or not. Every single thing feels like the difference between surviving and not—no matter how many times you tell me otherwise or how untrue that might be. Which is why losing my job was traumatic for me.

Yes, trauma. Trauma is when we experience something intense, dis-turbing, and sometimes life altering. Trauma can be major, but it can also be subtle. It's a concept that has arguably been overused to the point where it can be hard to explain what it really means or how it impacts us. Not everything bad that happens to someone codes itself in the body as trauma, but sometimes we experience trauma without realizing we have.

Perhaps the idea of workplace trauma sounds overwrought when talking about workplaces that are physically safe. (I mean, repetitive stress injury is real, but is it the same thing as running into a burning building?) But trauma doesn't rank itself; whether you want it to or not, and whether you think your experience deserves the label or not, trauma impacts your behavior in ways researchers are only beginning to uncover. As Bessel van der Kolk writes in his book *The Body Keeps the Score:*

> Trauma is not just an event that took place sometime in the past; it is also the imprint left by that experience on mind, brain, and body. This imprint has ongoing consequences for how the human organism manages to survive in the present. Trauma results in a fundamental reorganization of the way mind and brain manage perceptions. It changes not only how we think and what we think about, but also our very capacity to think.

Van der Kolk's work has come under scrutiny in recent years, but the role that trauma plays in our behavior continues to be a site of inquiry.

If you have experienced trauma, especially at work, it arguably changes how you perceive, understand, behave, and relate to work. The idea of workplace trauma is a newer concept, but research does suggest that things that happen to us at work can store themselves as trauma in our bodies. Not only does that impact our stress levels and burnout levels, but we take that trauma with us from job to job, reproducing it (there's a reason some well-known leaders are recognized behind closed doors as some of the worst, most toxic leaders). That way of working—treating our bodies and minds as expendable resources we sacrifice in pursuit of success and "greatness"—has functioned enough times that we do it over and over again.

Add to this the trauma we bring into the workplace from our personal lives, which also impacts how we show up to work—whether it be feeling exhausted from exposure to certain themes or being unable to process feedback because we already feel like we don't belong. In recent years, we've seen the growth of trauma-related and somatics training in the workplace, especially in nonprofits, where they make an effort to incorporate healing and learning about our trauma into their work.

After I lost my job and felt traumatized by it, I didn't fully internalize the lesson that I was largely OK. I had freelance work, I had a book deal, and I got a job a few months later. But instead of exhaling (*Look, you're fine!*), I immediately locked myself into a day-to-day hustle of overproducing, overperforming, and overachieving to prove that I belonged there. On some level, I was afraid of being fired again if I didn't go hard all the time. Every time there was talk about budget cuts, I'd start to panic—not knowing what my next move would be and worrying about how, despite the decent salary, I still didn't have enough in the bank to make it more than two months if I was out of work. I knew intellectually that there were friends in my life who could help me, should I need money—and more important, that I was valuable as an employee and could easily find another job. But the trauma had hardcoded into my response system the belief that my resources were always under threat, and that the only way to avoid danger was to, in the famous words of Rihanna, "work, work, work, work, work."

As I began to heal from the trauma of losing my job, I became more and more cognizant of how this cycle kept me anchored in myths about myself that benefited only my employers. It is very easy to exploit someone who fundamentally believes that the only way they can provide for themselves is by being exploited in some way. The stress of capitalism, the belief that you and you alone are responsible for your financial destiny and your ability to pay your student loans (or your mom's bills), keeps us in an abusive, nonconsensual relationship with work. What is success, what is ambition, what is loving what you do when work is tainted by the constant nagging reality that if you lose this job, you are fucked?

It's going to take more than a Pilates class to undo the ways we are bound up in the material pressures we face to provide for ourselves, while also having to smile, be nice, be hot, and be grateful.

How Did Self-Care Become So Stressful?

Of course, one solution to all this stress and burnout is self-care.

Self-care, though, has also become part and parcel of the girlboss agenda. Sure, mani-pedis, trips to Sephora, boozy group brunches, and scheduled retreats can be fun, but when does it stop? Our bodies themselves are now a product to be commodified, and self-care is another part of our lives at which we must excel. It's too much!

Take exercise: It's not a bad thing, but it's often less about health or relaxation for many women. It's also positioned as a way to increase our productivity and to help us attain and retain the beauty and body standards that we are told we should reach. Self-care is something that was actually supposed to be about taking care of ourselves, but it is now just as often another thing to be competitive about. We all know it's a ridiculous paradigm, but somehow, we all still buy into it.

In her 2021 book *Can't Even*, Anne Helen Petersen wrote that burnout "isn't a personal problem. It's a societal one—and it will not be cured by productivity apps, or a bullet journal, or face mask skin treatments, or overnight fucking oats." Later, she reflected on the burnout she experienced *after* publishing her seminal piece (which became the book) on burnout: "It took years to truly reflect, process, and alter my life in a way that would help me arrive at something like real self-care." But the mistake she made was she thought small things could fix the bigger problem. She believed that "a *massage* would somehow rectify the situation." In a conversation with psychiatrist Dr. Pooja Lakshmin, author of *Real Self-Care,* Petersen asks her about what Lakshmin has dubbed *faux self-care:* "wellness activities" like yoga, face masks, and spa days. "It's faux because it's not sustainable, not self-directed. It's faux because it exonerates the oppressive social structures that come from every direction and conspire with each other—patriarchy, white supremacy, toxic capitalism. It's faux because it places the burden on the individual instead of calling for systems reform," Lakshmin says.

As a culture, we have trouble resting. Every moment feels like it should be maximized: dating, exercise, self-care, and hobbies that can make us smarter, better, and more productive. We all show up to work in whatever emotional state we are in, and when work further exacerbates those feelings, we are forced to swallow our stress, squeeze what we can from our health, and deprioritize our wellness in the service of our jobs. And we think a few small moments of self-care will rectify this.

But if you are constantly afraid of messing up at work or losing your job, you don't have a lot of space for mental or physical healthcare. And when work piles on trauma or the microaggressions add up, the pressure compounds, and it leads to burnout, anxiety, health issues, and more. Work is supposed to trump all—and distract you from what it feels like to be a fully whole and functioning person.

This is exactly why *actual* self-care—not just mani-pedis and Peloton rides—is political. When Audre Lorde wrote in *A Burst of Light and Other Essays* that "caring for myself is not self-indulgence, it is self-preservation, and that is an act of political warfare," she wasn't simply making a statement about how we need to add a self-care routine. She was battling cancer and reflecting on how her illness was connected to overextending herself. In the sentence before that oft-quoted one, she writes, "I had to examine, in my dreams as well as in my immune-function tests, the devastating effects of overextension. Overextending myself is not stretching myself. I had to accept how difficult it is to monitor the difference."

Audre Lorde's self-care is not a fickle, superficial, or inconsequential act but a radical response to the harm that not caring for ourselves ultimately does. It silences us; it keeps us unhealthy; and it makes us die before our time—unrested, exhausted, and unable to be fully aware of the impact oppression has on our lives. Real self-care is radical because when we are our full, healthy selves, we can fight a system that would rather see us swallowed whole than thrive.

But having a life with any leisure is often demonized in working women and in people of color. A "woman of leisure" is someone we laugh at—an example of an almost retrograde feminism—and leisure itself is seen as the province of the rich. *The Theory of the Leisure Class,* written during the Gilded Age by Thorstein Veblen, compared the culture of the upper class, who were permitted to lie idle—to be nonproductive members of the industrial society—to that of the working class, who garnered their identities from their sense of industriousness.

To be at leisure as women, as poor people, as people of color, is a radical act that rejects basing our identity on our industriousness. To embrace a life of leisure has the potential to destabilize a system that relies on our burned-out, half-conscious participation.

Tricia Hersey was in seminary when she discovered what she calls the "liberating power of naps." She would sneak in quick naps and found herself revitalized and renewed. Since then, she's founded an organization, the Nap Ministry, and started a movement. Through workshops and immersive experiences, she takes the idea of rest to a site of agitation: "We believe rest is a form of resistance and name sleep deprivation as a racial and social justice issue."

In a 2022 essay, Hersey writes, "My rest as a Black woman in America suffering from generational exhaustion and racial trauma always was a political refusal and social justice uprising within my body." She adds, "This is about more than naps . . . It is about a deep unraveling from white supremacy and capitalism." She continues: "Rest pushes back and disrupts a system that views human bodies as a tool for production and labor. It is a counter narrative. We know that we are not machines. We are divine."

Vibe with this or not, there is a lesson here.

Capitalism benefits from us being dragged down, burned out, and exhausted. It won't shatter the system in and of itself, but what would it look like if we all just stopped trying so hard to be good at and do everything, simply acknowledging what was realistically possible, and were clear about what we really want? What if we had the space to have ups and downs, to rest, and to come back to ourselves and our loved ones better and more present? What if we had trauma-informed workplaces that allowed us the space to process, heal, and connect to the people around us and to our jobs?

At the core of the Great Resignation (or the "great breakup" women are having with corporate America), the mass drives to unionize, and all the other ways workers are advocating for themselves and demanding better working conditions, is the desire to live life on our own terms, have the time and space to be ourselves, to chill and to relax, to create and to enjoy. It's time to have workplaces that give us space to slow down, rest, seek pleasure, and focus as much on finding joy as we do on our careers, raising our children, and taking care of our loved ones.

My body took revenge on me, and I had no choice but to listen to it. I still struggle with balancing professional responsibilities with self-care while still being a functional and productive human being, but undoing the myth of having to do it all and be hot, thin, and pretty while I did so went a long way toward helping me find an authentic way to live.

And if we are listening to our bodies (and hearts and minds) and the message is to slow down . . . where does that put our ambition?

10

HAVING ENOUGH

I am often struck by the dangerous narcissism fostered
by spiritual rhetoric that pays so much attention to individual
self-improvement and so little to the practice of love
within the context of community.

—bell hooks

We are in the midst of a philosophical shift in how we relate to ambition.

My college roommate, Kara, is one of the most ambitious people I know. When we were undergrads, she was involved in every student group you can imagine in addition to her academic work. She was a die-hard campus activist (regularly arrested at protests), she was the president of the radio station, she was involved in the photography club—all while being a committed punk and hardcore fan who regularly attended shows. (This was a stark contrast to me, because I mostly refused to get out of bed the first two years of college.)

After graduating college, she backpacked to Nicaragua to help build a school. She then went to law school, during which she did a fellowship in Biloxi, Mississippi, after Hurricane Katrina to represent displaced people in housing cases. Later, she passed the bar and moved to Fresno, California, to defend low-income farmworker communities in environmental justice and civil rights cases. Most recently, she worked to protect vulnerable communities in the Bay Area from the threat of displacement. She was not just committed to social-justice work; she was also deeply ambitious.

On top of her impressive career accomplishments, Kara also managed to have a personal life: She got married, she got divorced, and after the divorce, she decided to have a child. Having a baby on her own and raising her mostly during a pandemic changed Kara by making her rethink what success meant to her.

One day I was visiting her and her daughter in Oakland, and while we were at the playground watching her daughter zip circles around the bouncy rubber mats on her scooter, she said, "I'm just not that ambitious anymore. I used to feel like I had to solve everything, and now I'm just happy leaving the office at four to spend the rest of the day with Arya."

I nodded, but I was perplexed. "I'm sure that'll change when she's older," I said confidently.

She retorted, "No, dude, I really don't think it will."

I was flummoxed. Kara had been my ambition partner since college. Our sense of self was rooted in a type of exceptionalism: We weren't normies like everyone else who just got married and had kids—we were motivated by values and theory and a commitment to be cool and change the world.

But if I looked at it as she seemed to be doing, where had all this ambition to change the world really gotten us? Her pivot was deeper than burnout or the natural life changes that happen as you get older, settle down, and sometimes have children. It was a recognition that she'd killed it at work and been a social-justice superstar, but she didn't have a ton to show for it: She didn't own a house, she didn't have any real savings, and she also hadn't seen the issues she had worked on coming to any major resolutions.

Many women seem to be rethinking ambition these days. As Ann

Friedman writes in *Elle,* "It's become apparent that many of the promised rewards of professional striving are never going to materialize. Why, some women are wondering, should I keep trying so hard?"

We are at an impasse in how to understand, think about, and make space for women's ambition—which has almost become an icky word. Jill Filipovic writes, "I certainly reflexively cringe when I hear [ambition] used pejoratively, a reaction to years of subtle (and often not-so-subtle) criticism of my own naked ambition and the disgust and rejection routinely leveled at women with the gall to try to achieve something." She continues: "That means I've been cringing a lot lately, because the Formerly Ambitious Woman is either a symbol of a kind of collective generational anti-capitalist enlightenment or a punching bag."

We're collectively bidding farewell to the try-hards, the hustle devotees, and the overachievers for the softer life we all know we want and deserve. But if women's ambition is outdated, what comes on the other side of that? A reversion to how things used to be? Because that's not exactly a solution, either. The anti-hustle, anti-girlboss ethos is manifesting in small ways—"lazy-girl jobs," a renewed obsession with cooking and homemaking, embracing a "bimbo" aesthetic—and much bigger, more deliberate and nefarious ways: stay-at-home girlfriends, "trad wives" (short for *traditional wife*), and other pivots to male dominance at home and at work. (Spoiler: male dominance never really went anywhere.)

Maybe every generation goes through this push and pull, this rediscovering of a more traditional life that they then fetishize, fantasizing about a "simpler" time. But that time is the stuff of fiction, and as Betty Friedan herself warned us, that dream for women has real limits spiritually, socially, and materially. Being a beautiful young support staff for your partner lasts as long as you are beautiful, young, and supportive (and have the mental energy to commit to that). When those things fade, what is left? It is a dubious proposition and goes hand in hand with denying women political agency, cultural power, or access to basic rights like reproductive healthcare.

Most young women don't want their rights to be rescinded; they just feel out of options. And embracing a politics of laziness, rejecting getting ahead at work, or "quiet quitting," while seductive, does assume you have access to a certain amount of wealth and stability (and probably someone who can pay your rent). Most of us don't have that. When working-class people, immigrants, or people of color (especially women of color and Black people) embrace the idea of being lazy, especially when it comes to work, all society's problems hang on their shoulders. Any misfortune they might experience is interpreted as self-inflicted, not a result of social and cultural, racial, and gendered dynamics. In his book *Bullshit Jobs,* David Graeber writes, "The ruling class has figured out that a happy and productive population with free time on their hands is a mortal danger . . . on the other hand, the feeling that work is a moral value in itself, and that anyone not willing to submit themselves to some kind of intense work discipline for most of their waking hours deserves nothing, is extraordinarily convenient for them."

We have established that the work-yourself-to-the-bone ethos that is supposed to be the righteous expression of our cutthroat ambition is not really great for us: It is bad for the environment, it is bad for workers, it is bad for our bodies, it is bad for our happiness, and it has not been as effective as we've wanted it to be in lifting us—women and people of color—as a social class. But that doesn't change the fact that women are ambitious. We have dreams beyond motherhood and wifedom; we have hobbies, interests, and passions. We are really freaking smart, and we have great ideas for movies and television shows; we are artists and writers, teachers, tech nerds, medical professionals. We have political aspirations.

Ambition is not just sitting home dreaming about being the first woman on the moon (though it may be for some). Ambition is real, it's tangible, it's a survival skill. We're very good at criticizing women's ambition and any of the strategies that are suggested for women to be equal or dominant players in the workplace. What we're not as good at is suggesting alternatives and considering other ways to live and feed ourselves.

Most young people are ambitious; they want to know where to put that energy, and they want to make an impact with it. My friend Kara is unique for my generation (and I don't just say that because she is my best friend): Most of our peers didn't commit their lives to changing the world like she had. But that's why I think she's an important barometer for the future of work, ambition, and the idea of "making it."

At the root of Kara's decision to step back from work is the fact that she had been pursuing her ambition for social change on her own. She has always embraced the collective, but at the end of the day she was working in isolation. Kara has long lived communally and believes in collective resistance, but even within that, she alone felt responsible for herself, her child, and the life she was building for them. She also realized that with a well-paying job, a young child, stable housing, an incredible friend group, and some disposable income, she had everything she needed.

Living in Alignment

Like Kara, I have also been driven by mission and purpose. I'm invested in social justice even when I've chosen to work in more corporate environments like *Teen Vogue*. In fact, what drew me to working there was the opportunity to bring my values to a new place. My motivation went deeper than just my background and training; I have long been connected to communities that are building movements to make the world a better place. I take every opportunity to elevate and infuse my work with the values I learned early on, working in nonprofits and among community organizers.

I come from a long line of people who did this work and a new generation of young people is now figuring out how to infuse their work with similar values. Recent college graduate and Rhodes scholar Jaz Brisack moved to Buffalo in 2022 after spending a year in the United Kingdom working on their fellowship. In Buffalo, they landed a job at a local Starbucks.

Jaz, radicalized by the teachings of the socialist Eugene Debs, was ready to help organize workers. Thanks to their efforts and those of their colleagues, theirs was the first Starbucks to have a union. They joined the many recent college-educated young people who are taking the very jobs they were counseled to avoid by going to college—hourly-wage service work, unpredictable and often without benefits. Rather than hemming and hawing about the lack of other opportunities for college graduates (and they have the right to hem and haw about that), they are bringing their political awareness to those roles and helping other workers agitate for change.

These moves, while brave, are being met with swift aggression from corporate leadership, which makes it clear that the fight to unionize is a long one. But the awakening has happened, and it gives us a clear path forward for how to begin creating equitable workplaces: Agitate for change when you can. The next step may not always be to unionize—many of us work in situations where the consequences of such moves would be dire—but if you work with other people, there is almost always an opportunity to work together for change, especially if you feel your workplace is inequitable.

These younger participants in the labor market, more than any other generation, believe they can change the world. They are socially conscious, politically aware, mindful of differences, and they want to create a better world for future generations. In fact, they have to, because there isn't an alternative. As such, they are demanding better in their workplaces—and, before that, some of them are demanding better at their colleges and universities. Institutions like Harvard Business School and Wharton at the University of Pennsylvania have started teaching courses on capitalism—not just the economics of it but its ethical implications in terms of scarcity and inequality.

Corporate social responsibility sometimes feels like a PR stunt, and it is usually a Band-Aid solution, like throwing inconsequential amounts of money toward a cause to say you did, or because you think it helped. But people are also taking up these causes in earnest, working to raise money and directing funding. Consulting agencies have popped up left and right (like Purpose, the one I worked at) to help businesses with their climate, racial, and gender initiatives and to help build equitable business strategies. There is an interest in giving back, and an entire ecosystem has been created around it, from impact investing and corporate philanthropy to, more locally, an increase in small donations supporting mutual aid for everything from hunger relief to helping people pay for top surgery.

There is, of course, a limit to how far you can go with an ethic of building wealth only to redistribute it. We regularly tout the value of stacking our own cash, as though we as humans are not corruptible by the changes that come with increased wealth. The "do good"–industrial complex, for all its noble intentions, relies on a few well-meaning rich people to solve the world's problems. This is rooted in a die-hard belief that, with a few tweaks, we can make the existing system work for us as individuals, especially if we work hard enough. This delusion is often what is stymieing our efforts at effectively overcoming inequality.

But it can be very self-defeating to simply say we can't do anything until capitalism is abolished. Resistance is, after all, the action of many people working in coordination—many people engaging in individual actions that create the conditions for collective benefit. The great union wins that gave us workweeks, lunch breaks, and the ability to file grievances for discrimination or harassment in the workplace were not rights won overnight but were the result of long organizing campaigns, education, and collective action.

What would it look like to channel our "hustle" energy into organizing our workplaces? Not just taking mental-health days and quiet quitting but talking to our colleagues about how we are treated, sharing our dreams and aspirations for the workplace, committing to starting businesses and collectives that are worker owned and operated, acknowledging that working to just fill our bank accounts is not enough, even when we still have to figure out how to sustain our lives.

And when that is too hard—as it often is—we can take respite in the realization that we alone can't fix the issues we are facing, but we alone can decide how much and in what ways we want to contribute to these systems.

My friend adrienne maree brown, a writer and pleasure activist, is someone I've long looked up to as a person who lives her values and is willing to make the sacrifices that sometimes takes. For as long as I've known her (which is almost twenty years), her work has been in commitment to her values: She trains social-justice leaders, writes about building movements, and creates science fiction universes that imagine new possible worlds and new ways of being.

I asked her how she's been so deliberate about the choices she makes when it comes to work. She told me she has one simple question she asks herself: "How much do I *actually* need?"

A few years ago, she founded a collective called the Emergent Strategy Ideation Institute to house her consulting work, but the organization grew, evolving into a collective of consultants, from facilitators to movement leaders. In thinking through how the organization functions, she also had to face her own relationship to money, abundance, and what she calls "financial karma."

"It's making me really think differently about even how my anti-capitalism works in practice. Because it's not enough for me to be theoretically against [capitalism]. What am I for on an economic-system level? What am I willing to practice? What am I willing to redistribute? What am I willing to share? Where do I need to structure security for myself so that I can have a generous spirit?" she says.

I have started to ask myself the same question: How much do I actually need? What's the baseline to live a comfortable, happy, and healthy life?

It can feel self-defeating to suggest that women get comfortable having less money or be more generous with what we have, but it's an interesting way to think about resources—a radical shift in how we imagine our progress—about accumulation, and about "having it all." Women already do have less money than our male counterparts, and that's even more true for Black women, Asian women, Indigenous women, and Latine women. We are also more likely to share our wealth or support other people with it. On some level, we are the blueprint: We are already living and sharing our resources collectively.

But, what if, instead of having it all, we all embraced having enough? What would our life look like then? What if we focused on our communities instead of just ourselves (as a deliberate practice, since often we already do)? What if we finally said, *Enough is enough. I have what I need—I do not need it "all." I refuse to do it all; stop trying to make me!* Wanting it all has pushed us to the edge of our abilities: We are struggling with mental-health issues, physical-health issues, environmental disasters, global human rights injustices, a prison-industrial complex, and more, almost solely because we have been sold a false bill of goods about what makes a happy, prosperous life. And the fight to get there defines every aspect of our being.

What if we just said, *I have enough. I don't need anything else.*

Rejecting capital accumulation might feel like it runs the risk of stalling women's progress. After all, as a class, women are behind in how much wealth we have. That is partially why hustle culture is so compelling, especially for historically disenfranchised women. Why should I not also get mine?

But our fight to accrue wealth and our inability to do so in a substantial way has already stymied our advancement. Our only solution is to figure out how to collectively overcome the very workplace scenarios we are talking about. As individual actors in the workplace, we are expendable—sure, we may be given some cookies and a slight raise for making it to management, but ultimately, if they don't like you, they will fire you. The problem with the individualistic sense of corporate feminism is that it is not how we build collective power.

Ours is not the first generation of people frustrated with our workplaces, but because that's true, there is guidance for how we might change them. As labor journalist Hamilton Nolan writes, "The impulse to react to your job's exploitation of you by doing what you can to exploit them with your own laziness is utterly human. But it is important, very important, that young people today who have become disillusioned with the bullshit lies of capitalism know that there is a better way. That way is to organize."

For us to truly have workplace flexibility—to not just spend our days tethered to our work-from-home computer jobs but to have the ability to structure our days as we want, to have boundaries and standards for what kind of work we do, and to know we won't just be fired at the drop of a hat—we need strong, equitable, nonsexist unions. We need paid family leave, equal pay, and for mothers not to get dinged for having children.

We're often told that the solution to systemic problems is personal: Work harder, ask for more, or, to quote the old adage, "Do what you love and never work a day in your life." Sometimes that advice helps us maneuver our way through a sticky situation or gets us the raise we so desperately deserve. But it's not a long-term solution that will equalize the workplace or bring true joy, balance, and happiness to our lives.

Labor journalist Sarah Jaffe rigorously untangles the idea that we should love what we do in her book *Work Won't Love You Back:* "The compulsion to be happy at work," she writes, "is always a demand for emotional work from the worker. Work, after all, has no feelings. Capitalism cannot love. This new work ethic, in which work is expected to give us something like self-actualization, cannot help but fail."

There is relief in this knowledge that work does not have to be our primary source of satisfaction. And we do not have to fix all the issues that plague our workplaces on our own. Sometimes we can just clock in; sometimes we can just live paycheck to paycheck; sometimes we can take jobs for the money, even when we know doing so means not living out our biggest hopes and dreams. But that doesn't mean there can't be moments when we can prioritize our colleagues, when we can advocate for raises together, when as supervisors we can fight to give everyone the biggest raise possible (because it is not even our own money). These little acts of recognition, of connection, of collective resistance can go a long way toward creating the culture of work we have long been craving.

And while I know trying to find myself through work is often a futile endeavor, I still struggle with not doing so. In the past few years, my foray into trying to live on my own terms has had mixed results. The hustle for money or the right gig is constant. Making ends meet and ensuring I have health insurance has been challenging. I don't have a lot of savings, and with an increased cost of living and the additional financial responsibilities I now shoulder, I've had to take several gigs just for the money. And even in those jobs that are supposed to be "just for the money," I find it extremely challenging to disconnect from the work or not get upset if it's going poorly. Work can't make you happy, sure, but when it makes you actively unhappy, it is awful.

So my quest to make work reasonable and enjoyable and impactful carries on, whatever the circumstance—whether it's set up to succeed or to fail. I simply can't help it, because I need meaning in my life; I need the work to feel like it's moving somewhere, whether it is writing something personal or editing a big piece that will move hearts and minds. For me to be able to do something, to get in that meeting or get on a call, I have to feel a spark: some sense of excitement, some opportunity. I regularly tell people I'm like a heat-seeking missile; it's just how I'm wired. I must have some amount of emotional investment, some amount of passion, some stake in the game. I need to see something flourish, to watch it grow, to see its impact.

But the question I am being forced to ask is, How does one sustain that passion without falling prey to the inherent selfishness of the modern workplace, or of overeager bosses who want to exploit our goodwill and our labor? And how do we temper our own naked desire to get ahead?

If work can't give us love, could we instead bring love to work? Arthur C. Brooks writes in *The Atlantic* that we often conflate finding happiness at work with finding our purpose. We believe, he writes, that if we find our purpose, we will be successful at what we do, and success will make us happy. But we're wrong to think that: Success, especially material success, does not lead to happiness. In fact, "pursuing success—whether you count that in money, power, or prestige—usually leads to less happiness, especially when the pursuit crowds out human relationships. It lowers satisfaction by putting you on the hedonic treadmill of never having enough. It makes you a success addict."

Which leaves him with the same question Jaffe asks in her book:

What is love? Brooks argues that to lead with love means, as the great philosophers have taught us, to love others. What does it mean to love others through our work? Reflecting on my own career, I realized that, for me, love in my work has meant advocating for my colleagues both personally and professionally. It's meant recognizing that people are whole beings with lives and worries and traumas, and that, while I can't fix all their problems, I can make it comfortable for them to share their loads with me rather than adhering to some arbitrary line of professionalism. It has meant working in collaboration with people, giving people credit where credit is due (rather than taking it, something a lot of managers do), and investing in their development. It entails working on issues in which I feel invested, or finding ways to get invested when I am not. It's also about working with integrity, even if I'm not met with integrity. It has at times meant being grateful for what I'm doing, and for loving what I do—even when sometimes I've needed to step away, because I couldn't love what I do and love myself simultaneously. And what I've learned from this is when I work with integrity, purpose, love, and in community, I am able to find happiness.

For the "knowledge" worker, there is no honest ambition without a recognition that a neoliberal desire to get ahead has convinced us that the only advancement that matters is our own. But if we bring love to work, if we commit to loving others on principle—believing that their growth, their future, and their earnings are as important as ours—that could fundamentally change how we think about work.

"Making it" is a myth to me not because I didn't make it. I *did* make it, and I'm still making it; I'm still on the hamster wheel. I still work too much. I still have such a hard time doing all the things that need to get done, let alone being able to think about the bigger picture. I have long been in a prison of my own ambition, stuck without a narrative for moving forward. And the change I seek—the change *we* seek—is not going to be accomplished with flowery day planners and how-to guides. It's going to come from deep personal and collective transformations. It's going to come by looking at ourselves and asking hard questions about what we actually need, what makes a joyful and satisfied life, what it means to truly live in our values, and how we can do that in the service of others. It sounds religious—and I'll be honest: It kind of is. But we are here, and we are ready for a new way of talking about work, our careers, and our ambitions.

And it's a clear way: There is no success without the collective, without love, and without one another.

It's our only path forward.

ACKNOWLEDGMENTS

To my agent, Sarah Burnes, thank you for your steadfast support and believing in me and my voice—you are truly the fiercest book sherpa. To my editor Jamia Wilson, thank you for advocating for this book and supporting it so wholeheartedly. How destined it is to work on it together so many years after we first met. And thank you, Miriam Khanukaev, for all the editorial support and advice on reaching the youths. Thank you, Carrie Frye, for helping me crack the coconuts of my story and giving me permission to tell it as fully as possible. Thank you, Megan Carpentier, for helping me through multiple iterations of this book and for the unrelenting fact-checking and gut check. Thank you, Natasha Lerner, for the final-hour research support. Thank you, MacDowell, for giving me the space to work on the soul of this project.

Thank you to my absolutely essential and insightful friend readers: Radhika, Nona, Emily, Syreeta, and Puja. Thank you, Phill, for giving me the fantastic title for this book and your support throughout. Thank you, Lindsay, for the creative and spiritual partnership. And the rest of the SATC crew, Tahirah and Asia, thank you for the sisterhood, the late-night soul sessions, and for always reminding me who this book is for. Thank you to my soul siblings: Henna, Tanaïs, Ajay, Zain, and Heems—I'm grateful to the ancestors for bringing us together. Thank you to my brain trust: Erin, Jamilah, Mathew, Zak, Aaron, and Sarah—IDs forever.

To my dear friends—Anjali, Kara, Neela, Lauren, Susie, Steven, Vanessa, Kelly, Ali, Shruti, Megan, Raquel, and Jane—thank you for all the pep talks and for letting me share your stories. Thank you to the women who gave me a chance: Malkia, Lindsay, Madhulika, Carla, Amanda, and Anna. Thank you to Cindi and the entire Meteor team— Ayesha, Shannon, Mik, Bailey, Tara, Katie, Rebecca—for giving me a work home while I was in the dregs of book writing (and for the health insurance).

Thank you to every team and every person who let me lead and gave me grace when I inevitably made mistakes.

To Peter and Mitu, thank you for providing me with a place to stay while I wrote and the endless support and prayer for mom and me. To my mother, thank you for being my biggest ally and advocate—I can do all this because of you.

To Michael—I hope wherever you are, you are proud of me, like I was of you. To my dearest Toto—you never got to give me that friend read you promised but I only hope you can see what I've done, and I hope I've made you proud. To Anthony—I will never have a better work husband. I wrote this for us, and I'm devastated you're not here to read it. Thank you to my father, who left this earthly realm before I even conceived of this project—but gave me so much guidance throughout it.

To Pete, thank you for loving me so good and for truly teaching me what it means to have enough and to luxuriate in all its glory.

NOTES

Introduction

xvi **"margin of maneuverability"**: Mary Zournazi, "Interview with Brian Massumi > Theorist > Montreal," Assembly International, December 14, 2011, www.assembly -international.net/Interviews/html/brian%20massumi.html, quoted in Jessica Dore, "Offering: January 2023," December 31, 2022, https://jessicadore.substack.com/p/ offering-january-2023.

Chapter 1: You Can't Have It All

3 **ready for justice:** Noreen Malone and Amanda Demme, " 'I'm No Longer Afraid': 35 Women Tell Their Stories about Being Assaulted by Bill Cosby, and the Culture That Wouldn't Listen," *The Cut*, July 27, 2015, www.thecut.com/2015/07/bill-cosbys-accusers -speak-out.html.

3 **The show** *Younger:* Darren Starr, *Younger*, TV Land, premiered March 2015.

4 *We Should All Be Feminists:* Chimamanda Ngozi Adichie, *We Should All Be Feminists* (London: Fourth Estate, 2014).

4 **parental leave policies:** Emily Steel, "Netflix Offers Expanded Maternity and Paternity Leave," *The New York Times*, August 4, 2015, www.nytimes.com/2015/08/05/business/ netflix-offers-expanded-maternity-and-paternity-leave.html.

4 **In 2015, Elizabeth Holmes:** Matthew Herper, "From $4.5 Billion to Nothing: Forbes Revises Estimated Net Worth of Theranos Founder Elizabeth Holmes," *Forbes*, June 1, 2016, www.forbes.com/sites/matthewherper/2016/06/01/from-4-5-billion-to-nothing -forbes-revises-estimated-net-worth-of-theranos-founder-elizabeth-holmes/?sh= f8c992363319.

4 **"since the dawn of time":** Charlotte Alter, "2014: The Best Year for Women since the Dawn of Time," *Time*, December 23, 2014, https://time.com/3639944/feminism-2014 -womens-rights-ray-rice-bill-cosby.

4 *#Girlboss:* Sophia Amoruso, *#Girlboss* (New York: Portfolio/Penguin, 2014).

5 **"Being anti-establishment":** Ryan, Erin Gloria, "Women at Work," *The New York Times*, May 16, 2014, www.nytimes.com/2014/05/18/books/review/sophia-amorusos -girlboss-and-more.html.

5 **The stats were exciting:** American Express OPEN, "2014 State of Women-Owned Businesses Report," National Association of Women Business Owners, 2014, www .nawbo.org/sites/nawbo/files/2014_state_of_women-owned_businesses.pdf.

6 *Having It All:* Helen Gurley Brown, *Having It All: Love, Success, Sex, Money, Even If You're Starting with Nothing* (New York: Simon & Schuster, 1982).

6 *Sex and the Single Girl:* Helen Gurley Brown, *Sex and the Single Girl* (New York: Bernard Geis Associates, 1962).

6 **"but she had brains":** Suzi Parker, "Helen Gurley Brown Turned Mouseburgers into Sex Kittens," *The Washington Post,* August 14, 2012.

7 **paralyzed by polio:** Brooke Hauser, *Enter Helen: The Invention of Helen Gurley Brown and the Rise of the Modern Single Woman* (New York: HarperCollins, 2016), 7–9.

7 **David Brown:** Christopher Reed, "David Brown Obituary," *The Guardian,* February 2, 2010, www.theguardian.com/film/2010/feb/02/david-brown-obituary.

7 **"deep-cleavage feminism":** Judith Thurman, "Helenism," *The New Yorker,* May 4, 2009, www.newyorker.com/magazine/2009/05/11/helenism-helen-gurley-brown-cosmo-girl.

7 **Jennifer Scanlon notes:** Jennifer Scanlon, *Bad Girls Go Everywhere: The Life of Helen Gurley Brown, the Woman Behind Cosmopolitan Magazine* (New York: Oxford University Press, 2009), 100–102.

8 **1963 interview with *Playboy:*** Richard Warren Lewis, "Playboy Interview: Helen Gurley Brown," *Playboy,* April 1963.

8 ***The Feminine Mystique:*** Betty Friedan, *The Feminine Mystique* (New York: W. W. Norton, 1963).

9 **"alienated subscribers":** Judith Thurman, "Owning Your Desire: Remembering Helen Gurley Brown," *The New Yorker,* August 15, 2012, www.newyorker.com/books/page-turner/owning-your-desire-remembering-helen-gurley-brown.

10 **according to *The New York Times:*** Jennifer Szalai, "The Complicated Origins of 'Having It All,'" *The New York Times,* January 2, 2015, www.nytimes.com/2015/01/04/magazine/the-complicated-origins-of-having-it-all.html.

10 **feature on Brown:** Carol Krucoff, "Wanting It All!" *The Washington Post,* November 10, 1982.

10 **"She offered a blueprint":** Moira Weigel, "Was She a Feminist? The Complicated Legacy of Helen Gurley Brown," *The New York Times,* July 14, 2016, www.nytimes.com/2016/07/17/books/review/helen-gurley-brown-biographies-enter-helen-and-not-pretty-enough.html.

11 **middle-class nuclear family:** "Nuclear family," Merriam-Webster.com, www.merriam-webster.com/dictionary/nuclear%20family.

12 **"long-term fortunes of the":** Cheryl Wetzstein, "Study: Modern Economies 'Rise and Fall' with Nuclear Families," *The Washington Times,* October 3, 2011, www.washingtontimes.com/news/2011/oct/3/modern-economies-rise-and-fall-with-nuclear-famili.

12 **"ultimately led to":** David Brooks, "The Nuclear Family Was a Mistake," *The Atlantic,* March 2020, www.theatlantic.com/magazine/archive/2020/03/the-nuclear-family-was-a-mistake/605536.

12 **"producers and reproducers":** Silvia Federici, *Caliban and the Witch* (New York: Autonomedia, 2004), 8.

13 **"To describe women's work":** Alice Kessler-Harris, *Women Have Always Worked: A Concise History* (New York: Feminist Press, 1981), 17.

13 **As Angela Davis has written:** Angela Y. Davis, *Women, Race & Class* (New York: Random House, 1981).

13 **"inordinate strength, with an ability":** Michelle Wallace, *Black Macho and the Myth of the Superwoman* (New York: Dial Press, 1978), 107.

14 **It is well documented:** Brent Staples, "How the Suffrage Movement Betrayed Black Women," *The New York Times,* July 28, 2018, www.nytimes.com/2018/07/28/opinion/sunday/suffrage-movement-racism-black-women.html.

14 **"From the onset":** bell hooks, *Where We Stand: Class Matters* (New York: Routledge, 2000), 102.

14 **"Simply put":** Kimberly Seals Allers, "Rethinking Work-Life Balance for Women of Color," *Slate,* March 5, 2018, slate.com/human-interest/2018/03/for-women-of-color-work-life-balance-is-a-different-kind-of-problem.html.

14 **In 1966, she founded:** Moira Donegan, "Betty Friedan and the Movement That Outgrew Her," *The New Yorker,* September 11, 2023, www.newyorker.com/magazine/2023/09/18/the-women-of-now-how-feminists-built-an-organization-that-transformed-america-katherine-turk-book-review-betty-friedan-magnificent-disrupter-rachel-shteir.

15 **"She made her plight":** bell hooks, *Feminist Theory: From Margin to Center* (New York: Routledge, 1984), 2.

15 **regressive economic policies of the Reagan administration:** Maurice A. St. Pierre, "Reaganomics and Its Implications for African-American Family Life," *Journal of Black Studies* 21, no. 3 (March 1991): 325–40; *JSTOR,* www.jstor.org/stable/2784341.

16 **60 percent in 2000:** Mitra Toossi, "A Century of Change: The U.S. Labor Force, 1950–2050," U.S. Bureau of Labor Statistics, May 2002, www.bls.gov/opub/mlr/2002/05/art2full.pdf.

16 **as of 2017:** Jocelyn Frye, "Valuing Black Women's Work," Center for American Progress, August 7, 2018, www.americanprogress.org/article/valuing-black-womens-work.

16 **77.8 percent:** Lauren Bauer and Sarah Yu Wang, "Prime-Age Women Are Going above and beyond in the Labor Market Recovery," Brookings Institute, 2023, www.brookings.edu/articles/prime-age-women-labor-market-recovery.

17 **her 1991 book:** Susan Faludi, *Backlash: The Undeclared War Against American Women* (New York: Crown, 1991), 3.

18 ***Time* magazine was criticizing:** Ginia Bellafante, "Feminism: It's All About Me!" *Time,* June 29, 1998.

18 **"As nineties feminism":** Lisa Levenstein, *They Didn't See Us Coming: The Hidden History of Feminism in the Nineties* (New York: Basic Books, 2020), 2.

18 **the incredibly successful:** Michele Goodwin, "The Long Shadow of Anita Hill's Testimony," *The Nation,* October 11, 2021, www.thenation.com/article/culture/anita-hill-30-years.

19 **She hailed from Oklahoma:** Roberto Suro, "The Thomas Nomination; A Law Professor Defends Integrity," *The New York Times,* October 8, 1991, www.nytimes.com/1991/10/08/us/the-thomas-nomination-a-law-professor-defends-integrity.html.

19 **In 1991, when Thomas:** Julia Jacobs, "Anita Hill's Testimony and Other Key Moments from the Clarence Thomas Hearings," *The New York Times,* September 20, 2018, www.nytimes.com/2018/09/20/us/politics/anita-hill-testimony-clarence-thomas.html.

20 **bolstered by "slick lawyers":** Neil A. Lewis, "Judge's Backers Take Up His Defense, Posing Motive and Method for Accuser," *The New York Times,* October 13, 1991, www.nytimes.com/1991/10/13/us/thomas-nomination-judge-s-backers-take-up-his-defense-posing-motive-method-for.html.

20 **"high-tech lynching":** "Thomas Denies Anita Hill Harassment Allegations" (video), September 18, 2018, *The Washington Post,* www.washingtonpost.com/video/politics/high-tech-lynching-thomas-denies-anita-hill-harassment-allegations/2018/09/18/370097aa-bbae-11e8-adb8-01125416c102_video.html.

20 **"a generation of women":** Rebecca Traister, *All the Single Ladies: Unmarried Women and the Rise of an Independent Nation* (New York: Simon & Schuster, 2016), 16.

20 ***To Be Real:*** Rebecca Walker, *To Be Real: Telling the Truth and Changing the Face of Feminism* (New York: Anchor Books, 1995).

20 ***The Vagina Monologues:*** Eve Ensler, *The Vagina Monologues* (New York: Villard Books, 2001).

21 **1998 cover of *Time*:** *Time,* June 28, 1998.

21 **Ginia Bellafante:** Ginia Bellafante, "Feminism: It's All About Me!" *Time,* June 29, 1998.

21 **mostly male writers:** "Ally McBeal," IMDb.com, www.imdb.com/title/tt0118254/fullcredits/?ref_=tt_cl_sm.

23 **vilification of "welfare queens":** Bryce Covert, "The Myth of the Welfare Queen," *The New Republic,* July 2, 2019, newrepublic.com/article/154404/myth-welfare-queen.

23 **much-needed financial assistance:** Andrew Glass, "Clinton Signs 'Welfare to Work' Bill Aug. 22, 1996," *Politico,* October 22, 2018, www.politico.com/story/2018/08/22/clinton-signs-welfare-to-work-bill-aug-22-1996-790321.

23 **"Everyone around me":** Syreeta McFadden, interview by Samhita Mukhopadhyay, August 13, 2021.

23 **2002 study:** Sylvia Ann Hewlett, "Executive Women and the Myth of Having It All," *Harvard Business Review,* August 2002, hbr.org/2002/04/executive-women-and-the-myth-of-having-it-all.

24 **egg- and embryo-freezing:** Netana Markovitz, "What You Need to Know about Freezing Your Eggs," *The Washington Post,* June 30, 2023, www.washingtonpost.com/wellness/2023/07/01/egg-freezing-process-cost-success-rate.

Chapter 2: Trickle-Down Feminism

25 **major player in social media:** Caroline McCarthy, "Facebook Hits 100 Million Users," CNET, August 26, 2008, www.cnet.com/culture/facebook-hits-100-million-users.

25 **"perfect fit":** Ken Auletta, "A Woman's Place," *The New Yorker,* July 4, 2011, www.newyorker.com/magazine/2011/07/11/a-womans-place-ken-auletta.

26 **who infamously said:** Suzanne Goldenberg, "Why Women Are Poor at Science, by Harvard President," *The Guardian,* January 18, 2005, www.theguardian.com/science/2005/jan/18/educationsgendergap.genderissues.

27 **$16 billion–plus:** Brad Stone and Miguel Helft, "Facebook Hires Google Executive as No. 2," *The New York Times,* March 4, 2008, www.nytimes.com/2008/03/04/technology/04cnd-facebook.html.

27 **In a 2010 TED talk:** Sheryl Sandberg, "Why We Have Too Few Women Leaders" (video), TED.com, December 2010, www.ted.com/talks/sheryl_sandberg_why_we_have_too_few_women_leaders.

28 *Lean In: Women, Work:* Sheryl Sandberg, *Lean In: Women, Work and the Will to Lead* (New York: Alfred A. Knopf, 2013).

29 **from Katy Perry to:** Emma Gray, "In the 2010s, Celebrity Feminism Got Trendy. Then Women Got Angry," *HuffPost,* December 26, 2019, www.huffpost.com/entry/celebrity-feminism-2010-taylor-swift_n_5dfbdc44e4b006dceaab16a7.

30 **"The neoliberal feminist":** Catherine A. Rottenberg, "The Rise of Neoliberal Feminism," *Cultural Studies* 28, no. 3 (2014): 418–37, https://doi.org/10.1080/09502386.2013.857361.

30 **"The movement originally":** Susan Faludi, "Facebook Feminism, Like It or Not," *The Baffler,* April 10, 2017, thebaffler.com/salvos/facebook-feminism-like-it-or-not.

31 **"Neoliberalism sees competition":** George Monbiot, "Neoliberalism—the Ideology at the Root of All Our Problems," *The Guardian,* April 15, 2016, www.theguardian.com/books/2016/apr/15/neoliberalism-ideology-problem-george-monbiot.

31 **the first to deeply investigate:** Kévin Boucaud-Victoire, "How Michel Foucault Got Neoliberalism So Wrong," interview with Daniel Zamora, *Jacobin,* September 6, 2019, jacobin.com/2019/09/michel-foucault-neoliberalism-friedrich-hayek-milton-friedman-gary-becker-minoritarian-governments.

31 **"Neoliberal rationality disseminates":** Wendy Brown, *Undoing the Demos: Neoliberalism's Stealth Revolution* (Princeton, N.J.: Zone Books, 2015), 31.

32 **"marketplace feminism":** Andi Zeisler, *We Were All Feminists Once: From Riot Grrrl to CoverGirl®, the Buying and Selling of a Political Movement* (New York: Public Affairs, 2016), 74.

33 **"If these obstacles persist":** Janet L. Yellen, "The History of Women's Work and Wages

and How It Has Created Success for Us All," Brookings, May 2020, www.brookings .edu/articles/the-history-of-womens-work-and-wages-and-how-it-has-created-success -for-us-all.

33 **they found in 2020 that:** Sundiatu Dixon-Fyle, et al., "Diversity Wins: How Inclusion Matters," McKinsey & Company website, May 19, 2020, www.mckinsey.com/featured -insights/diversity-and-inclusion/diversity-wins-how-inclusion-matters.

33 **Robin J. Ely and David A. Thomas:** Robert J. Ely and David A. Thomas, "Getting Serious About Diversity: Enough Already with the Business Case," *Harvard Business Review,* November/December, 2020, hbr.org/2020/11/getting-serious-about-diversity-enough -already-with-the-business-case.

34 **"even if I criticize":** Jia Tolentino, *Trick Mirror* (New York: Random House, 2019), 180.

34 **As Obama entered:** John Weinberg, "The Great Recession and Its Aftermath," Federal Reserve History, November 22, 2013, www.federalreservehistory.org/essays/great -recession-and-its-aftermath.

36 **"apologize for teaching":** Ashley Louise, interview by Samhita Mukhopadhyay, August 13, 2021.

36 **likely to hire other women:** Sue Duke, "To Close the Gender Gap, More Women Are Needed in Leadership," *Economic Graph,* LinkedIn, November 1, 2017, economicgraph .linkedin.com/blog/close-gender-gap-more-women-in-leadership.

37 **"These labels like":** Janice Gassam Asare, "Why Leaning In Doesn't Apply to Women of Color," *Forbes,* March 25, 2019, www.forbes.com/sites/janicegassam/2019/03/23/why -leaning-in-has-not-worked-for-women-of-color/?sh=6384469a1e41.

37 **"To women of color young":** bell hooks, "Dig Deep: Beyond Lean In," The Feminist Wire, October 28, 2013, thefeministwire.com/2013/10/17973.

37 **"This is simply":** Melissa Gira Grant, "Sheryl Sandberg's 'Lean In' Campaign Holds Little for Most Women," *The Washington Post,* February 25, 2023, www.washingtonpost .com/opinions/sheryl-sandbergs-lean-in-campaign-holds-little-for-most-women/2013/ 02/25/c584c9d2-7f51-11e2-a350-49866afab584_story.html.

37 **"It Girl of Silicon Valley":** Maureen Dowd, "Pompom Girl for Feminism," *The New York Times,* February 23, 2013, www.nytimes.com/2013/02/24/opinion/sunday/dowd -pompom-girl-for-feminism.html.

37 **"Plenty of women have":** Anne-Marie Slaughter, *Unfinished Business* (New York: Random House, 2015), 14.

37 **"I tell women":** Laurel Wamsley, "Michelle Obama's Take on 'Lean in'? 'That &#%! Doesn't Work.'" "Books," NPR, December 3, 2018, www.npr.org/2018/12/03/ 672898216/michelle-obamas-take-on-lean-in-that-doesn-t-work.

38 **"The feminist backlash":** Jessica Valenti, "Sheryl Sandberg Isn't the Perfect Feminist. So What?" *The Washington Post,* May 18, 2023, www.washingtonpost.com/opinions/dear -fellow-feminists-ripping-apart-sheryl-sandbergs-book-is-counterproductive/2013/03/01/ fc71b984-81c0-11e2-a350-49866afab584_story.html.

38 **"But anyone who had read her book":** Anna Holmes, "Maybe You Should Read the Book: The Sheryl Sandberg Backlash," *The New Yorker,* March 4, 2013, www.newyorker .com/books/page-turner/maybe-you-should-read-the-book-the-sheryl-sandberg -backlash.

39 **sold four million copies:** Judith Newman, " 'Lean in': Five Years Later," *The New York Times,* March 16, 2018, www.nytimes.com/2018/03/16/business/lean-in-five-years-later .html.

39 **"structures of imperialist":** hooks, "Dig Deep."

41 **"represents millions of dollars":** *The Devil Wears Prada,* directed by David Frankel (Los Angeles: 20th Century Fox, 2006).

46 **Condé Nast employees unionized:** Elahe Izadi, "Condé Nast Workers Win Recogni-

tion of Company-Wide Union," *The Washington Post*, September 9, 2022, www
.washingtonpost.com/media/2022/09/09/conde-nast-union.

49 **her 1915 book:** Anna Howard Shaw, *The Story of a Pioneer* (New York and London:
Harper and Brothers, 1915), 151.

49 **1.8 million more women:** Megan Cassella, "The Pandemic Drove Women out of the
Workforce. Will They Come Back?" *Politico*, July 22, 2021, www.politico.com/news/
2021/07/22/coronavirus-pandemic-women-workforce-500329.

49 **but by 2023:** Alicia Wallace, "There Are More Women in the Workforce than Ever
Before," "CNN Business," CNN, July 7, 2023, www.cnn.com/2023/07/07/economy/
women-labor-force-participation/index.html.

49 **vast differences in class experience:** Chabeli Carrazana and Jasmine Mithani, "Why the
Wage Gap Differs among Asian-American Women," *The 19th*, April 5, 2023, 19thnews
.org/2023/04/aapi-womens-equal-pay-day-wage-gap-ethnicity.

49 **straight white man:** Crosby Burns, "The Gay and Transgender Wage Gap," Center for
American Progress, April 16, 2012, www.americanprogress.org/article/the-gay-and
-transgender-wage-gap.

49 **10.4 percent of the CEOs:** Emma Hinchliffe, "Women CEOs Run 10.4% of Fortune
500 Companies. A Quarter of the 52 Leaders Became CEO in the Last Year," *Fortune*,
June 5, 2023, fortune.com/2023/06/05/fortune-500-companies-2023-women-10-percent.

49 **No Black women:** Judith Warner, et al., "The Women's Leadership Gap," Center for
American Progress, November 20, 2018, www.americanprogress.org/article/womens
-leadership-gap-2.

49 **Thasunda Brown Duckett became:** Shaun Harper, "One Black Woman Fortune 500
CEO Remains After Roz Brewer Vacates Walgreens Leadership Role," *Forbes*, September 12, 2023, www.forbes.com/sites/shaunharper/2023/09/08/one-black-woman-fortune
-500-ceo-remains-after-roz-brewer-vacates-walgreens-leadership-role/?sh=49d5fe452987.

49 **white and male:** Harper, "One Black Woman."

50 **breadwinners in their families:** Jennifer L. Glass, et al., "Children's Financial Dependence on Mothers: Propensity and Duration," *Socius* 7 (November 15, 2021), https://doi
.org/10.1177/23780231211055246.

Chapter 3: Girlboss, Interrupted

52 **"A #GIRLBOSS is someone":** Sophia Amoruso, *#Girlboss* (New York: Portfolio/
Penguin, 2014), 11.

54 **steady for years:** Lizette Chapman, "Women Founders Raised Just 2% of Venture
Capital Money Last Year," *Bloomberg*, January 11, 2022, www.bloomberg.com/news/
articles/2022-01-11/women-founders-raised-just-2-of-venture-capital-money-last-year
#xj4y7vzkg.

55 **heard about their experiences:** Victoria Masterson, "Here's What Women's Entrepreneurship Looks like around the World," World Economic Forum, July 20, 2022, www
.weforum.org/agenda/2022/07/women-entrepreneurs-gusto-gender.

55 **relationship to the office:** Ryan Waterman Aldana, "Generation Hustle: Young
Entrepreneurs Got Creative during the Pandemic," CNBC, August 3, 2021, www.cnbc
.com/2021/08/03/generation-hustle-young-entrepreneurs-got-creative-during-the
-pandemic.html.

55 **"We're a coven":** Ellen McCarthy, "Is 'the Wing' Too Hopelessly Manhattan for the
Working Women of Washington?" *The Washington Post*, April 10, 2018, www
.washingtonpost.com/lifestyle/style/the-wing-is-opening-its-exclusive-doors-to-dcs
-witches-but-will-they-accept-the-invitation/2018/04/09/c8950102-3aac-11e8-8fd2
-49fe3c675a89_story.html.

55 **One woman, Noël Duan:** Noël Duan, interview by Samhita Mukhopadhyay, August 11, 2021.

56 **raised $118 million:** Christine Lagorio-Chafkin, "The Wing Has $118 Million in Funding," *Inc.,* 2019, www.inc.com/magazine/201910/christine-lagorio-chafkin/wing -audrey-gelman-women-coworking-space-network-community.html.

56 **"Members and their guests":** Amanda Hess, "The Wing Is a Women's Utopia. Unless You Work There," *The New York Times Magazine,* March 17, 2020, www.nytimes.com/ 2020/03/17/magazine/the-wing.html.

56 **luggage company Away:** Zoe Schiffer, "Away Replaces CEO Steph Korey after Verge Investigation," *The Verge,* December 9, 2019, www.theverge.com/2019/12/9/21003787/ away-luggage-steph-korey-ceo-new-lululemon-stuart-haselden-replacement -investigation.

57 **Christene Barberich left:** Katie Robertson, "Refinery29 Editor Resigns after Former Employees Describe 'Toxic Culture,'" *The New York Times,* June 2020, www.nytimes .com/2020/06/08/business/media/refinery-29-christene-barberich.html.

57 **Leandra Medine:** Rachel Tashjian, "What Happened to Man Repeller?" *GQ,* December 4, 2020, www.gq.com/story/what-happened-to-man-repeller.

57 **"equal-opportunity asshole":** Claire Lampen, "Upper East Sider Realizes She's Privileged," *The Cut,* August 17, 2021, www.thecut.com/2021/08/leandra-medine-says -she-always-thought-she-was-poor.html.

57 **Yael Aflalo stepped down:** Kara K. Nesvig, "Reformation Founder Yael Aflalo Resigns After Allegations of Racism," *Teen Vogue,* June 14, 2020, www.teenvogue.com/story/ reformation-founder-yael-aflalo-apologizes-for-past-racist-behavior.

59 **After a series of investigations:** Rachel Metz, "Elizabeth Holmes Sentenced to More than 11 Years in Prison for Fraud," "CNN Business," CNN, November 18, 2022, www .cnn.com/2022/11/18/tech/elizabeth-holmes-theranos-sentencing/index.html.

59 **most notably John Carreyrou:** John Carreyrou, *Bad Blood; Secrets and Lies in a Silicon Valley Startup* (New York: Alfred A. Knopf, 2018).

59 **documentarians:** Alex Gibney, director, *The Inventor: Out for Blood in Silicon Valley,* HBO, 2019.

60 **gender discrimination lawsuit:** David Streitfeld, "Ellen Pao Loses Silicon Valley Bias Case against Kleiner Perkins," *The New York Times,* March 27, 2015, www.nytimes.com/ 2015/03/28/technology/ellen-pao-kleiner-perkins-case-decision.html.

60 **"Indeed, as Ms. Holmes's trial":** Ellen Pao, "The Elizabeth Holmes Trial Is a Wake-up Call for Sexism in Tech," *The New York Times,* September 15, 2021, www.nytimes.com/ 2021/09/15/opinion/elizabeth-holmes-trial-sexism.html.

60 **One woman founder:** Erin Griffith, "They Still Live in the Shadow of Theranos's Elizabeth Holmes," *The New York Times,* August 24, 2021, www.nytimes.com/2021/08/ 24/technology/theranos-elizabeth-holmes.html.

61 **"You need to make quick decisions":** Maurice Schweitzer, interview by Samhita Mukhopadhyay, August 12, 2021.

61 **weakening of American democracy:** Edward Sullivan and John Baird, "Bad Bosses Like Mark Zuckerberg Will Face a Backlash. America's Workers Are Fed Up," *USA Today,* August 17, 2022, www.usatoday.com/story/opinion/2022/08/17/mark -zuckerberg-employee-pressure-bad-leadership/10330735002/?gnt-cfr=1; Karen Tiber Leland, "Why Uber CEO Travis Kalanick Is a Toxic Boss and Must Go," *Inc.,* June 13, 2017, www.inc.com/karen-tiber-leland/how-uber-ceo-travis-kalanicks-toxic-boss -behaviors-could-cost-him-the-company.html; Kate Duffy and Sam Tabahriti, "Elon Musk Converts Some Twitter Offices into Bedrooms at San Francisco HQ in Light of 'Hardcore' Ultimatum," *Business Insider,* December 6, 2022, www.businessinsider.com/ elon-musk-converts-twitter-offices-bedrooms-headquarters-hardcore-san-francisco -2022-12.

61 **Being the only woman:** Anna Wiener, *Uncanny Valley* (New York: MCD, 2020), 113.

62 **"feel as though the rules":** Schweitzer, interview by Samhita Mukhopadhyay, August 12, 2021.

63 **"a gazillion-dollar company":** Renée Rouleau, interview by Samhita Mukhopadhyay, August 12, 2021.

63 **Renée Rouleau, Inc. was voted:** Will Anderson, "65 Companies Named Best Places to Work Winners for 2020," *Austin Business Journal,* May 15, 2020, www.bizjournals.com/austin/news/2020/05/15/2020-austin-best-places-to-work-all-winners.html.

65 **"an empowering term":** Cristina Flores, interview by Samhita Mukhopadhyay, August 13, 2021.

65 **"could get canceled or attacked":** Sky Conner, interview by Samhita Mukhopadhyay, August 14, 2021.

66 **"performative at best":** Claire Wasserman, *Ladies Get Paid: The Ultimate Guide to Breaking Barriers, Owning Your Worth, and Taking Command of Your Career* (New York: Gallery Books, 2021), x.

66 **"anti-Girlboss":** Ashley Louise, quoted in Samhita Mukhopadhyay, "The Demise of the Girlboss," *The Cut,* August 31, 2021, www.thecut.com/2021/08/demise-of-the-girlboss.html.

Chapter 4: The End of the Hustle

68 **In the late 1800s:** "hustle (v.)," *Online Etymology Dictionary,* www.etymonline.com/word/hustle.

68 **"Hustle—or a lack thereof":** Isabella Rosario, "When the 'Hustle' Isn't Enough," *Code Switch,* NPR, April 3, 2020, www.npr.org/sections/codeswitch/2020/04/03/826015780/when-the-hustle-isnt-enough.

69 **"For a variety of reasons":** Lester K. Spence, *Knocking the Hustle: Against the Neoliberal Turn in Black Politics* (Santa Barbara, Calif.: Punctum Books, 2015), xxiv–xxv.

69 **"rap explicitly exalts":** Spence, *Knocking the Hustle,* 2.

70 **"neoliberal turn":** Spence, *Knocking the Hustle,* 11.

70 **"Black elected officials":** Spence, *Knocking the Hustle,* 25.

70 **"the continued elevated":** Rich Lowry, "Biden's Covid-Relief Bill Is Bad Policy and Bad Faith," *National Review,* March 12, 2021, www.nationalreview.com/2021/03/bidens-covid-relief-bill-is-bad-policy-and-bad-faith.

71 **largely untrue:** Annelies Goger, et al., "Debunking Myths about COVID-19 Relief's 'Unemployment Insurance on Steroids,'" Brookings, May 12, 2020, www.brookings.edu/articles/debunking-myths-about-covid-19-reliefs-unemployment-insurance-on-steroids; Adam Chandler, "No, Unemployment Benefits Don't Stop People from Returning to Work," *The Washington Post,* May 13, 2021, www.washingtonpost.com/outlook/2021/05/13/unemployment-benefits-minimum-wage-work.

71 **"Many of us find":** Jenny Odell, *How to Do Nothing: Resisting the Attention Economy* (New York: Melville House, 2019), ix.

72 **working fifteen-hour weeks:** John Maynard Keynes, "Economic Possibilities for Our Grandchildren," *Essays in Persuasion* (London: Macmillan, 1931), 369.

72 **As Ezra Klein remarks:** Ezra Klein, "Transcript: Ezra Klein Interviews James Suzman," *The New York Times,* June 29, 2021, www.nytimes.com/2021/06/29/podcasts/transcript-ezra-klein-interviews-james-suzman.html.

72 **"Something is wrong":** Barbara Ehrenreich, *Nickel and Dimed: On (Not) Getting By in America* (New York: Picador, 2011), 199.

73 **of about $33,000:** "Fast Food and Counter Workers," U.S. Bureau of Labor Statistics, April 25, 2023, www.bls.gov/oes/current/oes353023.htm.

73 **need more space:** CBS New York Team, "Average Cost to Rent New York City Apartment up 18% over Last Year, Report Finds," CBS News, May 20, 2022, www .cbsnews.com/newyork/news/average-cost-to-rent-new-york-city-apartment-up-18-over -last-year-report-finds.

73 **"employers resist wage increases":** Ehrenreich, *Nickel and Dimed,* 203.

73 **with taxpayer dollars:** Hannah Miao, "Walmart and McDonald's Are among Top Employers of Medicaid and Food Stamp Beneficiaries, Report Says," CNBC, November 19, 2020, www.cnbc.com/2020/11/19/walmart-and-mcdonalds-among-top -employers-of-medicaid-and-food-stamp-beneficiaries.html.

74 **2023 Supreme Court decision:** Amy Howe, "Supreme Court Strikes Down Biden Student-Loan Forgiveness Program," *SCOTUSblog,* June 30, 2023, www.scotusblog .com/2023/06/supreme-court-strikes-down-biden-student-loan-forgiveness-program.

74 *Hustle Believe Receive:* Sarah Centrella, *Hustle Believe Receive: An 8-Step Plan to Changing Your Life and Living Your Dream* (New York: Skyhorse Publishing, 2016).

74 **Chris Guillebeau's *Side Hustle:*** Chris Guillebeau, *Side Hustle: From Idea to Income in 27 Days* (New York: Currency, 2017).

74 **rapper 50 Cent:** Curtis Jackson, *Hustle Harder, Hustle Smarter* (New York: Amistad Press, 2020).

75 **Oprah's rise to stardom:** "Oprah Winfrey," The Kennedy Center, 2010, www.kennedy -center.org/artists/w/wa-wn/oprah-winfrey.

79 **only 35 percent of American workers:** Kim Parker, "About a Third of U.S. Workers Who Can Work from Home Now Do So All the Time," Pew Research Center, March 30, 2023, www.pewresearch.org/short-reads/2023/03/30/about-a-third-of-us -workers-who-can-work-from-home-do-so-all-the-time.

79 **still working remotely:** Parker, "About a Third."

79 **By early 2023:** Parker, "About a Third."

79 **the service sector:** Heather Long and Andrew Van Dam, "U.S. Unemployment Rate Soars to 14.7 Percent, the Worst since the Depression Era," *The Washington Post,* May 8, 2020, www.washingtonpost.com/business/2020/05/08/april-2020-jobs-report.

80 **months of the pandemic:** Andrew Soergel, "ADP: More than 20 Million People Lost Their Jobs in April," *U.S. News & World Report,* May 6, 2020, www.usnews.com/news/ economy/articles/2020-05-06/adp-more-than-20-million-people-lost-their-jobs-in -april.

80 **In one study, 25 percent:** Kim Parker, et al., "Economic Fallout from Covid-19 Continues to Hit Lower-Income Americans the Hardest," Pew Research Center, September 24, 2020, www.pewresearch.org/social-trends/2020/09/24/economic-fallout -from-covid-19-continues-to-hit-lower-income-americans-the-hardest.

80 **most of the jobs lost:** Lydia DePillis, "With Surge in July, U.S. Recovers the Jobs Lost in the Pandemic," *The New York Times,* August 5, 2022, www.nytimes.com/2022/08/05/ business/economy/july-jobs-report-gains.html.

80 **15.7 percent:** Liana Christin Landivar and Mark deWolf, "Mothers' Employment Two Years Later: An Assessment of Employment Loss and Recovery During the COVID-19 Pandemic." *U.S. Department of Labor,* May 2022, www.dol.gov/sites/ dolgov/files/WB/media/Mothers-employment-2%20-years-later-may2022.pdf.

80 **According to *Forbes*:** Chase Peterson-Withorn, "How Much Money America's Billionaires Have Made during the COVID-19 Pandemic," *Forbes,* April 30, 2021, www .forbes.com/sites/chasewithorn/2021/04/30/american-billionaires-have-gotten-12-trillion -richer-during-the-pandemic/?sh=2db5ec77f557.

82 **A college senior at UCLA:** Mona Lee, interview by Samhita Mukhopadhyay, November 18, 2021.

84 **a trend that has:** "Quits Rate of 2.9 Percent in August 2021 an All-Time High," "The Economics Daily," U.S. Bureau of Labor Statistics, October 18, 2021, www.bls.gov/

opub/ted/2021/quits-rate-of-2-9-percent-in-august-2021-an-all-time-high.htm#:~:text
=In%20August%202021%2C%20the%20total,by%20242%2C000%20to%204.3
%20million.

84 **2022 Pew study:** Kim Parker and Juliana Menasce Horowitz, "Majority of Workers
Who Quit a Job in 2021 Cite Low Pay, No Opportunities for Advancement, Feeling
Disrespected," Pew Research Center, March 9, 2022, www.pewresearch.org/short-reads/
2022/03/09/majority-of-workers-who-quit-a-job-in-2021-cite-low-pay-no-opportunities
-for-advancement-feeling-disrespected.

85 **"pandemic epiphanies":** Alex Christian, "How the Great Resignation Is Turning into
the Great Reshuffle," BBC, February 25, 2022, www.bbc.com/worklife/article/20211214
-great-resignation-into-great-reshuffle.

85 **In a survey:** Ariel Edwards-Levy, "Nearly All American Women Agree the Pandemic
Changed Their Lives, but Their Experiences Vary Drastically. Here's Why," CNN,
March 31, 2022, www.cnn.com/2022/03/31/us/us-women-covid-pandemic-experiences
-as-equals-intl-cmd/index.html.

86 **rise in workplace organizing:** Sabrina Tavernise, "Are Unions Making a Comeback?"
The New York Times, May 2, 2022, www.nytimes.com/2022/05/02/podcasts/the-daily/
unions-amazon-starbucks.html?showTranscript=1.

86 **for union elections:** Tavernise, "Are Unions Making a Comeback?"

86 **going on strike:** Jacob Bogage, "Strikes Are Sweeping the Labor Market as Workers
Wield New Leverage," *The Washington Post,* November 17, 2021, www.washingtonpost
.com/business/2021/10/17/strikes-great-resignation.

86 **petitions for representation:** "Union Members—2022," U.S. Bureau of Labor Statistics,
January 19, 2023, www.bls.gov/news.release/pdf/union2.pdf.

86 **in nonunion jobs:** Greg Rosalsky, "You May Have Heard of the 'Union Boom.' The
Numbers Tell a Different Story," *Planet Money,* NPR, February 28, 2023, www.npr.org/
sections/money/2023/02/28/1159663461/you-may-have-heard-of-the-union-boom-the
-numbers-tell-a-different-story.

90 **Research suggests that Gen Z:** Garen Staglin, "The Future of Work Depends on
Supporting Gen Z," *Forbes,* June 22, 2022, www.forbes.com/sites/onemind/2022/07/22/
the-future-of-work-depends-on-supporting-gen-z/?sh=41a6aaf0447a.

90 **"salary floor of $80k":** "Careers," *Chani,* www.chaninicholas.com/careers.

91 **makes them more productive:** Shawn Achor and Michelle Gielan, "The Data-Driven
Case for Vacation," *Harvard Business Review,* July 13, 2016, hbr.org/2016/07/the-data
-driven-case-for-vacation.

91 **"Living in a capitalist":** Holly Corbett, "How One Tech Company Is Proving Why
Taking Care of Your Employees Is Profitable," *Forbes,* July 31, 2023, www.forbes.com/
sites/hollycorbett/2023/07/31/how-one-tech-company-is-proving-why-taking-care-of
-your-employees-is-profitable/?sh=626d8305278c.

Chapter 5: Having Too Much

93 **"creeping nonchoice":** Sylvia Ann Hewlett, "Executive Women and the Myth of
Having It All," *Harvard Business Review,* April 2002, hbr.org/2002/04/executive-women
-and-the-myth-of-having-it-all.

94 **As Reshma Saujani writes:** Reshma Saujani, *Pay Up: The Future of Women and Work
(and Why It's Different Than You Think)* (New York: Atria/One Signal Publishers,
2022), 26.

95 **"Knowing Catrin and myself":** Amy Siverson, interview by Samhita Mukhopadhyay,
May 17, 2002.

96 **"problem that has no name"**: Betty Friedan, *The Feminine Mystique* (New York: Norton, 1963), 57.

96 **"really powerless"**: Amanda Brown, interview by Samhita Mukhopadhyay, April 11, 2022.

96 **"It's adorable to see"**: Sadye L. Campoamor, interview by Samhita Mukhopadhyay, May 13, 2022.

97 **overlooked for promotions**: "The Motherhood Penalty," American Association of University Women, September 1, 2022, www.aauw.org/issues/equity/motherhood.

97 **kept out of C-suites**: Katherine Goldstein, "The Open Secret of Anti-Mom Bias at Work," *The New York Times,* May 16, 2018, www.nytimes.com/2018/05/16/opinion/workplace-discrimination-mothers.html.

97 **Jessica Valenti writes**: Jessica Valenti, *Why Have Kids?: A New Mom Explores the Truth about Parenting and Happiness* (Sacramento: New Harvest, 2012), 64–65.

98 **"If mothers and care workers"**: Angela Garbes, *Essential Labor: Mothering as Social Change* (New York: Harper Wave, 2022), 61.

98 **"reproductive labor"**: Garbes, *Essential Labor,* 53.

98 **"commensurately pay"**: Garbes, *Essential Labor,* 54.

99 **more likely than fathers**: Rakesh Kochhar, "Fewer Mothers and Fathers in U.S. Are Working Due to COVID-19 Downturn; Those at Work Have Cut Hours," Pew Research Center, October 22, 2020, www.pewresearch.org/short-reads/2020/10/22/fewer-mothers-and-fathers-in-u-s-are-working-due-to-covid-19-downturn-those-at-work-have-cut-hours.

99 **two million women**: Megan Cassella, "The Pandemic Drove Women Out of the Workforce. Will They Come Back?" Politico, July 22, 2021, www.politico.com/news/2021/07/22/coronavirus-pandemic-women-workforce-500329.

99 **under untenable circumstances**: Claire Cain Miller, "The Pandemic Has Been Punishing for Working Mothers. But Mostly, They've Kept Working," *The New York Times,* May 11, 2022, www.nytimes.com/2022/05/11/upshot/pandemic-working-mothers-jobs.html.

99 **was educational status**: Miller, "The Pandemic."

99 **competency as parents**: Derek P. Siegel, "Trans Moms Discuss Their Unique Parenting Challenges During the Pandemic—and What They Worry about When Things Go Back to 'Normal,'" *The Conversation,* May 20, 2021, theconversation.com/trans-moms-discuss-their-unique-parenting-challenges-during-the-pandemic-and-what-they-worry-about-when-things-go-back-to-normal-158857.

99 **pandemic baby bump**: Cara Tabachnick, "U.S. Birth Rates Drop as Women Wait to Have Babies," CBS News, January 12, 2023, www.cbsnews.com/news/u-s-birth-rate-decline-national-center-for-health-statistics-report.

100 **take care of *everyone***: Nidhi Sharma, et al., "Gender Differences in Caregiving among Family—Caregivers of People with Mental Illnesses," *World Journal of Psychiatry* 6, no. 1 (March 22, 2016): 7–17, www.ncbi.nlm.nih.gov/pmc/articles/PMC4804270; Kim Parker, "Women More than Men Adjust Their Careers for Family Life," Pew Research Center, October 1, 2015, www.pewresearch.org/short-reads/2015/10/01/women-more-than-men-adjust-their-careers-for-family-life.

100 **"The expectation that a woman"**: Jessica Grose, *Screaming on the Inside* (Boston: Mariner Books, 2022), 7.

101 **forcibly sterilized**: Abdallah Fayyad, "America's Shameful History of Sterilizing Women," *The Boston Globe,* September 18, 2020, www.bostonglobe.com/2020/09/17/opinion/americas-shameful-ongoing-history-sterilizing-women.

101 **Undocumented teen migrants**: Mica Rosenberg, "U.S. Court Rules Against Trump Administration in Immigrant Teen Abortion Case," Reuters, June 14, 2019, www.reuters

.com/article/us-usa-court-abortion-immigrant/u-s-court-rules-against-trump
-administration-in-immigrant-teen-abortion-case-idUSKCN1TF28A.

102 **Andrea Dworkin argued:** Andrea Dworkin, *Right-Wing Women* (New York: Tarcher-
     Perigee, 1983), 174.

102 **Shulamith Firestone wrote:** Shulamith Firestone, *The Dialectic of Sex: The Case for
     Feminist Revolution* (New York: William Morrow and Company, 1970), 65.

103 **Rich wrote her treatise:** Adrienne Rich, *Of Woman Born: Motherhood as Experience and
     Institution* (New York: W. W. Norton, 1976).

103 **As her own politics radicalized:** Maggie Doherty, "The Long Awakening of Adrienne
     Rich," *The New Yorker,* November 23, 2020, www.newyorker.com/magazine/2020/11/30/
     the-long-awakening-of-adrienne-rich.

103 **"We need to imagine a world":** Rich, *Of Woman Born,* 285–86.

103 **"Some problems we share as women":** Audre Lorde, "Age, Race, Class, and Sex:
     Women Redefining Difference," *Sister Outsider: Essays and Speeches* (Trumansburg,
     N.Y.: Crossing Press, 1984), 119.

104 **average age of marriage:** Constance Shehan, "How Roe v. Wade Changed Motherhood
     and Marriage," *YES!,* July 11, 2018, www.yesmagazine.org/social-justice/2018/07/11/how
     -roe-v-wade-changed-motherhood-and-marriage.

104 **entered the workforce:** Goldberg, Emma. "How Roe Shaped the World of Work for
     Women," *The New York Times,* May 7, 2022, www.nytimes.com/2022/05/07/business/
     roe-women-workforce-abortion-rights.html.

104 **women going to college:** Constance Shehan, "Roe v. Wade Gave American Women a
     Choice about Having Children—Here's How That Changed Their Lives," *The Conversa-
     tion,* May 19, 2021, theconversation.com/roe-v-wade-gave-american-women-a-choice
     -about-having-children-heres-how-that-changed-their-lives-161148.

104 **"It's not just that":** Lisa Belkin, "The Opt-Out Revolution," *The New York Times,*
     August 7, 2013, www.nytimes.com/2013/08/11/magazine/the-opt-out-revolution.html.

105 **"About a third":** Bryce Covert, "The Best Era for Working Women Was 20 Years Ago,"
     The New York Times, September 2, 2017, www.nytimes.com/2017/09/02/opinion/
     sunday/working-women-decline-1990s.html.

105 **Americans believe:** "Motherhood Today: Tougher Challenges, Less Success," Pew
     Research Center, May 2, 2007, www.pewresearch.org/social-trends/2007/05/02/
     motherhood-today-tougher-challenges-less-success.

105 **millions of women:** Megan Cassella, "The Pandemic Drove Women Out of the
     Workforce. Will They Come Back?" Politico, July 22, 2021, www.politico.com/news/
     2021/07/22/coronavirus-pandemic-women-workforce-500329.

105 **the pay gap:** Isabela Salas-Betsch and Beth Almeida, "Fact Sheet: The State of Women
     in the Labor Market in 2023," Center for American Progress, February 6, 2023, www
     .americanprogress.org/article/fact-sheet-the-state-of-women-in-the-labor-market-in
     -2023.

105 **their families at risk:** "Release: Nearly Two-Thirds of Mothers Continue to Be Family
     Breadwinners, Black Mothers Are Far More Likely to Be Breadwinners," Center for
     American Progress, May 10, 2019, www.americanprogress.org/press/release-nearly-two
     -thirds-mothers-continue-family-breadwinners-black-mothers-far-likely-breadwinners.

106 **"dichotomy between 'home' and 'work'":** Sarah Jaffe, *Work Won't Love You Back: How
     Devotion to Our Jobs Keeps Us Exploited, Exhausted, and Alone* (New York: Bold Type
     Books, 2021), 28.

106 **became a "natural resource":** Silvia Federici, *Caliban and the Witch: Women, the Body
     and Primitive Accumulation* (New York: Autonomedia, 2004), 97.

107 **a key component:** Elise Gould, et al., "Care Workers Are Deeply Undervalued and
     Underpaid: Estimating Fair and Equitable Wages in the Care Sectors," Economic Policy

Institute, July 16, 2021, www.epi.org/blog/care-workers-are-deeply-undervalued-and
-underpaid-estimating-fair-and-equitable-wages-in-the-care-sectors.

107 **Wages for Housework movement:** Jordan Kisner, "The Lockdown Showed How the
Economy Exploits Women. She Already Knew," *The New York Times Magazine,*
February 17, 2021, www.nytimes.com/2021/02/17/magazine/waged-housework.html.

107 **housework should be paid:** Kisner, "The Lockdown."

107 **"change their situation":** Louise Toupin, "The History of Wages for Housework," *Pluto
Press,* www.plutobooks.com/blog/wages-housework-campaign-history.

107 **"It would be possible":** Matt Bruenig, "The Case for Paying Parents Who Care for
Their Own Kids," *The New York Times,* April 9, 2022, www.nytimes.com/2022/04/09/
opinion/paying-parents-for-child-care.html.

108 **"What Bruenig is":** Jill Filipovic, "It's a Bad Idea to Pay Women to Stay Home," *Jill
Filipovic* (substack), April 12, 2022, jill.substack.com/p/its-a-bad-idea-to-pay-women-to
-stay.

108 **"payment for all":** Selma James, "Decades After Iceland's 'Day Off,' Our Women's
Strike Is Stronger Than Ever," *The Guardian,* March 8, 2018, www.theguardian.com/
commentisfree/2018/mar/08/iceland-global-womens-strike-protest.

108 **"Between 2020 and 2021":** Rebekah Barber, "Advocates and Families Push to Restore
Child Tax Credit amid Inflation," *The 19th,* November 28, 2022, 19thnews.org/2022/11/
child-tax-credit-families-poverty-inflation.

109 **"Mothering can no longer":** Garbes, *Essential Labor,* 64.

109 **one study published in *Organization Studies:*** Jennifer Merluzzi and Damon J. Phillips,
"Early Career Leadership Advancement: Evidence of Incongruity Penalties toward
Young, Single Women Professionals," *Organization Studies* 43, no. 11 (November 2022),
1719–43, https://doi.org/10.1177/01708406221081619.

110 **Black mothers, she says:** Dani McClain, *We Live for the We: The Political Power of Black
Motherhood* (New York: Bold Type Books, 2019), 4.

110 **"other-mother":** Patricia Hill Collins, *Black Feminist Thought* (New York: Routledge,
2000).

110 **much more communal one:** McClain, *We Live for the We,* 4.

110 **"raise a kid":** Dani McClain, interview by Samhita Mukhopadhyay, April 7, 2023.

111 **"the work that makes":** Ai-jen Poo, "The Work That Makes All Other Work Possible"
(video), TED.com, November 2018, www.ted.com/talks/ai_jen_poo_the_work_that
_makes_all_other_work_possible?language=en.

112 **"It's not that":** Mina Kim and Lakshmi Sarah, "'The Work That Makes All Other Work
Possible': Ai-jen Poo on Why Home Care Workers Are Infrastructure Workers," KQED,
June 15, 2021, www.kqed.org/news/11877838/the-work-that-makes-all-other-work
-possible-ai-jen-poo-on-why-home-care-workers-are-infrastructure-workers.

Chapter 6: The Diversity-Industrial Complex

116 **spending on DNI:** Global Industry Analysts, Inc., "With Global Spending Projected to
Reach $15.4 Billion by 2026, Diversity, Equity & Inclusion Takes the Lead Role in the
Creation of Stronger Businesses," PR Newswire, November 3, 2021, www.prnewswire
.com/news-releases/with-global-spending-projected-to-reach-15-4-billion-by-2026
--diversity-equity--inclusion-takes-the-lead-role-in-the-creation-of-stronger-businesses
-301413808.html.

117 **"firms where blacks are":** Michael A. Stoll, et al., "Why Are Black Employers More
Likely Than White Employers to Hire Blacks?" *Discussion Paper* no. 1236-01, Institute
for Research on Poverty, University of Wisconsin, Madison, August 2001.

117 **the World Economic Forum:** Sue Duke, "Key to Closing the Gender Gap? Putting More Women in Charge," World Economic Forum, November 2, 2017, www .weforum.org/agenda/2017/11/women-leaders-key-to-workplace-equality-closing-the -gender-gap.

117 **"We know of no evidence":** Robin J. Ely and David A. Thomas, "Getting Serious About Diversity: Enough Already with the Business Case," *Harvard Business Review,* November/December 2020, hbr.org/2020/11/getting-serious-about-diversity-enough -already-with-the-business-case.

118 **"visibility alone":** "Inclusion & Diversity in the American Fashion Industry," *Insider/ Outsider,* January 2019.

118 **"The more managers you have":** Erica Lovett, interview by Samhita Mukhopadhyay, February 14, 2022.

118 **"I have a hard time":** Maddi Eckert, "Civil Rights Leader Angela Davis Speaks at Bovard," *Daily Trojan,* February 23, 2015, dailytrojan.com/2015/02/23/civil-rights-leader -angela-davis-speaks-at-bovard.

118 **$7–$8 billion industry:** Bridget Read, "Inside the Booming Diversity-Equity-and- Inclusion Industrial Complex," *The Cut,* May 26, 2021, www.thecut.com/article/ diversity-equity-inclusion-industrial-companies.html.

119 **a provocative paper:** Victor Ray, "A Theory of Racialized Organizations," *American Sociological Review* 84, no. 1 (February 2019): 26–53, www.jstor.org/stable/48588888.

119 **"Racial inequality is not merely":** Ray, "A Theory."

121 **Away's social media post:** Tariro Mzezewa, "Posting a Black Square, but Not Black Faces," *The New York Times,* June 20, 2020, www.nytimes.com/2020/06/20/travel/travel -brands-black-lives-matter.html.

121 **Reddit cofounder Alexis:** Jackie Willis, "Reddit Replaces Alexis Ohanian with First Black Board Member," *ET,* June 10, 2020, www.etonline.com/reddit-replaces-alexis -ohanian-with-first-black-board-member-147904.

121 **The CEO of CrossFit:** Rachel Sandler, "CrossFit CEO Steps down after George Floyd Comments," *Forbes,* June 9, 2020, www.forbes.com/sites/rachelsandler/2020/06/09/ crossfit-ceo-to-step-down-after-george-floyd-comments/?sh=5c0e17c35ac8.

121 **Audrey Gelman stepping down:** Katherine Rosman, "Audrey Gelman, the Wing's Co-Founder, Resigns," *The New York Times,* June 11, 2020, www.nytimes.com/2020/06/ 11/style/the-wing-ceo-audrey-gelman-resigns.html.

121 **Yael Aflalo, the founder:** Kara K. Nesvig, "Reformation Founder Yael Aflalo Resigns After Allegations of Racism," *Teen Vogue,* June 14, 2020, www.teenvogue.com/story/ reformation-founder-yael-aflalo-apologizes-for-past-racist-behavior.

121 **James Bennet, head of:** Rishika Dugyala, "NYT Opinion Editor Resigns After Outrage Over Tom Cotton Op-Ed," *Politico,* June 7, 2020, www.politico.com/news/2020/06/07/ nyt-opinion-bennet-resigns-cotton-op-ed-306317.

121 **Adam Rapoport of Condé:** Kim Severson, "Bon Appétit Editor Adam Rapoport Resigns," *The New York Times,* June 8, 2020, www.nytimes.com/2020/06/08/dining/bon -appetit-adam-rapoport.html.

122 **wrote that she was:** Sonia Rao, "Bon Appétit Video Stars Leave the Test Kitchen Series Due to Alleged Racial Discrimination," *The Washington Post,* August 7, 2020, www .washingtonpost.com/news/voraciously/wp/2020/08/06/three-bon-appetit-video-stars -leave-the-test-kitchen-series-due-to-alleged-racial-discrimination.

122 **Most corporate board seats:** Emily Peck, "Share of Black Appointees to Fortune 500 Boards Declined Last Year," *Axios,* March 8, 2023, www.axios.com/2023/03/08/share-of -black-appointees-to-fortune-500-boards-declined-last-year.

122 **As of 2020:** "Black Women & the Pay Gap," American Association of University Women, www.aauw.org/resources/article/black-women-and-the-pay-gap.

122 **By the end of 2021:** Tracy Jan, et al., "Corporate America's $50 Billion Promise," *The Washington Post,* August 23, 2021, www.washingtonpost.com/business/interactive/2021/ george-floyd-corporate-america-racial-justice.

122 **in August 2020:** Matthew Lavietes, "'Watershed Moment': Corporate America Looks to Hire More Black People," Reuters, August 19, 2020, www.reuters.com/article/us-usa -race-hiring-idUSKCN25F2SY.

123 **In December 2020:** "Top Business Leaders Launch OneTen, Will Create 1 Million Jobs for Black Americans over 10 Years," Bank of America website, December 10, 2020, https://newsroom.bankofamerica.com/content/newsroom/press-releases/2020/12/top -business-leaders-launch-oneten--will-create-1-million-jobs-f.html.

123 **In an investigation:** Tracy Jan, et al., "Corporate America's $50 Billion Promise."

123 **"We don't want just":** Jan, et al., "Corporate America's."

123 **had hired only:** "OneTen Coalition Hires 17,000 Black Individuals into Family-Sustaining Jobs in First Year," PR Newswire, December 9, 2021, www.prnewswire.com/ news-releases/oneten-coalition-hires-17-000-black-individuals-into-family-sustaining -jobs-in-first-year-301441174.html.

123 **67 percent of Americans:** Juliana Menasce Horowitz, "Support for Black Lives Matter Declined after George Floyd Protests, but Has Remained Unchanged Since," Pew Research Center, September 27, 2021, www.pewresearch.org/short-reads/2021/09/27/ support-for-black-lives-matter-declined-after-george-floyd-protests-but-has-remained -unchanged-since; Juliana Menasce Horowitz, Kiley Hurst, and Dana Braga, "Views on the Black Lives Movement," June 14, 2023, Pew Research Center, www.pewresearch.org/ social-trends/2023/06/14/views-on-the-black-lives-matter-movement.

124 **one of the ways:** Kimberly Giles, "Why You Mistakenly Hire People Just Like You," *Forbes,* May 1, 2018, www.forbes.com/sites/forbescoachescouncil/2018/05/01/why-you -mistakenly-hire-people-just-like-you/?sh=60de67823827.

125 **In a 2018 paper:** Frank Dobbin and Alexandra Kalev, "Why Doesn't Diversity Training Work?" *Anthropology Now* 10, no. 2 (September 2018): 48–55, https://scholar.harvard .edu/files/dobbin/files/an2018.pdf.

125 **elevating and naming stereotypes:** Zulekha Nathoo, "Why Ineffective Diversity Training Won't Go Away," "Worklife," *BBC,* June 2021, www.bbc.com/worklife/article/ 20210614-why-ineffective-diversity-training-wont-go-away.

126 **A study from:** Juliet Bourke, "The Diversity and Inclusion Revolution: Eight Powerful Truths," *Deloitte Review* 22, January 22, 2018, www2.deloitte.com/us/en/insights/ deloitte-review/issue-22/diversity-and-inclusion-at-work-eight-powerful-truths.html ?utm_source=pocket_saves.

126 **In 2020, the company:** Gerrit De Vynck and Bloomberg, "Google Says It Will Hire More Black Workers at Senior Levels," *Fortune,* June 17, 2020, fortune.com/2020/06/ 17/google-hire-more-black-workers-diversity.

126 **showed that almost 9 percent:** Nico Grant, "Google Is Hiring More Black People but Struggling to Retain Them," *Bloomberg,* July 1, 2021, www.bloomberg.com/news/ articles/2021-07-01/google-is-hiring-more-black-people-but-struggling-to-retain-them ?embedded-checkout=true.

126 **attrition was a:** Derek Major, "Google Is Hiring More Black People, Retaining Them Is a Different Story," *Black Enterprise,* July 8, 2021, www.blackenterprise.com/google-is -hiring-more-black-people-retaining-them-is-a-different-story.

128 **"You need to see":** "Amber Ruffin/Viola Davis," *The View,* Season 25, episode 148, ABC, April 26, 2022.

128 **"I found that DEI":** Kim Tran, "The Diversity and Inclusion Industry Has Lost Its Way," *Harper's Bazaar,* March 23, 2021, www.harpersbazaar.com/culture/features/ a35915670/the-diversity-and-inclusion-industry-has-lost-its-way.

129 **DNI programs exist:** "Amber Ruffin/Viola Davis," *The View*, Season 25, episode 148, ABC, April 26, 2022.

129 **"We believe that the":** Combahee River Collective, "The Combahee River Collective Statement," 1977, www.blackpast.org/african-american-history/combahee-river -collective-statement-1977.

130 **"reject 'identity'":** Asad Haider, *Mistaken Identity: Mass Movements and Racial Ideology* (Brooklyn: Verso, 2018), 11.

130 **"If it is not":** Haider, *Mistaken Identity.*

130 **while identity politics hasn't:** Olúfẹ́mi O. Táíwò, *Elite Capture: How the Powerful Took Over Identity Politics (and Everything Else)* (London: Pluto Press, 2022), 9.

130 **This "elite capture" has:** Táíwò, *Elite Capture.*

130 **"Black women leaders":** Brittney Cooper, "Kamala Harris and Black Women Voters Helped Joe Biden Get Elected. Here's How America Can Do Right by Them," *Time*, November 8, 2020, time.com/5909002/kamala-harris-black-women.

131 **"To think that the":** Kaitlyn Greenidge, "The Bind of Being First," *Harper's Bazaar*, October 21, 2020, www.harpersbazaar.com/culture/features/a34426455/the-bind-of -being-first.

131 **"I don't think we should dismiss":** Victor Ray, interview by Samhita Mukhopadhyay, January 17, 2022.

132 **"a lone chief equity officer":** Sadye L. Campoamor, interview by Samhita Mukhopad-hyay, May 13, 2022.

Chapter 7: Not-So-Model Minority

137 **Karl Marx:** Karl Marx, *Economic and Philosophic Manuscripts of 1844*, trans. and ed. Martin Milligan (Mineola, N.Y.: Dover, 2007).

138 **"alienation is a form of living death":** Maria Popova, "MLK's Lost Lectures on Technology, Alienation, Activism, and the Three Ways of Resisting the System," *The Marginalian*, October 9, 2021, www.themarginalian.org/2021/10/07/mlk-massey -lectures.

138 **"shown woman solicited":** Simone de Beauvoir, *The Second Sex* (New York: Vintage Classics, 2015), 84–85.

139 **"Very quickly, I felt":** Dena Simmons, "How Students of Color Confront Impostor Syndrome" (video), TED.com, November 2015, www.ted.com/talks/dena_simmons _how_students_of_color_confront_impostor_syndrome.

140 **"no single piece of legislation":** Jay Caspian Kang, "The Enduring Importance of the 1965 Immigration Act," *The New York Times*, October 7, 2021, www.nytimes.com/2021/ 10/07/opinion/asian-americans-1965-immigration-act.html.

141 **"it can be argued":** Erika Lee, *The Making of Asian America: A History* (New York: Simon & Schuster, 2015), 285.

141 **"This screening process":** Cathy Park Hong, *Minor Feelings* (New York: One World, 2020), 13.

141 **"problem minorities":** William Petersen, "Success Story, Japanese-American Style," *The New York Times Magazine*, January 9, 1966, https://timesmachine.nytimes.com/ timesmachine/1966/01/09/356013502.html.

142 **"doubly privileged population":** Vijay Prashad, *Uncle Swami: South Asians in America Today* (New York: The New Press, 2012), 11.

142 **2022 Supreme Court case:** Harmeet Kaur, "How Asian Americans Fit into the Affirmative Action Debate," CNN, November 3, 2022, www.cnn.com/2022/11/03/us/ affirmative-action-asian-americans-qa-cec/index.html.

143 **Supreme Court ultimately ruled:** *Students for Fair Admissions, Inc. v. President and Fellows of Harvard College,* 600 U.S. 181 (2023), www.supremecourt.gov/opinions/22pdf/20-1199_hgdj.pdf.

143 **the Supreme Court gutted:** Nina Totenberg, "Supreme Court Guts Affirmative Action, Effectively Ending Race-Conscious Admissions," NPR, June 29, 2023, www.npr.org/2023/06/29/1181138066/affirmative-action-supreme-court-decision.

143 **"Most Americans seem to think":** Bertrand Cooper, "The Failure of Affirmative Action," *The Atlantic,* June 19, 2023, www.theatlantic.com/ideas/archive/2023/06/failure-affirmative-action/674439.

143 **"when you apply the normative definition":** Jay Caspian Kang, "It's Time for an Honest Conversation about Affirmative Action," *The New York Times,* January 27, 2022, www.nytimes.com/2022/01/27/opinion/affirmative-action-harvard.html.

143 **"Affirmative action is an imperfect":** Samhita Mukhopadhyay, "SCOTUS v. Affirmative Action," *The Meteor,* June 29, 2023, wearethemeteor.com/scotus-eliminates-affirmative-action.

144 **Ivies are filled with:** Shaun Harper, "Legacy Admissions at Harvard and Other Elite Institutions Advantage White Applicants, New Evidence Shows," *Forbes,* July 10, 2023, www.forbes.com/sites/shaunharper/2023/07/05/legacy-admissions-at-harvard-and-other-elite-institutions-privilege-white-applicants-new-evidence-reveals/?sh=5c75c83c593b.

144 **the consequences of feeling:** Maggie Wooll, "Connection Crisis: Why Companies Need to Build Workforce Connection," *Culture,* BetterUp, January 14, 2022, www.betterup.com/blog/connection-crisis-impact-on-work.

144 **40 percent of office workers:** Karyn Twaronite, "The Surprising Power of Simply Asking Coworkers How They're Doing," *Harvard Business Review,* February 28, 2019, hbr.org/2019/02/the-surprising-power-of-simply-asking-coworkers-how-theyre-doing.

145 **a study on loneliness:** Richard Eisenberg, "Who's Lonely at Work and Why," Next Avenue, February 25, 2020, www.nextavenue.org/whos-lonely-at-work-and-why.

145 **In the 2015 trial:** Nellie Bowles and Liz Gannes, "All-Male Ski Trip and No Women at Al Gore Dinner: Kleiner's Chien Takes the Stand in Pao Lawsuit," *Vox,* February 25, 2015, www.vox.com/2015/2/25/11559418/all-male-ski-trip-and-no-women-at-al-gore-dinner-kleiners-chien-takes.

145 **A jury found the firm not guilty:** David Streitfeld, "Ellen Pao Loses Silicon Valley Bias Case against Kleiner Perkins," *The New York Times,* March 27, 2015, www.nytimes.com/2015/03/28/technology/ellen-pao-kleiner-perkins-case-decision.html.

146 **"the everyday, subtle, intentional":** Andrew Limbong, "Microaggressions Are a Big Deal: How to Talk Them Out and When to Walk Away," NPR, June 9, 2020, www.npr.org/2020/06/08/872371063/microaggressions-are-a-big-deal-how-to-talk-them-out-and-when-to-walk-away.

146 **26 percent of:** Jillesa Gebhardt, "Study: Microaggressions in the Workplace," SurveyMonkey, 2019, www.surveymonkey.com/curiosity/microaggressions-research.

146 **And a Gallup study:** Camille Lloyd, "Black Adults Disproportionately Experience Microaggressions," Gallup website, July 15, 2022, news.gallup.com/poll/315695/black-adults-disproportionately-experience-microaggressions.aspx.

147 **The first study on:** Gustave A. Feingold, "The Influence of Environment on Identification of Persons and Things," *Journal of the American Institute of Criminal Law and Criminology* 5, no. 1 (May 1914): 39–51, https://doi.org/10.2307/1133283.

147 **In a more recent:** Zulekha Nathoo, "Why People of Colour Are Misidentified So Often," "Worklife," BBC, February 25, 2022, www.bbc.com/worklife/article/20210519-why-people-of-colour-are-misidentified-so-often.

Chapter 8: Impossible Compromises

156 **"Women are Over-Represented":** Michelle K. Ryan and S. Alexander Haslam, "The Glass Cliff: Evidence That Women Are Over-Represented in Precarious Leadership Positions," *British Journal of Management* 16, no. 2 (June 2005): 81–90, https://doi.org/10.1111/j.1467-8551.2005.00433.x.

158 **women are effective leaders:** Kevin Kruse, "New Research: Women More Effective Than Men in All Leadership Measures," *Forbes,* April 3, 2023, www.forbes.com/sites/kevinkruse/2023/03/31/new-research-women-more-effective-than-men-in-all-leadership-measures/?sh=7d7150bf577a.

158 **exhibit qualities:** Cassandra Frangos, "Female Leadership: The New Approach in the Workplace," *Forbes,* October 28, 2021, www.forbes.com/sites/cassandrafrangos/2021/10/28/female-leadership-the-new-approach-in-the-workplace/?sh=16a77f717c34.

159 **The phrase originally appeared:** Jane Hyun, *Breaking the Bamboo Ceiling: Career Strategies for Asians* (New York: Harper Business, 2005).

159 **"combination of individual, cultural, and organizational":** Jane Hyun, quoted in Liyan Chen, "How Asian Americans Can Break Through The Bamboo Ceiling," *Forbes,* January 20, 2016, www.forbes.com/sites/liyanchen/2016/01/20/how-asian-americans-can-break-through-the-bamboo-ceiling.

159 **"are overrepresented in low-paying occupations":** Michael Chui, et al., "Asian American Workers: Diverse Outcomes and Hidden Challenges," McKinsey & Company website, September 7, 2022, www.mckinsey.com/featured-insights/diversity-and-inclusion/asian-american-workers-diverse-outcomes-and-hidden-challenges.

159 **"Asians in tech":** Ellen K. Pao, "We Need to Talk about What It Means to Be 'White-Adjacent' in Tech," *Project Include,* Medium, May 14, 2021, medium.com/projectinclude/we-need-to-talk-about-what-it-means-to-be-white-adjacent-in-tech-f91fbcce7a42.

160 **sweeping 2023 study:** Emily Field, et al., "Women in the Workplace 2023," McKinsey & Company website, October 5, 2023, www.mckinsey.com/featured-insights/diversity-and-inclusion/women-in-the-workplace.

160 **"55% of the women":** Rasmus Hougaard, et al., "When Women Leaders Leave, the Losses Multiply," *Harvard Business Review,* March 10, 2022, hbr.org/2022/03/when-women-leaders-leave-the-losses-multiply.

161 **"privilege *and* exclusion":** Pao, "We Need to Talk."

162 **"We define the Professional-Managerial Class":** Barbara Ehrenreich and John Ehrenreich. "The Professional-Managerial Class," *Radical America* 11, no. 2 (March/April 1977): 7–31.

162 **"for the precarious academic":** Gabriel Winant, "Professional-Managerial Chasm," *N+1,* October 10 2019, www.nplusonemag.com/online-only/online-only/professional-managerial-chasm.

162 **"turned into an ultraleft slur":** Alex Press, "On the Origins of the Professional-Managerial Class: An Interview with Barbara Ehrenreich," *Dissent,* September 13, 2022, www.dissentmagazine.org/online_articles/on-the-origins-of-the-professional-managerial-class-an-interview-with-barbara-ehrenreich.

163 **"class consciousness":** Noreen Malone, "The Age of Anti-Ambition," *The New York Times Magazine,* February 15, 2022, www.nytimes.com/2022/02/15/magazine/anti-ambition-age.html.

163 **the Taft-Hartley Act:** Colin Gordon, "The Legacy of Taft-Hartley," *Jacobin,* December 19, 2017, jacobin.com/2017/12/taft-hartley-unions-right-to-work.

165 **"More often than not, our values":** Brené Brown, *Dare to Lead* (New York: Random House, 2018), 186.

166 "a culture of underreaction": Sarah Schulman, *Conflict Is Not Abuse: Overstating Harm, Community Responsibility, and the Duty of Repair* (Vancouver, B.C.: Arsenal Pulp Press, 2016), 21.

167 "Focus attention and energy": Adam Grant, *Give and Take* (New York: Viking, 2013), 256.

Chapter 9: Revenge Body

173 "thinner women simply": Aubrey Gordon, *What We Don't Talk About When We Talk About Fat* (Boston: Beacon Press, 2020), 66.

176 "We're often sat there": Vritti Rashi Goel, "Naomi Osaka Refuses to Do Press at French Open, Citing Importance of Mental Health," *CBS News,* May 27, 2021, www.cbsnews.com/news/naomi-osaka-french-open-press-conferences-mental-health.

176 "For me, I just want to": Liz Clarke, "Naomi Osaka Has Found Her Joy in Tennis in Time for the Australian Open," *The Washington Post,* January 15, 2022, www.washingtonpost.com/sports/2022/01/15/naomi-osaka-australian-open-preview.

176 Simone Biles, withdrew: Bill Chappell, "Read What Simone Biles Said After Her Withdrawal from the Olympic Final," NPR, July 28, 2021, www.npr.org/sections/tokyo-olympics-live-updates/2021/07/28/1021683296/in-her-words-what-simone-biles-said-after-her-withdrawal.

176 took home a bronze medal: Juliet Macur, "Gymnastics Updates: Simone Biles, in a Comeback, Takes Bronze on the Balance Beam," *The New York Times,* August 3, 2021, www.nytimes.com/live/2021/08/03/sports/gymnastics-olympics-biles-beam-final.

177 "arrogant spoiled brat": Barnaby Lane, "Piers Morgan Called Naomi Osaka an 'Arrogant Spoiled Brat' for Refusing to Speak to the Media, but People Were Quick to Point Out His Own Hypocrisy," *Insider,* June 1, 2021, www.insider.com/piers-morgan-slammed-for-calling-naomi-osaka-spoiled-brat-2021-6.

177 "petulant little madam": Jennifer Hassan, "Naomi Osaka Hailed for Bravery, Pilloried for 'Diva Behavior' amid French Open Withdrawal," *The Philadelphia Tribune,* June 1, 2021, www.phillytrib.com/naomi-osaka-hailed-for-bravery-pilloried-for-diva-behavior-amid-french-open-withdrawal/article_0cd8cbef-2c7c-591f-a2b6-e437affd5712.html.

177 "diva-like": Hassan, "Naomi Osaka."

177 "selfish sociopath": Brenley Goertzen, "Charlie Kirk, Piers Morgan Slam Simone Biles as a 'Selfish Sociopath' and 'Shame to the Country,'" *Salon,* July 28, 2021, www.salon.com/2021/07/28/charlie-kirk-piers-morgan-slam-simone-biles-shes-a-selfish-sociopath-shame-to-the-country.

177 "high levels of psychological distress": Scott Keeter, "Many Americans Continue to Experience Mental Health Difficulties as Pandemic Enters Second Year," Pew Research Center, March 16, 2021, www.pewresearch.org/short-reads/2021/03/16/many-americans-continue-to-experience-mental-health-difficulties-as-pandemic-enters-second-year.

178 "experienced high levels of psychological distress": John Gramlich, "Mental Health and the Pandemic: What U.S. Surveys Have Found," Pew Research Center, March 2, 2023, www.pewresearch.org/short-reads/2023/03/02/mental-health-and-the-pandemic-what-u-s-surveys-have-found.

178 83 percent of American: "Workplace Stress," The American Institute of Stress, February 15, 2023, www.stress.org/workplace-stress.

178 Approximately one million: Caitlin Mazur, "40+ Worrisome Workplace Stress Statistics [2023]: Facts, Causes, and Trends," Zippia, February 11, 2023, www.zippia.com/advice/workplace-stress-statistics.

178 led to a mental-health crisis: Jeffrey Pfeffer and Leanne Williams, "Mental Health in the Workplace: The Coming Revolution," McKinsey & Company website, Decem-

ber 8, 2020, www.mckinsey.com/industries/healthcare/our-insights/mental-health-in
-the-workplace-the-coming-revolution.

178 **"have considered downshifting"**: Rachel Thomas et al., "Women in the Workplace,
2021," McKinsey & Company, November 16, 2021, www.mckinsey.com/~/media/
mckinsey/featured%20insights/diversity%20and%20inclusion/women%20in%20the
%20workplace%202021/women-in-the-workplace-2021.pdf.

178 **A 2023 study from Future Forum**: Morgan Smith, "Burnout Is on the Rise
Worldwide—and Gen Z, Young Millennials and Women Are the Most Stressed,"
CNBC, March 14, 2023, www.cnbc.com/2023/03/14/burnout-is-on-the-rise-gen-z
-millennials-and-women-are-the-most-stressed.html.

178 **"to fail, wear out"**: Herbert J. Freudenberger, "Staff Burn-Out," *Journal of Social
Issues* 30, no. 1 (winter 1974): 159–65, https://doi.org/10.1111/j.1540-4560.1974.tb00706.x.

178 **The World Health Organization**: "Burn-out an 'Occupational Phenomenon':
International Classification of Diseases," World Health Organization, May 28, 2019,
www.who.int/news/item/28-05-2019-burn-out-an-occupational-phenomenon
-international-classification-of-diseases.

179 **"1. emotional exhaustion"**: Emily Nagoski and Amelia Nagoski, *Burnout: The Secret to
Unlocking the Stress Cycle* (New York: Ballantine Books, 2019), xi.

179 **"Burnout isn't special anymore"**: Eve Ettinger, "Have We Been Thinking About
Burnout All Wrong?" *Bustle,* March 7, 2022, www.bustle.com/wellness/burnout
-definition-what-we-get-wrong.

180 **highest levels of burnout**: Danielle Abril, "Service Workers Say Their Jobs Have Only
Gotten Worse since the Pandemic," *The Washington Post,* May 25, 2023, www
.washingtonpost.com/technology/2023/05/25/service-workers-job-burnout.

181 **"We might think"**: Jonathan Malesic, "Mental-Health Days Are Only a Band-Aid for
Burnout," *The Atlantic,* November 14, 2022, www.theatlantic.com/family/archive/2022/
11/workplace-burnout-mental-health-days/672111.

182 **Trauma is not just**: Bessel van der Kolk, *The Body Keeps the Score* (New York: Penguin
Books, 2015), 21.

182 **come under scrutiny**: Danielle Carr, "How Trauma Became America's Favorite
Diagnosis," *Intelligencer,* July 31, 2023, nymag.com/intelligencer/article/trauma-bessel
-van-der-kolk-the-body-keeps-the-score-profile.html.

182 **trauma in our bodies**: Lexi McMenamin, "Why Long-Term Workplace Trauma Is a
Real Phenomenon," "Worklife," BBC, February 28, 2022, www.bbc.com/worklife/
article/20210415-why-long-term-workplace-trauma-is-a-real-phenomenon.

183 **trauma into their work**: Samhita Mukhopadhyay, "Doing the Work While Doing the
Work," *The Nation,* July 12, 2023, www.thenation.com/article/society/social-justice
-trauma-healing.

184 **burnout "isn't a"**: Anne Helen Petersen, *Can't Even: How Millennials Became the
Burnout Generation* (Boston: Mariner Books, 2021), xxix.

184 **"It took years"**: Anne Helen Petersen, "The Tyranny of Faux Self-Care," *Culture Study*
(substack), February 22, 2023, annehelen.substack.com/p/the-tyranny-of-faux-self-care.

184 *Real Self-Care:* Pooja Lakshmin, *Real Self-Care: A Transformative Program for Redefining
Wellness (Crystals, Cleanses, and Bubble Baths Not Included)* (New York: Viking, 2023).

185 **"It's faux because"**: Anne Helen Petersen, "The Tyranny of Faux Self-Care."

185 **"caring for myself"**: Audre Lorde, *A Burst of Light and Other Essays* (Ann Arbor:
Firebrand Books, 1988), 130.

186 *The Theory of the Leisure Class:* Thorstein Veblen, *The Theory of the Leisure Class*
(London: Macmillan, 1899).

186 **"We believe rest"**: "About," The Nap Ministry, thenapministry.wordpress.com/about.

186 **"My rest as a Black woman"**: Tricia Hersey, "Rest Is Anything That Connects Your

Mind and Body," The Nap Ministry, February 21, 2022, thenapministry.wordpress.com/2022/02/21/rest-is-anything-that-connects-your-mind-and-body.

187 the "great breakup": Holly Corbett, "The 'Great Breakup' and Why Women Leaders Are Leaving Companies at Higher Rates," *Forbes,* October 18, 2022, www.forbes.com/sites/hollycorbett/2022/10/18/the-great-breakup-and-why-women-leaders-are-leaving-companies-at-higher-rates/.

Chapter 10: Having Enough

190 "It's become apparent": Ann Friedman, "What Comes After Ambition?" *Elle,* August 18, 2022, www.elle.com/life-love/opinions-features/a40835443/women-rejecting-traditional-ambition-2022.

190 "I certainly reflexively cringe": Jill Filipovic, "An Ambitious Woman After the End of Ambition," Jill Filipovic (substack), February 2, 2023, jill.substack.com/p/an-ambitious-woman-after-the-end.

191 "The ruling class": David Graeber, *Bullshit Jobs* (New York: Simon & Schuster, 2018), xviii–xix.

192 Jaz, radicalized by: Greg Jaffe, "A Rhodes Scholar Barista and the Fight to Unionize Starbucks," *The Washington Post,* February 12, 2022, www.washingtonpost.com/nation/2022/02/12/rhodes-scholar-barista-fight-unionize-starbucks.

193 many recent college-educated: Noam Scheiber, "The Revolt of the College-Educated Working Class," *The New York Times,* April 28, 2022, www.nytimes.com/2022/04/28/business/college-workers-starbucks-amazon-unions.html.

193 Institutions like Harvard Business School: Emma Goldberg, "Have the Anticapitalists Reached Harvard Business School?" *The New York Times,* November 28, 2022, www.nytimes.com/2022/11/28/business/business-school-social-justice.html.

195 "really think differently": adrienne maree brown, interview by Samhita Mukhopadhyay, April 5, 2022.

195 We are also more likely: Sarah Jane Glynn, "Breadwinning Mothers Continue to Be the U.S. Norm," website for the Center for American Progress, September 22, 2023, www.americanprogress.org/article/breadwinning-mothers-continue-u-s-norm.

196 "The impulse to react": Hamilton Nolan, "American Workers Are Burned Out and Tired. There's a Solution: Unions," *The Guardian,* September 6, 2022, www.theguardian.com/commentisfree/2022/sep/06/american-workers-are-burned-out-and-tired-theres-a-solution-unions.

197 "The compulsion to be": Sarah Jaffe, *Work Won't Love You Back: How Devotion to Our Jobs Keeps Us Exploited, Exhausted, and Alone* (New York: Bold Type Books, 2021), 15.

198 "pursuing success": Arthur C. Brooks, "The Only Career Advice You'll Ever Need," *The Atlantic,* May 18, 2023, www.theatlantic.com/ideas/archive/2023/05/career-advice-happiness-know-thyself/674087.

INDEX

ABOUT THE AUTHOR

SAMHITA MUKHOPADHYAY is the former executive editor of *Teen Vogue* and former executive editor at *Feministing*. As a writer, her work has appeared in *New York* magazine, *The Cut*, *Vanity Fair*, *Vogue*, *The Atlantic Monthly*, and *Jezebel*. Born in New York City, Mukhopadhyay lives between Putnam County and Brooklyn.

ABOUT THE TYPE

This book was set in Garamond, a typeface originally designed by the Parisian type cutter Claude Garamond (c. 1500–61). This version of Garamond was modeled on a 1592 specimen sheet from the Egenolff-Berner foundry, which was produced from types assumed to have been brought to Frankfurt by the punch cutter Jacques Sabon (c. 1520–80).

Claude Garamond's distinguished romans and italics first appeared in *Opera Ciceronis* in 1543–44. The Garamond types are clear, open, and elegant.